KU-278-534

BEYOND ROMANTICISM

LIVERPOOL JOHN MOORES UNIVERSITY
HOPE STREET LIBRARY
68 HOPE STREET LIVERPOOL L1 9EB
TEL. 051 231 3104/3105

Books are to be returned on or before
the last

[illegible] a substantial challenge to traditional views of the Romantic period and provides a sustained critique of 'Romantic ideology'. The debates with which it engages have been under-represented in the study of Romanticism, where the claims of history have never had quite the same status as they have had in other periods, and where confidence in poetic literary value remains high.

This volume attempts to demystify 'the Romantic' by specifying the particular problems of knowledge, configurations of representation and conjunctions of discourse which have been reified historically into 'Romanticism'. It directs critical attention towards the historical constructions which gave rise to the term, and to the erasures which this dominantly aesthetic construction has found necessary in order to assert its independence.

Individual essays examine the philosophical underpinnings of Romantic discourse; they survey analogous and competing discourses of the period such as mesmerism, Hellenism, orientalism and nationalism; and analyse both the manifestations of Romanticism in particular historical and textual moments, and the texts and modes of writing which have been historically marginalized or silenced by 'the Romantic'.

Stephen Copley is a Lecturer in English at the University of Wales College of Cardiff, and **John Whale** is a Lecturer in English at the University of Leeds. They have, respectively, published widely on the subjects of the eighteenth century and Romanticism.

LIVERPOOL JMU LIBRARY
3 1111 00572 9536

BEYOND ROMANTICISM

New approaches to texts and contexts 1780–1832

Edited by

Stephen Copley and John Whale

ROUTLEDGE

London and New York

First published 1992
by Routledge
11 New Fetter Lane, London EC4P 4EE

Simultaneously published in the USA and Canada
by Routledge
a division of Routledge, Chapman and Hall, Inc.
29 West 35th Street, New York, NY 10001

© 1992 Routledge
Introduction © Stephen Copley and John Whale
Individual chapters © respective authors

Typeset in 10 on 12 point Bembo by
Falcon Typographic Art Ltd., Edinburgh & London
Printed in Great Britain by
Clays Ltd, St Ives plc

All rights reserved. No part of this book may be reprinted or reproduced or utilized in any form or by any electronic, mechanical, or other means, now known or hereafter invented, including photocopying and recording, or in any information storage or retrieval system, without permission in writing from the publishers.

British Library Cataloguing in Publication Data
Beyond Romanticism: new approaches to texts and contexts 1780–1832.
1. English literature. Romanticism, history, 1780–1832
I. Copley, Stephen. II. Whale, John C.
820.9145

Library of Congress Cataloging in Publication Data
Beyond Romanticism: new approaches to texts and contexts, 1780–1832 / edited by Stephen Copley and John Whale
p. cm.
Includes bibliographical references and index.
1. English literature — 19th century — History and criticism.
2. English literature — 18th century — History and criticism.
3. Romanticism — Great Britain. I. Copley, Stephen.
II. Whale, John C.
PR457.B38 1992
820.9'145—dc20 91-16163

ISBN 0-415-05200-9 (hbk)
ISBN 0-415-05201-7 (pbk)

CONTENTS

CONTRIBUTORS

Stephen Bygrave is a lecturer in the Department of English and Literature at King's College, London. He is the author of *Coleridge and the Self* (1986) and articles on eighteenth-century fiction and poetry. He is currently working on a study of Kenneth Burke, *Kenneth Burke: Ideology and Rhetoric.*

Stephen Copley is a lecturer in the School of English at University of Wales College of Cardiff. His publications include *Literature and the Social Order in Eighteenth-Century England* (1983) and articles on literature and polite culture in eighteenth-century England and Scotland.

Harriet Guest is a lecturer in the Department of English and Related Literature at the University of York. She is the author of *A Form of Sound Words: The Religious Poetry of Christopher Smart* (1989). She is working on two projects: a book on British perceptions of India and the South Pacific in the late eighteenth century, and a book on eighteenth-century women's writing.

Paul Hamilton is a Professor of English at the University of Southampton, and is the author of *Coleridge's Poetics* (1983), *Wordsworth* (1986) and numerous articles on the Romantic period.

Robin Jarvis is a lecturer in literary studies at Bristol Polytechnic. He is the author of *Wordsworth, Milton and the Theory of Poetic Relations* (1991) and a number of articles on Romantic poetry. He is currently working on a study of pedestrianism in Romantic writing.

Vivien Jones is a senior lecturer in the School of English at Leeds University. She is the author of studies of Henry James and Jane Austen, and editor of *Women in the Eighteenth Century: Constructions of Femininity* (1990).

Nigel Leask is Director of Studies in English at Queen's College, Cambridge, and is the author of *The Politics of Imagination in Coleridge's Critical Thought* (1988). His forthcoming book is entitled *Anxieties of Empire: British Romantic Writing and the East.*

Angela Leighton is a lecturer in the Department of English at the University of Hull, and is the author of *Shelley and the Sublime* (1984), *Elizabeth Barrett Browning* (1986) and articles on nineteenth-century poetry and feminist theory. She is currently completing both a critical study and an anthology of nineteenth-century women's poetry.

Susan Matthews is a lecturer in the Department of English at Roehampton Institute. She is the author of articles on eighteenth-century and Romantic literature, and is currently completing a book on Blake.

Jane Moore is a lecturer in the Centre for Critical and Cultural Theory at University of Wales College of Cardiff. She is co-editor of *The Feminist Reader: Essays in Gender and the Politics of Literary Criticism* (1989), and author of articles on feminist theory.

Michael Rossington is a lecturer in the Department of Literature at The Open University. He is currently writing books on Shelley and myth and Shelley criticism, and editing *The Cenci.*

John Whale is a lecturer in the School of English at Leeds University, and is the author of *Thomas De Quincey's Reluctant Autobiography* (1984) and essays on Burke, Hazlitt, Wollstonecraft and Pope. His next book, *Imagination Under Pressure,* is a study of the relation between aesthetics and politics in Romantic prose.

ACKNOWLEDGEMENTS

The editors would like to thank the contributors for their support, enthusiasm and patience through all the stages of the book's production and particularly Vivien Jones and Mike Rossington for their helpful suggestions. Our thanks also to Jill Gittins and Tom Cooper for their work on the Bibliography.

1

INTRODUCTION

Stephen Copley and John Whale

I

A 'new' eighteenth century has recently been announced. In justification it has been claimed that literary criticism of the period on both sides of the Atlantic has resisted theory. To make such a claim for the Romantic period would be thought absurd. Romantic criticism has long been theoretically sophisticated: over the past twenty years it has represented the peak of applied deconstructive and poststructuralist critical practice. With its classic expressions of individualism Romantic literature offered itself as a prime site for deconstruction's rigorous questioning of self-presence. This is not to suggest, of course, that Romantic studies have been equally theorized on both sides of the Atlantic. In Britain the Romantics industry never was apocalyptic in the American manner and still has a strong traditional identity: recent opposition to the predominantly empirical British Romantic establishment has itself tended to remain empirical in nature.

Within this opposition, two important strands can be distinguished. The first is best represented by Marilyn Butler's achievement in questioning the Romantic canon. As a fiction specialist, she originally dealt with figures such as Edgeworth, Peacock and even Austen, which Romanticism often excluded solely on the grounds of genre. The focus of her work set her apart from her highly theorized American counterparts in the 1970s, and her outsider status was confirmed by the fact that she was primarily a contextualizer rather than an interpreter. Her earlier work depended on the self-evident effects of contextualizing, and the labelling of movements within the framework of a largely traditional history of ideas, and culminated in the admirably clear and, at the same time, specialized study *Romantics, Rebels and Reactionaries* in 1981.

Her important contribution to the debate on Romanticism in this period was to extend it, multiply it and sub-divide it. Her recent work has shown signs of a more explicit engagement with theory. However, it still largely depends for its impact on adding to the list of authors in the Romantic period. If this is indeed a subversive strategy in the politics of canon-formation, its empiricism has more in common with traditional British scholarship than with a radical assault on positivism as Marjorie Levinson has rather extravagantly claimed.[1] Marilyn Butler has provided a more varied authorial and socially orientated diet in the Romantic period. Her revivalism is scholarly and pragmatic, and her revisionism remains firmly based on the criteria of literary merit.

The other strand of oppositional work deployed its empiricism strategically in pursuit of explicitly political ends. Within the British New Left, such important figures as E.P. Thompson and Raymond Williams saw a preoccupation with theory as a negation of political engagement. This stance left its legacy in a distinctly British form of radical historical criticism, soft-voiced and sceptical in its encounter with theory, but strongly engaged in its reading of Romantic texts and projects.

John Barrell is one of the most impressive representatives of this approach. His work across different cultural practices – painting, aesthetics, poetry, social theory and landscape – has always been more strategically ordered than Butler's. The exclusions it 'remedies' (the case of Clare, for example) indicate a questioning perception of the notion of 'culture' itself, rather than the liberal eclecticism of Butler. Most importantly, perhaps, his intense concentration on the discourse of civic humanism across the eighteenth century to its demise in the Romantic period reads in his different books both as a meticulous scholarly description and as a radical polemical construction, available to those willing to take hold of its implications. Barrell's political enterprise has been worked out in the intensive and strong-minded empiricism of scholarship. Whilst dealing with theories of culture and society he has rarely invoked theory in a self-conscious way on behalf of his own methodology.

Now that the political possibilities of deconstruction and post-structuralism are being significantly reassessed, young critics in the Romantic period also have an opportunity for revaluing work which has, albeit empirically, extended or seriously qualified the idea of a Romantic canon. It is a situation which could benefit from a consideration of both early and late Raymond Williams. At a time when new developments in the literary use of history have led to a widespread revision of critical practices his is an important example of a particularly productive mediation of cultural study and political analysis. Invoking this British context provides a convenient reminder of the different contexts which produce Romantic studies: the fractures, instabilities and limits of Anglo-American Romantic scholarship.

The contributors to this volume do not necessarily draw on the same intellectual or political history. Rather, they represent some of the new voices and methodologies which are now contributing to the rapidly changing face of Romantic studies on both sides of the Atlantic. In a variety of forms of committed criticism they challenge past claims for Romantic transcendence and see the value of exploring the period's cultural productions outside the prevailing – often narrowly literary – terms of Romanticism. Significantly composed of both Romantic insiders and outsiders, this volume gives voice to a new generation of younger British critics.

II

The dominant force in American Romantic criticism in the 1970s and early 1980s was clearly Paul de Man. His influence – exerted through such essays as 'The rhetoric of temporality' and 'The intentional structure of the Romantic image' – was instrumental in making the Romantics one of the prime sites of applied deconstruction. No longer could critics write innocently or confidently about such supposed dualisms of Romantic thought and practice as nature and supernature, subject and object, and, most particularly, symbol and allegory. Gone were the unified verbal icons of the New Criticism and the systematic myth-makings of Bloom and Abrams. Romantic poetry was now to be read intertextually – though predominantly still poet against poet, the literary against itself. As Arden Reed claimed in the introduction to his significantly titled *Romanticism and Language* 'deconstruction offers a way to interrogate the ideologies by which earlier critics had underwritten Romanticism while still allowing for, if not encouraging, a sustained reading of that literature' (Reed 1984: 17). This draws attention both to the subversive power of applied deconstruction within the academy and to its ambiguous, even collusive relationship with the literary. The iconoclasm of its disfigurings remained ill-defined. At the same time, the question of its ability to move beyond the narrowly 'literary' is raised with his admission, in the same introduction, that: 'Perhaps the most powerful approach on the margin of this volume is the historical, and it is at least worth raising the question how far an historical outlook is compatible with such close reading as is practised here' (Reed 1984: 18). Dissatisfaction with what was thought to be de Man's legacy of 'formalist' poststructuralism was also voiced in terms of its failure to account for the role of the reader in the literary transaction. Again the cry was for a widening of the perceived deconstructionist boundaries; at some level an opening out to the 'world', even if in terms of textual transactions. Tilottama Rajan's 'Displacing poststructuralism: Romantic studies after Paul de Man' (Rajan 1985: 474) concludes with an appeal which reaches beyond reader-response theory to a recognition of reading as a 'self-differing appropriation and enactment of the text', of reading itself as 'dialogical' – to use Bakhtin's term.

In the wake of Paul de Man and the high point of deconstruction, Romantic critics on both sides of the Atlantic have now turned to new methodologies: theories of audience, genre, the new historicisms; and, as with deconstruction, have made them their own. Just as the Yale critics moved from Romantic text to 'pure' theory, so too, in the new phase, Romantic studies are rejigging themselves in the quest for ideas, and in the light of the recent 'return to history' which has taken place generally in literary studies. Characteristically, in this process Romantic criticism continues its struggle simultaneously to define and be rid of itself, a doubleness symptomatic of the continuing dialectical relationship between Romantic construction and Romantic critique. Even the most flamboyant new voices in the recent debate continue to wrestle with a definition of 'the Romantic' at the same time as claiming to have found a way out of its ideology. In this way there remains a danger that an incipient colonialism can be effected where a denial is thought to be taking place, so that definitions of 'the Romantic ideology', the modern and the assumption of a 'postmodern condition' can easily begin to merge.

Perhaps the most obvious turning point in the new phase came from an unexpected quarter: Jerome McGann's *The Romantic Ideology* (1983) which produced the buzz phrase of 'the Romantic ideology'. Strangely, McGann's hardening of Romanticism into an ideology, using Heine's model of historical self-consciousness, was surrounded with an appreciation of the human qualities to be found in Romantic texts. As Clifford Siskin[2] has astutely pointed out, ideology in this context was being used in a peculiarly specific way which could actually have the effect of glorifying 'the Romantic': the attempt to put limits on Romanticism so as to contain it resulted in a dangerous act of reification.

When the new historicisms have encountered Romantic studies they have found it impossible to invoke a centralized object of power (Klancher 1989: 77). Romanticism can itself lay claim to be a counter-culture, even a marginalized resistance movement. Critics of Romanticism can 'assume neither a new historicist's identification of power and culture, nor their Romantic opposition'. So, while there is a danger of assuming a watertight and centralized system of power (the negative possibility arrived at by some of their Renaissance counterparts), the possibilities of a transgressive potential have to be even more carefully screened.

In this respect the rethinking of 'history' in Romantic studies can be seen as a point of contestation with the Renaissance – with what has been so confidently named the 'New Historicism'. It is not surprising, therefore, that Marjorie Levinson should open her own *Rethinking Historicism: Critical Readings in Romantic History* with: 'We have had more than enough reflections on "the new historicism"' (Levinson 1989: 1). Her statement is characteristically shocking and paradoxical. She sees the critic in the position of 'Schlegel's prophet looking backwards' (ibid.: 21), recognizes the impossibility of escaping the bind of history and so performs a double-act which turns it against itself. In this respect she takes the new historicists to task for attempting to redeem the time – for imagining the possibility of a freedom of choice either from the privileged academy or by projection back onto the poets of the past. Similarly, Jon Klancher identifies a collusion between Renaissance New Historicism and forms of postmodernism as they 'probe the delicate semiosis of history, culture, and power' (Klancher 1989: 77). Where one 'discloses power' the other displays and worships it; and 'the risk lies', according to Klancher, 'in making historical criticism a transhistorical echo of the politics of the present' (ibid.).

If Klancher is scathing about New Historicism and urgent in his plea that English Romantic studies take on the issues raised by 'cultural materialism', Gayatri Spivak has launched a more general attack on the New Historicism as 'a sort of academic media hype mounted against deconstruction' (Spivak 1989: 280). She seriously questions the New Historicism's often glib, or strategic, assumptions of a materialist analysis; its unjustified claim to be dealing with a 'something else' beyond text. More particularly, she sees the very term 'history' only possible as 'catachresis' – an improper use of words – or, in her terms, 'a metaphor without an adequate literal referent' (ibid.: 279). Her position resists the claim for a theoretical difference assumed by the New Historicism, and vigorously maintains a continuity with de Manian deconstruction and, even if rather ambiguously and negatively, with her own distinctly un-postmodern version of Foucault. Like both Foucault and de Man she offers the possibilities of a 'literal' reading, a practice which attempts to resist the authoritarianism or the self-righteous moralizations of a symptomatic reading of the text. For her the text is to be lover or accomplice rather than patient or analysand. For example, in her stimulating analysis of sex in *The Prelude* she explains:

> In these pages I have read a poetic text attempting to cope with a revolution and paternity. I have not asked the critic to be hostile to poetry or to doubt the poet's good faith; although I have asked her to examine the unquestioning reverence or – on the part of the poets themselves – the credulous vanity that seems to be our disciplinary requirement.
>
> (Spivak 1987: 76)

At the same time as providing an illuminating and creatively disruptive negotiation of a canonical Romantic text Spivak provides a helpful reminder, in face of the persuasively new, of the continuing debate and argument which must take place between deconstruction, poststructuralism and historicism.

III

Part of the historical conundrum which besets properly self-conscious Romantic studies is the already doubled nature of the Romantic construct – not only in terms of subject/object and transcendence, but also in its institutional history. Appearing after the event, and in the wake of its literary objects, the Romantic is always already retrospective. The implications of this rebound even on the claims of a critic like McGann who sets so much store by a liberating self-consciousness. In this sense, Romantic criticism's relationship to theory might be said to include the overbearing claims of pre-empting it.

In this context, a familiar strategy in Romantic criticism is to go to where the binaries are often thought to begin – in the philosophical discourse of the knowledge of the object. Invoking epistemological and ontological questions rather than 'material histories' can give the impression of going straight to the heart of the matter instead of setting out on a perilous voyage of discovery. Once again, however, all the hazards of replicating a familiar Romantic site must be faced. The critic remains in danger of simply swapping the role of questor for that of contemplative thinker; and, in any case, the expectation of release or transcendence only duplicates an act of (bad) faith.

In the 1980s there have been various exciting attempts to find meaningful others with which to prize open or escape from the claims of what is often considered to be an all-embracing 'Romantic ideology'. Many of these might be better thought of as related to larger movements in literary practice and theory, rather than specifically to the claims of Jerome McGann's *Romantic Ideology* (1983) – even if one accepts his claim that lack of self-consciousness had typified much Romantic criticism. These others – notably the body – have been used, as is so often the case of others, to reflect back on what Thomas McFarland, with self-conscious and unabashed idealism, has referred to on more than one occasion as the mountain range of Romanticism (McFarland 1987: 15–24). Material histories have repeatedly been ushered in to speak against Romantic transcendence. Once again, however, a potential problem arises in that either these outsiders can be invoked in a way which defies the logic of poststructuralism's pervasive textuality; or, even if they don't, they can be reappropriated too easily on the grounds of the old Romantic argument. Slavery, bodies, ruins, revolution and political economy can be seen as the very things which provide the springboard for such Romantic transcendence, and are thereby included in the very fabric of its idealizing power.

More recently there have been attempts to reassess Romanticism by posing it against other cultural institutions, notably the national, civic, military and imperial structures of culture with which it is implicated and which it is supposedly matched against. At their most sophisticated such studies locate the exchanges, or the transferences, which take place between these cultural sites rather than simply bringing them to light. Straightforward discovery is no longer the point. The usability of institutional counters is precisely that they can be seen to possess a discursive rather than an object quality. At this point they meet up with the wealth of Foucauldian discourse analyses which many critics are currently producing. And it is precisely the discursive quality of these analyses which takes them out of the imperative to define the Romantic. Discursivity might be seen as a way of escaping the push to transcendence.

Recent interest in political economy and the sublime represents a return to old areas of enquiry, but with new poststructuralist horizons. Revaluation of the sublime came in the late 1970s, within the Romantic period, with Thomas Weiskel's pioneering study *The Romantic Sublime* (1976). It was further sophisticated by the general influx of post-Freudian and Lacanian theory beginning in the late 1970s, and received an impetus from Lyotard's *The Postmodern Condition* in the early 1980s. The sublime provides many possibilities for those who would interrogate the Romantic, precisely because such a discourse of absolute power can be challenged on account of its limitations and exclusions. From a feminist perspective it exposes the aesthetic relationship as one of mastery and subjection and figures woman as its most precious exclusion. Significantly, though, the power relations of sublimity, being inherently unstable, reflect back the mastery/subjection roles somewhat precariously. For all the rhetoric of domination and annihilation, and given the dynamics of sublime power, actual mastery, and thereby male autonomy, is never, one might suggest, quite graspable.

From this gender perspective, the Burkean example has often proved helpful. Sublimity, as defined in the *Enquiry*, through the distinction between sublimity and beauty, is inherently structured on difference – on a system of social relations and on a specific exclusion. In this way the high points of Romanticism can be said to rest on some inherently unstable strata and some precarious infolds. Similarly, the long-established connection between Burke's *Enquiry* and his *Reflections* also provides an obvious way of introducing a political base to the sublime effusions of power in later Romantic poetry.

Some of the most challenging work now taking place on the culture of the Romantic period characteristically spreads itself across discourses rather than specializing in one or the other, thereby breaking down categories in an attempt to harness deconstructive procedures to a sense of history. Writing about a slightly earlier period Peter de Bolla has provided a powerful example of the possibilities opened up by such an approach in *The Discourse of the Sublime* (1989). Refusing to privilege the aesthetic or regard the economic merely as a form of contextualization for it, he insists instead on reading the discourses which constitute the reality of mid-eighteenth-century Britain – a network which might be extended infinitely to include 'theology, ethics, politics, aesthetics, education, gaming etc.' (de Bolla 1989: 7–8). At the same time he reads them in their historical specificity as products of the Seven Years War. His enterprise may carry its own dangers: there is, for instance, no end to the inter-discursive relations it may be called on to investigate. On a different subject and with different horizons Clifford Siskin encounters the same dilemma in his extensive *The Historicity of Romantic Discourse* (1988). In seeking to demystify the Romantic, Siskin runs the risk of monumentalism; in an attempt to limit it historically he could be seen as extending it.

If the subject of many exciting new studies can be described as being discursive and their nature as necessarily and in a complex sense inter-disciplinary there are nevertheless two specific areas of study which already have produced, and are likely to continue to produce, some of the most stimulating and challenging enquiries to bear down on a transcendent Romanticism: feminism and critiques of orientalism.

The impact of feminism on the Romantic period has already been considerable. Characteristically, its challenge has taken both a pragmatic and a theoretical form; working both from within the Romantic canon and from outside it. At the level of canon-formation it has begun to shift attention significantly, remedying exclusions and creating a new agenda. The critical attention now being given to Wollstonecraft and her contemporaries is indicative of the change already taking place. Recent studies of the Gothic and sensibility have significantly altered both the ways in which texts of the period are studied and the selection of the texts themselves. And in their different ways critics such as Mary Poovey, offering a trenchant sociological analysis of women writers, and Mary Jacobus, performing a rigorous and sustained critique of sexuality in Wordsworth's *The Prelude*, have begun to change the face of the Romantic period.

Ann K. Mellor's *Romanticism and Feminism* (1988) makes a valuable attempt to reconstitute the canon by a 'renewed attention and appreciation [of] the hundreds of female and male writers working in the early nineteenth century, all those novelists, essayists, journalists, diarists, and letter-writers who had narratives to tell other than those plotted as "natural supernaturalism" or "the romantic sublime" or "romantic irony"' (Mellor 1988: 8). Such positive attempts to by-pass the canonical Big Six have, of course, to guard against the risk of reinforcing the principles of canon-formation which they attempt to challenge, by falling back on simple insider/outsider empiricism. Those marginalized figures standing outside the Romantic canon are there precisely because of the excluding power of the prevailing narratives. The constitution of the canon must be read, like other constitutions, as a dynamic of representation and exclusion. It is susceptible to change and capable of being rewritten.

Ever since Said's influential *Orientalism* (1978) the subject has provided a useful and challenging base for analyses of the Romantic ideology and the origins of Romanticism. For most Anglo-American Romanticists in the field of English literature, this should result in a chastening and productive double othering: of Europe as much as of the Orient. It is likely to be the exponents of feminism and the critics of orientalism who will provide the most productive challenge to the established Romantic order and who will offer the most helpful critiques of Romanticism's restrictive binaries of culture and society, art and politics, self and other.

More recently, the bicentenary of the French Revolution has provided an invaluable opportunity for Romantic criticism to put its new-found historical pretensions to the test, and to sound out the usefulness of the new historicisms: to see history as narrative and political crisis as rhetorical event and to debate the merits of a cultural materialism over the New Historicism. There is more at stake here than the excitement of bicentenary celebrations. The urgency of this debate extends beyond English faculties and must be measured against the strong revisionist tendencies in the discipline of history itself. The success of historians such as Jonathan Clark and Simon Schama in challenging and attacking left-wing radical assumptions demands a concerted and suitably sophisticated response.

NOTES

1 See Marjorie Levinson (ed.) (1989) *Rethinking Historicism: Critical Readings in Romantic History*, pp. 4–7.
2 See Clifford Siskin (1988) *The Historicity of Romantic Discourse*, pp. 56–63.

2

'A SHADOW OF A MAGNITUDE': THE DIALECTIC OF ROMANTIC AESTHETICS

Paul Hamilton

Definitions of Romanticism appear to be back in favour with critics and theorists, provided they focus on questions of ideology. To identify Romantic ideology is easier than to escape it, although escape is usually presented as the prerequisite for an accurate definition uncompromised by Romanticism's image of itself. In this essay I suggest both the difficulty of escaping Romantic ideology in its broadest descriptions, and the extent to which its prime category of the aesthetic might already contain the political debates which Romantic ideology is often thought to elide. The latter proposition is thus neither the happy acceptance of an aesthetic sublimation of politics, found in M.H. Abrams, Harold Bloom and others; nor is it the idea that the aesthetic is merely the artifice for universalizing the historically relative political interests of a particular class – a view associated with but by no means encompassing Jerome McGann's New Historicism. Instead, I wish to argue that the aesthetic is, in Paul de Man's description of Kant's *Critique of Judgement*, 'epistemological as well as political through and through' (de Man 1983: 140).[1]

I

De Man's late work on the politics of the aesthetic may seek to compensate for his repression throughout his academic career of early, unmentionable politics. Far from being original, though, it reiterates a common view of the aesthetic as the place where we negotiate, by persuasion rather than deduction, metaphysical and ethical assumptions underpinning knowledge. On the Kantian model, we would abandon the judgement we display in aesthetic ascriptions (beautiful, sublime, ironic, etc.) if we could not persuade others of its universal validity. Yet this universal validity is not something automatically given but 'found', a consensus which has to be argued for critically through a rhetorical process which creates a common culture. This is not part of science, but a civil agreement outside its discourse; one which, for Kant, creates a society agreeing the aims of conceptual thought and so empowering discourse in general – epistemological and political through and through. As Terry Eagleton points out in *The Ideology of the Aesthetic*, there is a clear affinity of the aesthetic with that 'civil society' later described by Gramsci (Eagleton 1990: 19–20). The strength of its civil society safeguards an ascendant class's hegemony against changes in scientific or economic paradigms. Both civil society and the aesthetic are metadiscursive, and so remain unshaken by disruptions at the discursive level; but they are also the sphere in which the Wittgensteinian 'point' or teleology of any discourse can be discussed, a sphere which must be re-occupied for any revolutionary orientation of society to take place.

Competing definitions or non-definitions of Romanticism, from Lovejoy onwards, move towards a realization that they are battling over the aesthetic in Gramsci's sense of civil society; a cultural hegemony which is appropriated and redeployed, rather than replaced, in the act of criticizing it. In the critical tradition which leads from Russian and Prague formalists to deconstruction, to define the aesthetic is to denaturalize it; to make it strange, even incoherent, by exposing its devices. Equally, within this idiom, to defamiliarize the aesthetic is to repeat what it does and so make more of the same. The critical difference is the reproduction of power. It is our own forgetfulness of the aesthetic's political genealogy, its history of such rearticulations of itself, that permits us to absorb its circle within linguistics and grammatology concerning whose political potential we then misleadingly argue as if from scratch.

I've mentioned Gramsci, but this political understanding of the aesthetic is common to Hannah Arendt and others cited by de Man, Benjamin, Lukács, Adorno and Althusser. In Eagleton's account, Gramsci's ideas are typically those of the aftermath of failed revolution. Gramsci participates in that movement in twentieth century Marxism, highlighted by Perry Anderson, in which brilliant annexations within cultural studies mask the failure of intellectuals to achieve success off their home ground and in the materialist sciences of the economic base (Anderson 1976). Changing rather than merely understanding the world, the discourse of *Capital* had been offered by Marx as the revolutionary inversion of this now revived idealist heritage of Romantic philosophy. In calculating a relative autonomy for themselves, modern intellectuals have not only exonerated their remove from unphilosophical praxis but have made that very distance, their own intellectual character, the subject of their discourse. Viewed so starkly, this reflexivity appears to justify the oldest and most familiar accusations of impracticality and abstraction levelled against intellectuals. The Romantic genealogy of the aesthetic, though, politicizes this reflexivity by proposing a model in which it can only reproduce ideology by criticizing it. Its history then records a dialectic between the ideological containment of criticism and the critical transgression of ideology. Like all dialectics it is tensed between restrictions which ensure that its self-criticisms do not threaten its identity, and the revolutionary alternatives which these criticisms nevertheless inspire.

I will deal with the latter possibility in my final section. However, in first of all demonstrating the continuity of the Romantic pattern of self-criticism in our modern, largely American theoretical tradition, my claim is also that even in its restricted form the Romantic aesthetic's dialectic makes it much more informative than the repetitive exercise in containment it might otherwise seem to be. Look, for example, at the way in which the configuration of the aesthetic is gendered throughout this history. Within Kant's philosophy, the aesthetic takes on power without responsibility, joining his scientific to his moral philosophy through a kind of judgement itself somehow excluded from this otherwise mutually exclusive pair. The result looks strongly analogous to feminization within patriarchy. The supreme aesthetic example in Hegel's *Phenomenology*, that of Antigone, develops this feminist impulse into an active challenge to the state, but one which would have lost its unanswerable authority were it ever to furnish statutes in the daylight world of government and legislature. The aesthetic character of this bind shows that politics can sublimate injustice. Hegel's state gains enormously from the subordination of women on grounds of their otherwise inordinate political importance. Justice is so much on women's side that their grasp of its universality rivals the jurisdiction of those institutions which legitimately dispense justice on their behalf. The role of Hegel's aesthetic here in naming this contradiction 'tragedy' doesn't elide the political but makes palatable the ineluctable separation of its civil and executive forms. In much conservative thought, such unrepresentable interests are what give political point to state apparatuses and establish their correct orientation. A society in which women and their familial interests had to sue for equal political representation in order to gain political redress would be one gone awry: the society would be discredited rather than the women justified. We can find this reactionary scenario repeated from Hegel through Nietzsche's *The Gay Science* to contemporary anti-feminism. The sophistry comes from Romantically isolating women as citizens only of civil society, and never of both civil society and the state.[2]

Feminist configurations of the aesthetic can be studied in Romantic examples as varied as the fissured allegiances of Keats's *Lamia* and Coleridge's distinction between cultivation and civilization in *On the Constitution of the Church and State*. Following Karen Swann (Swann 1988), we can see how the irony of Byron's later poems, cavalier if ever irony was, stereotypes as male his narrator's insouciant attitude towards the authority he craves. Assumed indifference to a constitutionally female muse endorses male sexual ascendancy as effectively as would harassment of her. Similarly, the desire or Hegelian *Begierde*, that motivates Shelley's universal literary history in *A Defence of Poetry* ('Veil after veil may be undrawn and the inmost naked beauty of the meaning never exposed' – Shelley 1988: 291) is inexhaustible. It is never definitely 'acknowledged' or realized and is thus exalted and denatured by the incommensurability of its power. For Shelley, to consummate the male desire otherwise infinitely extended in voyeuristic or readerly mode would be to allow the undressing object which figures poetry to become the subject. For her, further divestments of meaning – and why should she stop? – could have a significance outlasting male desire. Or why, we might ask, should the logic of Shelley's erotics of poetic history require her desire to end with his? Shelley's aesthetic treatise matches a male principle of interpretation to a female principle of structural ambiguity by keeping them equally 'unacknowledged' in discourse. But the effect is surely different in each case: the male interpretative desire expands to achieve an unlimited authority which the female figure is thereby never permitted for herself. Every meaning will have her interpreter. In his odes, Keats's symbols for poetry, 'urn' and 'nightingale', fake the same bad infinity. Unravished and untrodden, his figures symbolize an infinite desire nevertheless measured by their friendliness to man, seen and heard only in his successive interpretations.

From Thomas Love Peacock to McGann, the stock reason given by critics for suspecting Romanticism of peddling a reactionary ideology is the fact that it internalizes. In particular, its internalization of politics is often thought of as an intrinsically conservative strategy. Yet the examples we have just looked at articulate rather than sublimate sexual politics: we witness a philosophy of poetry losing its political innocence rather than a politics being aesthetically unrealized. Recent welcome demystifications of Romantic ideology have tended to neglect this possibility in their eagerness to attribute to Romanticism simpler oppositions between a private realm of internalized ideals and a political realm of hard, materialist praxis. Equally, internalization is why Romanticism is such a rich source or precursor to psychoanalysis which claims to restore a political dimension to internalization. Internalization becomes not a bowdlerized translation of external political forces, but a power structure showing on its own terms the mechanisms by which the prohibitions necessary for acceptance into the symbolic order are enforced. This upsets the earlier conservative judgement: the politics of the repressions which make communication and society possible are a 'mental fight', prototypes of the power relations stabilizing civil society. Aesthetic writing figures the different versions of this hegemony, exposing the patriarchal variable in psychoanalytic equations from Freud, through Lacan to Kristeva, Cixous, Irigaray and others.

The most enlightening criticism of Romantic internalization comes from McGann. Here is one of his earlier formulations:

> The poetic response to the age's severe political and social dislocations was to reach for solutions in the realm of ideas. The manoeuvre follows upon a congruent Romantic procedure, which is to define human problems in ideal and spiritual terms. To characterize the Romantic period as one marked by 'epistemological crisis' is to follow Romanticism's own definition of its historical problems.
>
> (McGann 1983: 71)

The familiar 'crisis of representation', the dilemma of logocentrism, the deconstruction of all material categories of the natural into arbitrary modes of legitimation – all betray a contemporary linguistic idealism which is bound to see Romanticism in what McGann calls its 'own' terms. I hope it is less easy to see why a critical difference should necessarily be lost because of this. Can't continuity work through active critique rather than supine complicity? Again, that is a Romantic idea. My aim here is to show the dialectical strength and instability of the Romantic response, which would be that to see an idealist continuity is not to fudge or lose a critical difference: in fact, as I have been arguing, critical difference constitutes the idealist continuity.

This aim receives support from Clifford Siskin's recent book, in which he tries to do away with critical perspective by proposing a generic account of Romanticism (Siskin 1988). He produces a postmodern literary history of Romanticism, in the strongest possible sense of the word 'literary': a history, therefore, that shows how its historical content is never presented independently of the literary conventions out of which that content is constructed. Literary history is thus genre- or kind-based through and through. Siskin puts his claim for what he calls 'a new literary history', then, not as a claim either to discover or to deconstruct historical truth, but to identify the stories which frame and make possible the appearance of historical truth in any character whatsoever.

> A history of genre imposes a historical narrative on single forms, treating each one as an independent, organic unity evolving naturally towards greater sophistication. The result is usually a Romantic developmental tale such as *the* Novel's rise or *the* Lyric's flowering. A generic history, however, uses genre to construct history rather than the other way round.
> (Siskin 1988: 10)

Siskin differs from McGann in suggesting that the critical ascendancy supposedly gained by identifying the narrative framework of other critical efforts is itself 'a Romantic developmental tale'. The implication is that Siskin's own writing is enabled by a tale of another kind (genre), and so is not ideologically Romantic. The threat that his success in describing Romanticism might be evaluative or even critical is to be allayed by his belief that his historical difference from the Romantics must be read in another way, just because to read it critically or evaluatively would be to read it Romantically. Nevertheless, Siskin still replicates the literary, generic character of the writing he historicizes, and so still models a Romantic aesthetic redeploying itself through self-difference. There seems to be no escape from the Romantic circle embracing the critical idea.

Philippe Lacoue-Labarthe's and Jean-Luc Nancy's influential book, *The Literary Absolute* (1988), corroborates this conclusion by revealing the object of the critical idea, literature, to be comparably entrapped. Literature is Romantic through and through: the object of a discipline different from philosophy, but a difference determined by philosophy's incapacity to get on terms with the ideas of totality ('Ideas') which it typically raises. Literature's symbolic function is to excuse Kantian philosophy's failure by locating its idealist self-presentation '*outside* philosophy'. But then literature's apparent autonomy is merely the aesthetic displacement of philosophical incoherence. On this unabashedly Romantic reading, literature seems invented to be the palliative of the damaged self-esteem of a certain kind of idealist philosophy. Equally, this philosophy 'must effectuate itself – complete, fulfil, and realize itself – as poetry' (Lacoue-Labarthe and Nancy 1988: x, xiv, 36). Philosophy creates literature to escape from its own limiting devices; literature redeems aesthetically, as Schlegelian irony, the embarrassing poverty of those devices, thus endowing with philosophical gravitas its own poetic licence.

But Siskin lets us see how a more spectacular option is available to the Romantic dialectic we have been tracing. He quotes Foucault's view that ideology and its critique are mutually incriminating. Out of the window at the same time goes any notion of scientific definition which isn't story-relative. Instead, Foucault is interested only 'in seeing historically how effects of truth are produced in discourses which are themselves neither true nor false' (Foucault 1980: 118). Accordingly, if one wants to preserve the notion of criticism, then one must 'see historically' by telling a Romantic story. Again, my further point is that to tell the Romantic story is to tell a tale of truth being rendered unstable by its very definition – therefore a tale of power over received knowledge, a tale which thus comes full circle to coincide with Foucault's thought as a type of the aesthetic politics in which we plot discursive jurisdiction. This coincidence must mean, though, that Romanticism may generate a critical idea so powerful in redefining and reorientating knowledge that it redescribes itself as cultural materialism. The critical difference no longer reproduces power within an idealist economy but breaks out of Romantic isolation and into discursive *Realpolitik*.

This wilder option, which collapses idealism into materialism, is the one taken by Marx in *The German Ideology* when he describes the class required to set in motion a revolution to eliminate class – a position which goes along with a Marxist view that we need intellectuals to demonstrate their own impossibility. Their intellectual ascendancy is a product of material circumstance; their advantages do not belong to them but we need them to tell us this. Foucauldians like Paul Bové can see nothing in this ploy save a tyranny of 'the humanistic project' (Bové 1986). But Eagleton should be understood as repeating a classical Marxist manoeuvre in his conclusion to *Literary Theory* when he describes as 'the embarrassment for literary criticism that it defines for itself a special object, literature, while existing as a set of discursive techniques which have no reason to stop short at that object at all' (Eagleton 1983: 201–2). The literary object focuses the techniques needed for dissolving its own aesthetic specificity, and so propels its critic out of Romantic isolation once again.

At the end of this essay I will argue that the Marxist option exists embryonically within some Romantic writing. The irony theorized by the Romantics, and so taken up by their successors, by-passes this most radical moment. Instead, we inherit at best reaffirmations of the aesthetic dialectic such as Friedrich Schlegel's notion of a socially reconstituting irony in which, as Gary Handwerk summarizes it, 'ethical irony takes the incompatibility characteristic of all irony as an impetus towards the searching out of consensus' (Handwerk 1985: 4). In the next section I will use the example of the Russian formalists to show how influential that model was, and to stress once more the political content scanted by most commentators. Then I will return to the alternative, incipiently but definitely there in the sonnets by Keats I will focus on, and even more unjustifiably neglected.

II

What should the historicist's story of the continuity of Romanticism sound like? We might begin by asking how we should read the classic disagreement between Arthur Lovejoy and René Wellek over the discrimination of Romanticisms, a dispute still cited regularly at the start of literary histories of the period. The difference of opinion spans twenty-five years. Lovejoy's paper, 'On the discrimination of Romanticisms', was first published in 1924 in *Publications of the Modern Language Association* and reissued in Lovejoy's *Essays on the History of Ideas* in 1948. Wellek's essay, 'The concept of Romanticism in literary history', followed in 1949. Lovejoy argues that Romanticism in literature and philosophy is not identifiable as a set of topics, techniques or modes of expression but as a resistance to such categorization, and Wellek argues that it does possess defining criteria. This dispute establishes with some precision the differences over a quarter of a century between an American critical tradition and the European one about to enrich it. For the moment we can regard England as having sunk below the Atlantic, rising momentarily in this story only in 1937, when Wellek again looked like the man most likely to succeed in defining critical positions, this time in opposition to Leavis. For it is the confidence in saying what things are which Wellek brings with him from Europe, whose literary theorists were now showing the influence in their writings of the scientific assurance of Russian and Czech formalists, even if they were not professedly affiliated to them. Their aesthetic theories of defamiliarization, achieved through the linguistic study of literary functions, claim to provide the first exact account of literary history.

Wellek acknowledges the influence of 'Roman Jakobson, Jan Mukarovsky, and the other members of that splendid group [the Linguistic Circle]' in 'Prospect and retrospect' at the end of his recent book *The Attack on Literature* (1982).

> In the Prague years I came more and more under the influence of my older colleagues at the circle and of their models, the Russian formalists. But again I withheld full allegiance. In a review of the Czech translation of Shklovsky's *Theory of Prose* in 1934 I voiced many misgivings about the extremes of his mechanical formalism, and in a paper on Jakobson's and Mukarovsky's history of Czech versification I questioned their views on literary evolution.
>
> (Wellek 1982: 153)

Wellek's admission of influence goes hand in hand with his distancing from full allegiance; and later he stresses his lack of commitment to any critical school he learned from.

> Looking back on my work I am struck with my detachment from all the phases I went through: historical scholarship,

> symbolist criticism in the wake of Salda and Gundolf, the American New Humanism, the Prague School shaped by Russian formalism, the Leavis group, the American New Criticism.
>
> (Wellek 1982: 157)

Nevertheless, Wellek first published a Czech article on the formalists in 1936. His first contribution to an American critical manifesto in 1941 was a reworking of this piece to which he again returned in *Concepts of Criticism* with a chapter on 'The concept of evolution in literary history' (Wellek 1936, 1941, 1963).[3] He therefore begins his American career by commending the methods of Russian and Prague formalists and by holding up their formal definitions as the goal of a literary criticism 'which has not yet developed satisfactory methods which would enable us to describe a work purely as a system of signs' (Wellek 1941: 97, 117). Furthermore, his renewed exposition of the formalists and their agenda in 1963 could have been inspired by a formalist awareness, and hence distance from, the institutionalizing of current critical methods: the very descriptive success which Wellek desired eventually looks like a mechanical routine itself in need of critical rejigging. Wellek tries to distinguish his own discontent from Mukarovsky's belief that 'in history there is only one criterion of interest: the degree of novelty' (Wellek 1963: 45). But Gerald Graff, in his genealogy of critical institutions in America, *Professing Literature*, finds it natural to use Wellek as a prime identifier of what Graff calls 'the routinization of Criticism' (Graff 1987: 226–53). As soon as criticism takes on an institutional shape there arises a theoretical drive to see its practice as a limiting device. As it becomes accepted and academically naturalized, even this awareness in its turn will be theorized and so defamiliarized. Graff wonders how the cycle may be broken, but he does not attribute to it the formalist genealogy to which Wellek's percipience is the clue.

Of course the Prague School's theory had its own problems: it was formal and linear and immediately productive of counter-examples which jumped its chronologies. However, it did make a literary trope, irony, the constitutive motor force in laying out its sequence. And in this, with Wellek as an unconscious carrier, it had a destination to reach in American deconstructive theory to which Wellek is very much opposed. Yet, in this updating of the Kantian crisis, the accuracy in saying what things are is dialectically related to showing how they fail to be, how their existence is inauthentic, either through *mauvaise foi* or the logocentric constraints revealed by grammatology as the embarrassment of western philosophy. The language most people automatically revert to if sketching deconstructive method is existentialist. There is also the native tradition of New Criticism and its links with later American close-reading practices, relations cited, on the one hand, as a conclusively damaging irony by Frank Lentricchia (Lentricchia 1980: xiii), and on the other hand unworriedly accepted by the Yale critics, save de Man. But within the terms of the original migration as I am describing it, with the European idea of a recuperative ironic trope concealed within historical procedures for literary discrimination, it is only to be expected that deconstruction would adopt the terms of existentialism or New Criticism within an ironical exposé of their critical certainties. Literary historians like Wellek, therefore, are set fair to gain the whole world for their catalogues only if they lose the immortal soul of their subject.

In other words, history as irony appears to be too professionally embarrassing to acknowledge. Nevertheless, the alternative, in Wellek's case, is considerable disillusion: attacks on contemporary theory go along with a learned pessimism about his own practice, doomed to mortality and a melancholy sureness of repetition. Wellek, in 'The fall of literary history' (Wellek 1982), a title reversing that of a book he wrote describing the precedents for his own professional ambitions, concludes with this verdict on his own efforts:

> there is no evolution in the history of critical argument. . . . Possibly a similar conclusion is required for the history of poetry itself. 'Art', said Schopenhauer, 'has always reached its goal.' Croce and Ker are right. There is no progress, no development, no history of art except a history of writers, institutions, and techniques. This is, at least for me, the end of an illusion, the fall of literary history.
>
> (Wellek 1982: 77)

To which one wants to reply, that if Wellek is now driven to admit the analogy between poetry and criticism he can also dispense with the need for any goal. He has in effect opted for the ironic side of formalist theories of literary evolution at the expense of the scientific side: what Jan Mukarovsky calls 'unstructured aesthetic', the 'unpredictable', 'deautomatizing', 'enlivening' half of an 'unceasing antinomy' with its normative, rule-bound scientific counterpart (Mukarovsky 1964: 31–69). There is perhaps a distinction between the discredited concept of evolution and the emergent one of ironic reproduction which could save critical theory, and which is implicit in Wellek's final musings, however undesirable he might find this.

Implicit, therefore, in Wellek's belated reply to Lovejoy is a buoyant functionalism, a scientific sureness of address to the subject in hand. Lovejoy's diversitarianism is 'mistaken. There is, on the contrary, a profound coherence and mutual implication between the romantic views of nature, imagination and symbol' (Wellek 1949: 171–2). This confidence in definition, though, seems to me to be a reflex of Wellek's acquaintance with the theories of the Russian and Prague formalists. Implicit in the laying bare of literary devices characteristic of *their* analyses is a modernist rhetoric in which literary history ironizes itself in reproductive form. By that I mean the way in which formalist theories keep crossing generic boundaries and categories: making strange the perceived world turns out to have been the identification of the literary representations which otherwise naturalize the world for us. This defamiliarization in turn exposes the historically relative position from which those conventions have become visible. At every level of explanation, the previously dominant level is proffered ironically – that is, not conclusively, but with an uncommitted reserve capable of producing an understanding of it in a sense opposite to the routine one. So, a novel changes the lights for us, and criticism of that novel shows how the lighting works, only to have its technology revealed as being similarly relative to this kind of illumination, as the next master-narrative looms up over the horizon suitably focused or targeted in its turn. Literature and its criticism converge. Literature generates itself out of past forms, rejuvenating or demystifying them by exposing the conventions which legitimate them. Literature becomes in this way an ironic history of itself, inviting the corollary that the critic's literary history must be another version of the same. By unmasking the distinctive features of a literature, criticism participates in the same function by which that literature propagates itself.

Geoffrey Hartman promotes this movement in his chapter 'Literary commentary as literature' in *Criticism in the Wilderness*:

> For in the period that may be said to begin with Arnold – a period characterized by increasing fears that the critical would jeopardize the creative spirit, and self-consciousness the energies of art – literary criticism is acknowledged at the price of being denied literary status and assigned a clearly subordinate, service function. There is no mysticism, only irony, in the fact that literary commentary today is creating texts – a literature – of its own.
>
> (Hartman 1980: 213)

Again, there is the idea at work that criticism becomes creative through an ironic, disillusioned view of its own past: and Hartman quotes T.S. Eliot's accusation that Arnold 'overlooks the capital importance of criticism in the work of art itself'. Certainly, the last thing Wellek could have thought he was doing when tightening up Lovejoy's definition was opening up the *mise-en-abyme* we know so well today. The discipline which Lovejoy appeared to have invented, the history of ideas (in *The Great Chain of Being* and *Essays*), studied European thought in a grandly impartial way, as though individual ideas could be followed in their typical transformations through history with absolute judiciousness. But this American philosophical detachment perhaps had to change with the influence of European scholars out of favour with their own governments or fleeing the impending holocaust. Many viewed scientism and objectivity as reflective notions which, far from being unproblematically available to the intellectual, had to be kept negotiable, answerable to personal and professional responsibilities, and free of possibly totalitarian dogma. One of them, Leo Spitzer, attacked Lovejoy precisely on this point, arguing that Lovejoy could only have mistaken Spitzer's inheritance of Romantic *Geistesgeschichte* for a prefiguration of 'Hitlerism' because his own history of ideas was constitutionally blind to its own polemical relativism.[4]

Writing on institutions in the opening chapters of *Framing the Sign*, Jonathan Culler (1988) builds on Graff's genealogy and becomes more precise than Hartman about criticism's literary character. He sees contemporary literary theory as renewing the function of avant-garde literature. Again, the means he ascribes are formalist: the avant-garde is constituted by defamiliarization of the devices and conditions of possibility of previous methods and thus becomes a history of itself. Yet this professional reflexivity is not narrowness of focus or reductive abstraction from larger issues; it stages an authentic confrontation with the ideology by which criticism is always contained. Furthermore, Culler, like Graff and other American-based theorists now writing in the genealogical idiom (Peter Hohendahl, Jonathan Arac, Jon Klancher), thus resumes the Romantic dialectic for which I am claiming precursor status here. As Friedrich Schlegel put it in his 'Ideen': 'Whatever can be done while poetry and philosophy are separated has been done and accomplished. So the time has come to unite the two' (Schlegel 1984: 108). This much more overt mingling of the two disciplines explicitly relates philosophical insight to poetic output. Extending Schiller's description of the kinds of poetry, it makes criticism sentimental rather than naive, the genealogical reflection of what Schiller took modern literature to be. The Hegelian idiom is much more strictly philosophical in its claims, but, just as much, it sets up the model in which the very description of things puts in motion an immanent logic by which they can turn into something else. For Hegel, this is the manifestation of *Geist*, or the noumenal world as it is capable of being subsumed within the phenomenal world: an absolute will or notion explains the teleology producing change in the phenomenal world.

Our later descriptions of Romantic thought can dispense with Hegel's teleology. It is not so clear that they can give up the idea that criticism perpetuates itself in a manner analogous to the ironic reproduction of literature; or that we can conceal the power relations directing an apparently politically innocent epistemology. Hegel may mask politics with the absolute terms of *Geist*, but the machinery of local government in the *Phenomenology* and the *Aesthetics* always remains visible. And it is the aesthetic example which restores the political profile to that ironic reserve from which power over existing knowledge is demonstrated. Once more we return to the example of Antigone in the *Phenomenology*. The woman's voice becomes that 'of the everlasting irony [in the life] of the community', her 'ridicule' telling powerfully on the side of youth and innovation at the expense of 'the earnest wisdom of mature age' (Hegel 1977: 288).

III

Antigone's dilemma is dramatized in a tragedy. Institutionalized within art, her powerless authority defines an extradiscursive site where such contradictions conventionally remain unresolved. For a tough-minded theorist of the avant-garde, this aporia has to be sought out and given its proper name: 'social ineffectuality stands revealed as the essence of art in bourgeois society, and thus provokes the self-criticism of art' (Bürger 1984: 27). In Peter Bürger's account, an abrasive avant-gardism breaks with Romantic reflexivity and attacks the institution of art. Instead of Culler's avant-garde, whose exposure of the possibilities of art simply sets up the next aesthetic *frisson*, and whose critical reconstitution of its object is replicated by theory, we meet a revolutionary response, one intent upon destroying the institution it defamiliarizes. Bürger's avant-garde improves on Hegel's eventual supersession of art by philosophy to 'return aesthetic production', in Eagleton's words, 'to its humble, unprivileged place within social practices as a whole' (Eagleton 1986: 137). Or, rather, the avant-garde effort falls short of completing this project and so leaves Bürger's critical theory something to do.

In this final section I want to suggest that even Bürger's Marxist cultural materialism, explicitly severed from any aesthetic, is still stalked by a Romantic prescience. To do this, I will consider two Romantic definitions of the aesthetic, exemplified by the Elgin marbles, one by Keats and one by Benjamin Robert Haydon; one, Keats's, puzzlingly full of an unspecified reserve; the other, Haydon's, the naive target of the political critique possibly implied by Keats's lack of a redemptive irony. The full provocation of Keats's critique is articulated in a recent account by Marjorie Levinson of a desirable historicism:

> the idea is to sidestep historicism's Hobson's choice of contemplation or empathy: in the Romantic idiom, knowledge or power. If there is one single insight peculiar to the postmodern condition, it might be the realisation that both these attitudes, however different the methods they endorse, are still in the service of a rigged dialectic: a subjectively privileged and also armored affair. Moreover, by rewriting 'knowledge' as possession *of* the object, and 'power' as possession *by* the object, we begin to appreciate both high ambitions as reflections of the commodity form.
>
> (Levinson 1989: 2)

The first of Keats's two sonnets on the experience of viewing the Elgin marbles, 'On Seeing the Elgin Marbles', shows a revealingly fraught use of catalogue. Precisely what might be the connection between the sestet's listed items brings into play the alternatives of knowledge and power. The aesthetic object, the Elgin marbles, is one whose exemplary knowledge has been facilitated by a questionable power (an imperialist Britain or Lord Elgin's pillaging the Parthenon), exposing its commodity structure in the way Levinson wants. The universal aesthetic object – the classic – is thus ironized by what is implied by having the power to see it (in London). It becomes the sign of an imperial hegemony, reflecting critically upon the culture using it to endorse its humanism in this way. This is the same rough, conflictual passage through definition and irony to civic awareness which I've been trying to plot. Levinson's more radical version suggests what I characterized as the Marxist attempt to use the cultural criticism generated by irony to step outside the ironic narrative altogether: to escape its aesthetically constitutive alliance of knowledge and power, and take up residence in a different materialist practice. But how far can Keats anticipate the self-effacement of aesthetic distinction desired by Eagleton and Bürger?

Keats's two sonnets make most sense when the sonnet to Haydon ('To Haydon, with a Sonnet Written on Seeing the Elgin Marbles') is taken as a commentary on the sonnet purely about the marbles. The second sonnet then repeats the first's efforts to define an aesthetic object. Like the first, it fails, but this time in a way that makes the expected recuperation of the lost aesthetic through irony even harder to credit. The first sonnet mourns the failure of the narrator to live up to a conception of his own vocation, 'godlike hardship', and takes comfort in the 'gentle luxury' of being released from that degree of aspiration. Yet its final catalogue dismisses emotional equilibrium and insists on conflict, apparently licensing the juxtapositions of the final simile:

> Such dim-conceived glories of the brain
> Bring round the heart an undescribable feud;
> So do these wonders a most dizzy pain,
> That mingles Grecian grandeur with the rude
> Wasting of old Time – with a billowy main –
> A sun – a shadow of a magnitude.
>
> (Keats 1978: 93, lines 9–14)

The sonnet establishes a likeness between experiencing poetic ambition ('dim-conceived glories') and seeing the marbles ('a most dizzy pain'). Unexpectedly, seeing the marbles turns out to be a distressing experience; its complexities suggest that the introspective poet who agonizes over aesthetic means has still to confront the problematic of aesthetic ends. Aesthetic difficulties don't finish with poetic achievement but are replicated in the critical experience of spectator or reader. Apollo subliminally figures the poet's assumption, to be belied by his audience, that were he to succeed he would communicate a kind of 'godlike' seeing whose success was guaranteed because, like an observing sun, it produces the light it needs to see by. Godlike seeing returns as a crux in the Hyperion poems. Here, the meaning might be that viewing the marbles makes the poet aware that his ambitions are either blasphemous or unrealistic. More likely, though, following the title's insistence on 'looking', the sonnet's point is the climactic description of the confusing rather than unifying benefits conferred on the consumer by the highest artistic excellence. The emulative poet's conflict only prepares for the spectator's disjunctive phenomenology: 'That mingles Grecian grandeur with the rude / Wasting of old Time – with a billowy main – / A sun – a shadow of a magnitude.'

The meaning of these condensed oppositions can be partly unpacked by reading them through Haydon's own response on seeing the marbles, and through his interpretation of the controversy surrounding their purchase for the nation. Haydon understood that act as a blow against the system of private patronage which neglected artists who, like him, attempted 'the Higher Walk of Art' – an epic, 'historic art' not tailored to the ornamental requirements of the aristocracy. Haydon believed that his articles in *The Champion* and *The Examiner*, attacking Richard Payne Knight and authenticating the marbles, contained 'thoughts and truths which neither nobility nor patrons ever forgave' (Haydon 1960: I, 267; 1926: I, 232). The nobility, or their spokesmen, the hated connoisseurs, had been able to turn their prejudices against 'high' art into self-fulfilling prophecies, 'when by resolute reliance on their own power & in the ability, if properly fostered, of the Artists, the higher walk would at once be released from its neglect and at once elevated to take its natural Station' (Haydon 1960: I, 267). In the case of the marbles, though, here at last was art of the highest calibre being accorded the proper treatment and exhibited in a public institution. It was almost as if Haydon's longed-for 'Minister of Taste' had stepped in 'so that Works might be for ever [in the] public inspection of all the World', free of capricious patronage and open to democratic judgement. The marbles had forged a unique link between 'Artists' and 'People', championed on the People's behalf in the press by artist–polemicists such as Haydon, and finally endorsed by their government to the discomfiture, Haydon thought, of the connoisseur lobby. Political and professional aspirations towards the establishment of a public sphere were fulfilled at one stroke. Artists' suspicions of recent attempts to achieve this, such as the lately established British Institution (1806), were allayed. Despite its non-exclusive membership in comparison to the Royal Academy, the British Institution had Payne Knight as one of the founding governors. '*Owners*', Constable was to call them, and in his opinion they were ruining British art (Constable 1968: VI, 105). In rosy retrospect, Haydon explained his spat with a patron in 1823 as still deriving from the fact that in the dispute over the marbles, 'the Connoisseurs, as a body, will never pardon me who destroyed the value of their judgement' (Haydon 1960: II, 410; I, 8).

Inevitably, there are some supplementaries to the main theme of Haydon's hectic tale, qualifying his innocent notion that 'the remains of Athens have fled for protection to England', as though miming the myth of a necessary progress of poetry from east to west. In fact, Napoleon's cultural imperialism was what was embarrassingly mimed by England. The conundrum of Keats's puzzling inventory comes from a not unsurprising difficulty in finding a language adequate to the multiple and mixed meanings of 'high' art in this context. His meaning comes out more as a still muffled critique of the circumstances under which unequivocal endorsement is expected. The 'dizzy pain' of the spectator *is* separable from the 'indescribable feud' around the heart of the emulative artist. The artist's difficulties, as the poem testifies, can always be taken ironically, salvaging success from their own expressivity. The motivating 'dim-conceived glories of the brain' can evoke the obscurity of Burkean sublimity, the other main Romantic palliative of poetic difficulty. Keats, though, abandons self-righting buoyancy, the phoenix of Romantic irony, for an irrecuperable confusion besetting the contemplator of a paragon of aesthetic success. He cannot explain as well as describe such giddiness: the critique which would be implied by the acceptance of an inessential art breaks too rapidly with the unity of the 'old Antique'. The sonnet registers the surpassing of received standards of unity by an art whose catalogue historicizes its own transcendent effect. The self-sufficiency of the bourgeois poet, whose efforts are always self-validating despite falling short of traditional mastery, makes for a life of irony.[5] But this life is doubly and critically ironized if there is shown to be no alternative to it: if the authority desired and pictured in fragments of ironic compensation remains ungraspable because it is *not* unified, but *is* just that ideological opportunism which can force a group of disparates temporarily into society.

The advice given to Haydon by the despised patrons and connoisseurs on whom he depended was that 'the Higher Walk of Art' led to destruction. This might have warned him against exploring the sources of ideological legitimacy, the 'end of Art' or 'perfection' so directly addressed in this 'Higher' vocation, in expectation of its essential grounding (Haydon 1960: I, 267). Instead, the ancient 'grandeur' of Greece, the meaningful society of fragments, is valorized by the political prestige of those who can enforce it: the marbles are 'reverenced & envied by Foreigners, because they do not possess them', as Haydon's *Diary* ingenuously concedes. The Homeric sea and renascent sun conjure up a popular franchise whose radicalism is dependent on a fallen, Napoleonic ideal. The Greek aesthetic remains the secondary phenomenon, the 'shadow' of these primary, substantial issues. Power presumes over knowledge. To define the aesthetic is above all to have the means to define it, and is thus primarily to describe a political ascendancy, something other than the aesthetic.

Keats could not produce this theory of cultural materialism. He writes from within the dialectic of the Romantic aesthetic, but his treatment of the marbles threatens it. Hence the second sonnet, to Haydon, on the marbles regrets the first's inability to 'speak / Definitively on these mighty things'. Its conclusion discredits the spectator's position as clueless – 'For when men stared at what was most divine / With browless idiotism, o'erweening phlegm' – and revives but delegates the artistic response in an image of Haydon's prayerfulness – 'Thou hadst beheld the Hesperan shrine / Of their star in the East, and gone to worship them'. The image of the Magi is presumably alien to the Keats reported by Haydon to have taken Shelley's side against him in 'a theological ambush' (Haydon 1960: I, 439; II, 253–4). It refers the imagined unity of Haydon's response to another, religious discourse. A unified response to the marbles, then, can only be preserved in Haydon's religiosity because neither the poet nor the spectator of the first sonnet could realize it aesthetically. Given this plot, the implausibility of the religious conclusion can hardly be recuperated as poetry, however 'Hesperean' that Christian shrine. Keats again has slipped the leash of Romantic irony. He may not be in a position to state an alternative, but it is his prophetic achievement to have made the Romantic aesthetic run out of excuses.

APPENDIX

On Seeing the Elgin Marbles

My spirit is too weak – mortality
  Weighs heavily on me like unwilling sleep,
  And each imagined pinnacle and steep
Of godlike hardship tells me I must die
Like a sick eagle looking at the sky.
  Yet 'tis a gentle luxury to weep
  That I have not the cloudy winds to keep
Fresh for the opening of the morning's eye.
Such dim-conceived glories of the brain
  Bring round the heart an undescribable feud;
So do these wonders a most dizzy pain,
  That mingles Grecian grandeur with the rude
Wasting of old time – with a billowy main –
  A sun – a shadow of a magnitude.

To Haydon, with a Sonnet Written on Seeing the Elgin Marbles

Forgive me, Haydon, that I cannot speak
  Definitively on these mighty things;
  Forgive me that I have not eagle's wings –
That what I want I know not where to seek:
And think that I would not be overmeek
  In rolling out upfollow'd thunderings
  Even to the steep of Heliconian springs,
Were I of ample strength for such a freak.
Think too that all those numbers should be thine;
  Whose else? In this who touch thy vesture's hem?
For when men star'd at what was most divine
  With browless idiotism – o'erweening phlegm –
Thou hadst beheld the Hesperean shrine
  Of their star in the east, and gone to worship them.

(Keats 1978: 92–3)

NOTES

1 Idealist positions are conveniently summarized by M.H. Abrams in 'Construing and deconstructing' (Abrams 1986: 127–83); they are also epitomized by Harold Bloom's conclusion in his paradigmatic 'The internalization of the Quest Romance' that 'the Romantic poet turned away, not from society to nature, but from nature to what was more integral than nature, within himself' (Bloom 1971: 26). On the Historicist side, Jerome J. McGann's *The Romantic Ideology* (McGann 1983) and Marilyn Butler's *Romantics, Rebels and Reactionaries* (Butler 1981) are already classics and unignorable starting points for recent good Historicist work. Tony Bennett's *Formalism and Marxism* (Bennett 1979) is still important, although Terry Eagleton's *The Ideology of the Aesthetic* (Eagleton 1990) bids to be the most comprehensive treatment of the subject since Lukács and Adorno.

2 See especially *The Gay Science* (Nietzsche 1974: 59); Derrida tries to rescue this aesthetic compliment to women from Nietzsche's misogyny in *Spurs/Eperons* (Derrida 1979). Alice A. Jardine trenchantly exposes the negations this traditional philosophical valorization of the woman involves in *Gynesis: Configurations of Women and Modernity* (Jardine 1985: 159–227). She asks: 'are we here only brushing up against a new version of an old male fantasy: that of escaping the laws of the fathers through the independent and at the same time dependent female?' (ibid.: 207).

3 See Bucco 1981: 21–2.

4 Spitzer's attacks on Lovejoy are full of a Romantic emphasis on the untranslatable (extradiscursive) particularity of the aesthetic and the reflexive narrative of criticism. In contrast, he characterizes the history of ideas as a discipline which unjustifiably arrogates poetic meaning to itself, and which, although 'wholly given up to historical relativism . . . has not yet learned to see the relativity of its own procedures' (Spitzer 1941: 604). Lovejoy's response, predictably, is to add Spitzer to his list of 'Romanticisms' (Lovejoy 1944: 217). Erich Auerbach's comparable differences with Eric Curtius are usefully elucidated by Geoffrey Green (1982: 3–5; 73–4). See also *The Intellectual Migration: Europe and America, 1930–1960* (Fleming and Bailyn 1969).

5 See Marjorie Levinson's discussion of Keats's 'allegorical' life (Levinson 1988: 125–7 and *passim*); see also my discussion (Hamilton 1989: 135–7).

3

LAND OF THE GIANTS: GAPS, LIMITS AND AUDIENCES IN COLERIDGE'S *BIOGRAPHIA LITERARIA*

Stephen Bygrave

I

In 1983 the Bollingen Foundation with Routledge and Princeton University Press published, in two volumes, the first full-dress scholarly edition of Coleridge's *Biographia Literaria* since that of John Shawcross in 1907. The introduction and apparatus of that edition located Coleridge's famous but notoriously difficult adumbration of a theory of 'Imagination' within a genealogy which, though it was largely that of Kant and his successors, stretched back to the pre-Socratics: one offshoot of the edition was a book by its joint-editor making clear the teleology that completed itself with Coleridge.[1] In the same year Paul Hamilton's *Coleridge's Poetics* and Jerome McGann's *The Romantic Ideology* offered re-orientations of Romantic aesthetics implicitly critical of the way such a project would tend to repeat the suggestive but historically compromised and ideologically duplicitous terms of the *Biographia* itself. Hamilton and McGann are alike in their revisionary ambitions but maybe not in much else, and Hamilton's own essay in the present volume measures their difference. It's a difference, perhaps, between wanting to rewrite Marx's *German Ideology* for contemporary purposes and wanting to *include* Marx's inversion of a whole idealist tendency within an account of what would still have to be called 'Romanticism'.

McGann saw a paradigm of the Romantic ideology in the claims for wholeness, aesthetic transcendence and unarguable 'principles' made by Coleridge; to him it was Byron and Shelley who, seeing no transformation of the present and responding with, respectively, cynicism and utopian projection, were exemplary. Hamilton's subsequent work has interrogated the notion of Romantic ideology as false consciousness which can be gone beyond. Readers of Romantic texts necessarily produce a kind of meta-Romanticism, which results most fruitfully in the sort of dialectical critique of Romanticism by which our own reception of its topics (the subject–object relation for example) can be acknowledged and which forms material for reflection upon them. This was implicit in Hamilton's book on Coleridge, which recuperated the 'emancipatory impulses' to a common language from Coleridge's own repression or retraction of those impulses.

Biographia Literaria was first published in two volumes in 1817, at the time of Coleridge's closest relations with the already much more marketable Byron. While it is evidently transitional in its revision of a set of premises from which much Romantic criticism still borrows its criteria, it can also seem, retrospectively, to be poised between first and second generations, or in McGann's terms, between 'phases', both of which are secondary – revisionary rather than visionary – but the later of which *knows this*. Furthermore, the fact of publication in two volumes has invited alternative responses: *Biographia* is exemplary in confronting philosophy with poetry, or it is symptomatic in failing to bring them together, proclaiming an epistemological and social wholeness which it cannot demonstrate.

An influential description of the latter kind is that by Marilyn Butler who sees the *Biographia* as a lay sermon to the propertied classes, reactionary not only in its abjuration of the levelling Wordsworth but also in its recall to religion and its appeal to the culture of counter-revolutionary Germany. For Butler, the *Biographia* is 'the masterpiece of the counter-revolutionary phase, updated to meet the needs of a time where a more active conservatism was called for' (Butler 1981: 166). Such a description, in its historicizing zeal, can have little time for attention to the elaborateness of surface in Coleridge's text or would see its rhetorical gamesomeness as ideologically mystifying in itself. Nigel Leask who, like Hamilton, stresses the dependence of Coleridge's radicalism on native models rather than on events in France or on German metaphysics has usefully complicated this description. In Leask's account, German literature was seen as Jacobin in 1800, safely conservative by 1815;

Kant remained by reputation a republican and an atheist (Leask 1988: 82). Butler's sly participle 'updated', though, seems to allow for the lapses of time as well as of rhetoric which the *Biographia* flaunts. By lapses of time I do not mean only the retrospection of the narrative. The edition does clarify the history of writing and publication of the *Biographia*. Wordsworth's preface to the *Lyrical Ballads* of 1800 is treated, it suggests, as a stalking-horse for the preface to his *Poems* of 1815, Coleridge having originally conceived the *Biographia* as a preface to his own *Sibylline Leaves*. The gap between volumes of *Biographia* is initially little more than an accident of publishing history. J.M. Gutch, the Bristol printer, found enough for two volumes, then considered that the second volume would be too short. Coleridge rapidly expanded the critique of Wordsworth in chapter 22 and added 'Satyrane's letters' from *The Friend* and the critique of *Bertram* in chapter 23 for publication in July 1817.[2]

Whatever the contingent reasons, the gap between the volumes of the *Biographia* seems emblematic of a separation of philosophy from 'practical criticism', speculation from practice, culture from politics evident in the later writings. This gap is adverted to in the *Biographia* just at the point where its cancellation or its transcendence is also announced. The chapters on Imagination must at least hold out the possibility of totalization. As a whole the *Biographia* has twenty-four chapters and thus the thirteenth, which closes volume II, ought to be the pivot or bridge; and yet it's a pretty wobbly bridge, consisting of the letter from a putative friend complaining about the disconnection apparent to that point, followed by a summary of conclusions, the progress towards which, it is promised, will be revealed in a forthcoming work which never forthcame. Those remarks 'desynonymizing' Imagination from Fancy (a distinction first adumbrated in chapter 4 and one which rejoins a lengthy eighteenth-century debate) and then within Imagination itself distinguishing primary and secondary types seem themselves the product of a rhetorical gamesomeness which shies from the ideological work it has to do. This is in line with the proffered definitions of Imagination itself which is associated with an Absolute that is at once both formative and amorphous. In the seventh of the 1811–12 lectures on Shakespeare and Milton, Coleridge refers to the generation of 'conceits' in Shakespeare's language as

> an effort of the mind, when it would describe what it cannot satisfy itself with the description of, to reconcile opposites and qualify contradictions, leaving a middle state of mind more strictly appropriate to the imagination than any other, when it is, as it were, hovering between images. As soon as it is fixed on one image, it becomes understanding; but while it is unfixed and wavering between them, attaching itself permanently to none, it is imagination.
>
> (Coleridge 1960: II, 103)

Here Imagination is, in the *Biographia*'s terms, an 'intermediate faculty which is at once both active and passive' (Coleridge 1983: I, 124). It is also a faculty that can be named only after the event. Imagination entails a deferral: in this phenomenal moment, subject and object, poet and reader, lose their distinctiveness, and yet the residue here is itself a process. The critic or philosopher is enjoined to distance and belatedness, not to description but to establishing the grounds for a description. What would be prospective, a philosophy of mind, can only be retrospective, an aesthetic. Yet the correlation of imagination with civic virtue – its absence 'render[s] the mind liable to superstition and fanaticism' (Coleridge 1983: I, 30) – allows the exemplary figure of Milton to be recuperated as a model of postrevolutionary contentment, since he had the misfortune to live 'in an age in which he was as little understood by the party *for* whom, as by that *against* whom, he had contended' (ibid.: I, 37). The nebulosity of both instances I have quoted promises a correction or clarification outside the instance itself. Hence the need for the certainties of geometry as an analogy. It is from geometry that Coleridge takes the term 'postulates' in chapter 12:

> Geometry . . . supplies philosophy with the example of a primary intuition, from which every science that lays claim to *evidence* must take its commencement. The mathematician does not begin with a demonstrable proposition, but with an intuition, a practical idea.
>
> (Coleridge 1983: I, 250)

Kant draws authority from geometry in attempting to found a science of Reason, and I shall return to the analogy, but I want here to draw attention to a paradox which has consequences for reading the *Biographia*. Claiming that his propositions derive from 'postulates' on the analogy of geometry (as elsewhere on 'principles') commits

Coleridge to showing the process of derivation, yet he can only promise to do so while actually grounding his arguments on such terms as postulate or principle (or idea, or symbol) which themselves brook no argument. The Coleridgean 'idea' is distinguished from the way the term is used in English empiricism, and is to be associated rather with post-Kantian versions of the *Ding an sich*, an irreducible element. Thus it depends upon an unmediated intuition: 'An IDEA, in the *highest* sense of that word, cannot be conveyed but by a *symbol*; and, except in geometry, all symbols of necessity involve an apparent contradiction' (Coleridge 1983: I, 156). By the time of *On the Constitution of the Church and State* (1829) the two estates can be defined, so the book's sub-title promises, 'according to the idea of each'. An 'idea' is defined as

> that conception of a thing, which is not abstracted from any particular state, form, or mode, in which the thing may happen to exist at this or that time; nor yet generalized from any number or succession of such forms of modes; but which is given by the knowledge of its *ultimate aim*.
>
> (Coleridge 1976: 12)

The 'idea' serves at once as prior ground, 'ultimate aim' and immanent activity.[3]

All the critics I have mentioned so far helpfully contextualize (provide grounds for) this paradox but in taking for granted a description of the text as fragmentary, aporetic, their accounts may not bear much relation to what it is like to read a text which self-consciously anticipates the demurrals of its reader. I don't think that this is to fetishize the language of the text but to point up the biases inherent in McGann's adjuration that we find a point of vantage outside the self-representations of Romanticism. For example, Leask remarks that the letter in chapter 13 'replaces a metaphysical with a rhetorical idiom . . . translating the *Biographia* from a philosophical to a literary-critical idiom' (Leask 1988: 132–3). If this describes Coleridge's procedures it uses something like his own terms to do so, tacitly repeating the gap between the two volumes. Now the course of his discussion, in which is traced the translation of Imagination from civic to religious imperative, shows the inevitably conservative consequences of this division of intellectual labour so its repetition may bespeak its institutional reification: 'One Life', but at least two departments. Every reading of the *Biographia* seems necessarily to involve a redescription and it may then be helpful simply to describe the stages by which Imagination comes to occupy its pivotal position.

One option which has seemed available is to consider the *Biographia* as a kind of Shandean autobiography, a reflexive text of which the 'subject' is always the reader, the 'object' always itself. In this reading, the gap between the volumes would be closed by a concern with the phenomenology of poetry unifying them both into an 'organic Whole' (Coleridge 1983: I, 234). (Elsewhere Coleridge calls poetry 'the *identity* of all other knowledge' [Coleridge 1936: 343].) Such a reading depends though on the desperation of the gesture by which Coleridge says of Wordsworth's philosopher–narrators 'nothing but biography can justify this' (Coleridge 1983: II, 133). 'I have wandered far from the object in view', he says at the beginning of chapter 4 (Coleridge 1983: I, 69), though we don't know what that object is, following this with a partisan history of philosophy. That this is his own philosophical development only becomes clear again at the start of chapter 9, largely a pre-emptive defence against the charge of plagiarizing Schelling, and it's the tenth, avowedly 'a chapter of digressions and anecdotes' (ibid.: I, 168), which returns to the autobiographical. Given the revisionary account of Wordsworth which occupies most of the second volume, though, it may be beguiling to see the *Biographia* as the growth of a philosopher's mind. Where *The Prelude* locates its fall in France, Coleridge's fall would be Wordsworth, the text being a process of accommodation to a present wich would be all sequel – so chapter 5, for example, suddenly reveals itself not as autobiographical reminiscence but as present time. Coleridge's opening paragraph avows that 'the least of what I have written concerns myself personally', and that 'I have used the narration' (ibid.: I, 5). This use is asserted to be an allegorical or exemplary one: 'Every other science pre-supposes intelligence as already existing and complete: the philosopher contemplates it in its growth, and as it were represents its history to the mind from its birth to its maturity' (Coleridge 1983: I, 297). This allegorical usage must depend upon a teleology which is apparent only from the present, or which can be constructed retrospectively. Hegel's *Aesthetics* and *Philosophy of History* structure their account of world history on a biographical model – the Orient, childhood; Greece, adolescence; Rome, manhood; culminating in German culture as an old age which, unlike the diminutions of old age in nature, is an epoch of maturity and strength. Though there are hints of such a model in Coleridge, biographical events are not taken to be merely contingent, to provide terms for the allegory. Abstractions must be grounded in the individuals or communities that use them (even if such users have to be invented). Coleridge's early radical pamphlets and *The Watchman* continually appeal to a consensual 'truth' from which even those who would subscribe to it – chiefly ministers of state – have deviated. But he omits those writings from the list of publications said to constitute his 'whole publicity' which he gives in chapter 3 (Coleridge 1983: I, 53) and the account of the *Watchman* and *Friend* tours rewrites their protagonist as Don Quixote. In autobiographical terms, then, the *Biographia* might be seen as revising an earlier revisionary appeal (to an ideal community whose members all obey the laws of association or are embodied as Lakeland shepherds) in favour of an appeal to a community which is posited as audience as well as example and which can be seen as it sees itself, as a consensual maturity.

Biographia Literaria claims for itself, and is claimed to exemplify, the unity of philosophic and aesthetic speculation with 'practical criticism' (the latter a term which it coins). I want to go on to contend that the *Biographia* has an interest in maintaining the very gap which it claims to bridge, and that it is in the production of such a gap that the text is most exemplary since it continues to be reproduced. The gap is not only between the 'philosophical' and 'critical' volumes of a single text. It can be theorized historically in terms of Coleridge's movement away from the Christian Commonwealth radicalism of the 1790s to a much more conservative use of the same classical republican discourses. I shall argue that this movement, analogous to the apparently concomitant movement away from poetry, is due to Coleridge's conviction that the landed interests – and the paternalistic and aristocratic order they maintained – were in danger of internal collapse through voluntary capitulation to materialist assumptions which might readmit Jacobinism by the back door. The *Biographia*'s insistence on 'speculative philosophy' then is not – or is not merely – obscurantist and elitist, as it is often taken to be, but an attempt, congruent with the educative project of the later *Church and State*, to revitalize a constitutional 'Idea' through appeal to its 'principles'. Such a description of course depends on the provisional acceptance of a vocabulary that is fraught with problems. The circularity inherent to 'idea' we have seen, and the first paragraph of the *Biographia* again adverts to the problem of 'principles'. Autobiography will serve to introduce 'the statement of my principles in Politics, Religion, and Philosophy, and the application of the rules, deduced from philosophical principles, to poetry and criticism' (Coleridge 1983: I, 5). The actual direction, as we have also seen, might be the reverse of what it is claimed to be here.

For such reasons the *Biographia* is often taken to be cautionary rather than exemplary (a claim the epigraph seems to make for the text itself), and can thus be examined as it were pathologically. In the second part of this essay I shall try to read the *Biographia* symptomatically. One means of doing so is through the text's own metaphors of sickness, diagnosis and recovery which are turned explicitly against their employment by Wordsworth and implicitly against other metaphors of logical and geometric certainty. The *Biographia* attempts to accommodate a vocabulary of Reason and interests to a Neoplatonic vocabulary which is likewise immune to sensualism and materialism but which is also durably native. The most famous example of such an attempt is its announcement of a totalizing discourse of Imagination. However I want rather to explore the implications of a suggestion from the earlier, transcended discourse: 'truth soon changes by domestication into power' (Coleridge 1983: I, 5).

II

Since such a suggestion is reflexive, claiming exemplary (or heuristic) status for its own abstract discourse, this exploration will entail some account of the career of the 'Idea' in Coleridge's thinking; and Kant must figure largely in such an account as he figures as hero in the *Biographia*. The *Biographia*'s autobiographical pilgrimage ends at the point where, as Coleridge says in chapter 9, the work of Kant 'took possession of me as with a giant's hand' (Coleridge 1983: I, 153). Two related points need to be made about this 'possession'. First, that it is the mediating, limiting aspects of Kant's project that Coleridge finds liberating. Thus his reading of Kant must self-consciously read against the grain – or, again, allegorically. Second, this kind of reading is necessary because of the political and historical determinants of the writing. To put it crudely, though Coleridge remains an idealist in insisting on the priority of ideas to circumstances, he does not take the further step to claiming the transcendence of metaphysical speculation over historical circumstances. Metaphysical systems, their rise and fall, influence and may coincide with the rise and fall of states (Coleridge 1972: 14–15; 103) but it is not, in the case of his own writings, that Coleridge's durable 'thought' is swallowed by an unfortunately idealist vocabulary.

At the beginning of chapter 9, Coleridge reports his own question: 'is a system of philosophy, as different from mere history and historic classification, possible?' (Coleridge 1983: I, 141). His answer – to argue back to principles and forward to boundaries – is Kantian. This is because the question itself is Kantian. Kant is the apotheosis of an Enlightenment project of developing an epistemology that would represent 'ideas' rather than the 'mere history' of ideas. To do so entails definition by, and limitation, even reduction, to a set of rules that would have a similar status as the rules of geometry. The later *Critique of Judgement* then allows for representation of the suprasensible – those things of which the first *Critique* said we could have no knowledge – within the aesthetic. The beautiful is unreal: the cost of the autonomy of art is its ineffectuality. In the *Biographia* I think that Coleridge wants to incorporate this extension of the possibilities of representation without its corollary. If this is so, it would suggest that Coleridge anticipates the equation of the aesthetic with the mystifying made by some recent critics of Romanticism. To 'demystify' the aesthetic by regarding it as a rather pure form of ideology is not however to render it powerless. Rather, that 'domestication' of which Coleridge speaks might describe the way in which Kant's aesthetic is meant to function – to bridge the cognitive and the ethical; that is, to join them while keeping them apart. Coleridge says that at the time he was living at Stowey 'the *idea* of the Supreme Being appeared to me to be as necessarily implied in all particular modes of being as the idea of infinite space in all the geometrical figures by which space was limited' (Coleridge 1983: I, 200). A limit or boundary implies an unlimited boundlessness within which it is constructed. Yet 'the *idea*' is categorically abstract, distinct from its historical embodiments. The 'idea' is set against the material world, the world of appearances, yet is only discernible *through* appearances; it underlies rather than transcends phenomena.

Reason must limit itself if it is to be a science. All experience (the world of appearances) necessarily follows the laws of the understanding, the totality of which is the possibility of experience. This, the Kantian settlement, depends upon abjuring any claim to knowledge of the referent, the thing-in-itself. Coleridge is not the least of the post-Kantians who themselves questioned that limit, that founding postulate. It is only the signifying functions (the categories of experience) that we can possibly know. The boldness and the exhaustiveness of the Kantian project are finally the same thing: to question limits will also be to redraw them. (Kant himself saw his work as rebutting scepticism, the limitation of which is that it will always fall back on its first assumptions.) The effect of that 'giant's hand' might then be to crush rather than to uplift those who were beckoned by it. Coleridge had to posit the leaving of a gap in the Kantian system. His letter to Humphrey Davy of 9 October 1800 refers to a projected 'Essay on the Elements of Poetry' which 'would in reality be a *disguised* system of Morals & Politics' (Coleridge 1956–71: I, 632). Such covert or allegorical radicalism, Coleridge believes, was forced on Kant too. Since Kant had to speak '*mythically* or equivocally' (Coleridge 1983: I, 157), Coleridge will complete and 'clarify' what he dared not say. Kant's obscurities are 'hints and insinuations referring to ideas, which KANT either did not think it prudent to avow, or which he considered as consistently *left behind* in a pure analysis, not of human nature in toto, but of the speculative intellect alone' (Coleridge 1983: I, 154). While the hint is of the exigencies under which Kant wrote, such a hint also seems elitist, suggesting possession of a secret. And in a passage taken almost verbatim from Schelling the suggestion becomes an insinuation of guild monopoly:

> Whoever is acquainted with the history of philosophy, during the two or three last centuries, cannot but admit, that there appears to have existed a sort of secret and tacit compact among the learned, not to pass beyond a certain limit in speculative science.
>
> (Coleridge 1983: I, 147–8)

Such a plot can come to seem providentially resolved in that the 'abandonment' of such speculation to 'the illiterate and the simple' in turn permits the mystics, Boehme, Fox and others, to arise from among them, but the adjuration is to the guardians of the temple, the priests who first drove out the faithful and let in the money-lenders. Though Burke might have exorcized the spirit of Jacobinism 'from the higher and from the literary classes', it has, 'like the ghost in Hamlet', gone underground (Coleridge 1983: I, 192). An article for *The Courier* in October 1814 had prefigured the *Biographia*'s suspicions of the philosophical closed shop in its descriptions of working-class organizations as a conspiratorial freemasonry, a less visible Jacobinism under a 'control . . . in which every man is made his brother's keeper, and which arming the hand and fixing the eye of all against each, merges the free-will of the individual in the merciless tyranny of the confederation' (Coleridge 1978: II, 388–9). On the other hand, a letter of 1817 refers to the gentry as 'the *Quality Cousin* of Jacobinism' (Coleridge 1956–71: IV, 710). This apparent even-handedness certainly suggests that the ostensible audience Coleridge is addressing is the innovating 'personal interest', the business and professional classes of *Church and State*; and I have suggested that the separation of powers necessary to civil society might find an allegorical repetition in the *Biographia*. However there is a wavering in the terms of address. The landed gentry has hurt itself by the protectionist Corn Law of 1815 so that although Coleridge remains convinced of the primacy of landed property he is convinced too that it should give responsibilities as well as rights to its possessors. At the time of the *Biographia* he is, in effect, addressing an audience he has not yet invented – the third party which, supported by an active commercial class and a static landowning one, will balance both. As J.G.A. Pocock has suggested (Pocock 1985: 190, 282), *Church and State* stands in a post-Enlightenment line starting with Burke in which commerce does not expand and support the progress of 'manners' but rather threatens it, and therefore a national church and a 'clerisy' require property of their own in order to function as the 'counterweights'. Such claims can be grounded in an account of the continuity for Coleridge of 'idea' and 'principles' within the very different events and objects that reveal them. One way of exemplifying this is by seeing in Coleridge's career not the replacement of poetry by metaphysics but the gradual replacement of Wordsworth by Burke as well as by Kant.

The Friend insists on conceiving the subject of a state as moral, a person rather than a thing, an end rather than a means. (So 'prudence' for example is not the utilitarian expediency of Paley, but the practice of reason, the action of the moral law.) Reason alone generates political axioms that have the same status as ideas of space and extension in geometry: 'as there is but one System of Geometry, so according to this Theory there can be but one Constitution and one System of Legislation' (Coleridge 1969: II, 105). Such a Kantian vocabulary will therefore need continual modification as a basis for political practice, according to the habits and customs pertaining in a particular culture. Burke as well as Herder would stand as authority for the claim that an ancient language enshrining habits and customs composes a national 'culture' which is superior to tampering with a constitution, and will outlast it; but alongside this there is in the *Biographia* a more inclusive Hegelian claim: 'Christendom, from its first settlement on feudal rights, has been so far one great body, however imperfectly organised, that a similar spirit will be found in each period to have been acting in all its members' (Coleridge 1983: II, 29). 'Spirit' here is not for all time but of an age, yet this unanimity is newly evident to Coleridge at the time of his dictating the *Biographia*, when 'Englishmen of all classes are restored to their old English notions and feelings' (Coleridge 1983: I, 189). 'Spirit', the protagonist of chapter 12 of the *Biographia*, which 'in all the objects which it views, views only itself' (Coleridge 1983: I, 278), is, like the definitions of poetry advanced against Wordsworth, an entity which is not required to answer to laws not of its own making. This reflexiveness however – 'the principle of our knowing is sought within the sphere of our knowing' (Coleridge 1983: I, 284) – means that the laws it discovers will be those of its own principles.

Poetry speaks for a culture. Shakespeare figures in a familiar role as the transmitter of solidarity and reconciliation for the national culture. Yet Coleridge's famous announcement that he has 'snapped [his] squeaking baby-trumpet of Sedition' (Coleridge 1956–71: I, 240), his turn towards constitutional defence rather than attack, is followed by the announcement of his abandonment of (or by) poetry. The former is confirmed by the new French constitution, drawn up by the Triumvirate in 1799 and unfavourably contrasted with the balance of interests in Britain; the latter can be ascribed to the Wordsworth that Coleridge constructed. In December 1800 Coleridge wrote, to Thelwall: 'As to Poetry, I have altogether abandoned it, being convinced that I never had the essentials of poetic Genius, and that I mistook a strong desire for original power' (Coleridge 1956–71: I, 656). Then, three days later, in a letter to Francis Wrangham: 'our literary occupations . . . are still more distant than our residences – He is a great, a true Poet – I am only a kind of Metaphysician' (Coleridge 1956–71: I, 658). This does seem to acknowledge a theoretical as well as an empirical distinction of these roles which is both cancelled and maintained by the *Biographia*. Wordsworth's failure to fulfil Coleridge's prescription does not prove the inefficacy of the prescription. Yet the continued claims for the appeasement of these roles are confronted with Coleridge's continued disclaimers – the repeated insistence for example that not everyone can be a philosopher. The revision of Wordsworth's preface which occupies most of the second volume asserts the poetic symbol, broadly defined, against literalist interpretations of the programme for 'the language really used by men'. Coleridge stresses as a contrary 'truth' a poetic 'genius' which is beyond the language community, a thing *per se* which stands alone. The symbol is therefore claimed as a kind of self-sufficient metaphor. In wishing to distinguish an expressive from a discursive function of language, then, Coleridge tends to posit a language without contingency, like the logic of geometry. This is prefigured by the claim Kant makes for the normative function of geometry and physics in the preface to the second edition of *The Critique of Pure Reason*, recommending that metaphysics imitate the revolution they have undergone.

There is of course a lengthy history of recourse to geometry as an analogy for epistemological certainty.[4] Kant had argued in his inaugural dissertation of 1770 that mathematics could be concerned only with appearances and was thus insufficient as a paradigm for Reason. By the time of the first *Critique* he wants to identify laws of the understanding to which even laws of nature will be subject, and pure mathematics (geometry) functions as both paradigm and example of the synthetic *a priori* on which transcendental philosophy rests. Synthetic judgements are those which, unlike analytic judgements, cannot be contradicted (Kant 1953: 17–24) and the limits of the understanding can be plotted only by investigating the very existence, the scope and validity of synthetic *a priori* judgements. Even space and time must be established by necessary relation to the objects of experience, and the grounding principles of mathematics are those which begin in the 'concepts' of the understanding rather than in the 'intuitions' yielded by objects. (Arithmetical calculations would be an example of the latter.) To deny that the axioms of (Euclidian) geometry are synthetic *a priori* judgements would be to deny the possibility of perceiving space and time (Kant 1933: 192–201). Constructing figures and numbers *makes sense* (*Sinn*) of *a priori* concepts. The law rests on its circularity, or even tautology; nevertheless it is crucial for Kant's rebuttal of Hume. Synthetic *a priori* judgements are arrived at by necessity and not by custom, originating in the 'pure understanding' and not deduced from experience (Kant 1953: 10). Hume's separation of mathematics (analytic) from metaphysics (synthetic) would (for Kant) logically lead to his denying the axioms of pure mathematics or to the redundancy of metaphysics. The assault on scepticism and associationism, for which Hume is the adversary for Kant, and of which the axioms of geometry are the crucial case, is certainly paralleled (or narrativized) in the *Biographia*.

We move from the sublime to – well, to the sublime when Coleridge cites an authority nearer home at the start of the *Biographia*, Bowyer having taught him at school that 'poetry . . . had a logic of its own as severe as that of science; and more difficult, because more subtle, more complex, and dependent on more and more fugitive causes' (Coleridge 1983: I, 9). The 'severe' but unsystematic 'logic' connoted by the term poetry can be connected with Coleridge's attacks on the claims of political economy to be a science in *The Friend*, but it also recapitulates the terms of address from Wordsworth. In the *Biographia* mathematics is described as 'the only province of knowledge which man has succeeded in erecting into a pure science' (Coleridge 1983: I, 297–8). In Wordsworth's *Prelude* it features as the name for a desire for that which is non-contingent and which cannot betray; that it is also non-organic, however, reveals it as metonymic of, rather than alternative to, the 'Reason' which the revolutionary state had promised to erect as law and reveals it, further, to be similarly deluded. In Book X of *The Prelude* the 'sick' Wordsworth (at 'the crisis of that strange disease' in the 1850 version [Wordsworth 1959: 419; 1850: XI, 306]), 'Turned towards mathematics, and their clear / And solid evidence' (ibid.: 418; 1805: X, 903–4) and then to Coleridge, who lent 'a living help / To regulate my soul' (ibid.: 906–7). Nevertheless, James K. Chandler makes the case convincingly that in *The Prelude* Coleridge figures mostly as patient rather than doctor: to 'represent the English mind in disarray, in illness, and in need of rescue' (Chandler 1984: 239).

This is consistent with Coleridge's self-diagnosis, and his own 'crisis' is resolved by an insistence upon the continuity of internal principles surviving the breaks seemingly enforced by external events. So for example he can reprint the 1795 *Moral and Political Lecture* with its equivocations over Robespierre and its insistence on '*bottoming* on fixed Principles' (Coleridge 1969: I, 326) in the 1818 *Friend*. The rhetoric is consistent, and Coleridge becomes less inclined to separate an admiration for Burke's rhetoric from the political ends which it serves. The British constitution can be defended as a balance of property interests, by favourable comparison both to Jacobin France and to ancient Rome, on which the Republic purported to model itself. Coleridge allies himself to a mixed constitution in which a hereditary, land-owning aristocracy would countervail the financiers who provided loan-broking services for Pitt's government. These are the arguments of the eighteenth-century 'Country Party' and can be connected with Coleridge's movement away from Unitarian radicalism and towards the established church, again by virtue of its capacity to provide a counterweight to the executive and legislature, and by favourable contrast to the French church. Counter-balances are not to be supplied by legislation (seen as interference which would deny free agency and thus be immoral) but by education and religion. The national church must be seen in constitutional not doctrinal terms and is to be distinguished from the Christian church. As such, its constitutional function can be that of such a counterweight. So, in *Church and State*, the educative 'clerisy' the church maintains has the potential to mediate between the people (whom it ought to 'cultivate') and the court and state (to whom it was too exclusively 'clinging'). Coleridge has moved a long way from the assertion of 1796 that property is the origin of all evil (Coleridge 1956–71: I, 213–14): property is essential to the church if it is to remain as a moral alternative to the (quite legitimate) property interests of legislature and executive and thus to become the agency of its own 'idea'. There is also a softening in Coleridge's attitude towards non-landed (commercial) wealth. The National Debt for example can be defended as the 'cement' of the state, a material repetition of cultural unity (Coleridge 1969: I, 233). (Again, this is in contradistinction to the apparent destruction of commercial interests by revolutionary France.) Hence the terms of praise for the current and most recent ministries, of Lord Liverpool and Spencer Perceval, in the *Biographia*:

> the concentration of the national force to one object; the abandonment of the *subsidizing* policy, so far at least as neither to goad or bribe the continental courts into war till the convictions of their subjects had rendered it a war of their own seeking; and above all, in their manly and generous reliance on the good sense of the English people, and on that loyalty which is linked to the very heart of the nation by the system of credit and the interdependence of property.
>
> (Coleridge 1983: I, 212–13)

Once again an assertion of equilibrium implicitly demands to be set against a disequilibrium evident from reading a text whose declared fulcrum is absent, or is present only in summary. The providential rhetoric here is consistent with the rescindment of the 1800 preface in the *Biographia*'s second volume:

> The feelings with which, as Christians, we contemplate a mixed congregation rising or kneeling before their common maker: Mr. Wordsworth would have us entertain at *all* times as men, and as readers and by the excitement of this lofty, yet prideless impartiality in *poetry*, he might hope to have encouraged its continuance in *real life*.
>
> (Coleridge 1983: II, 130)

Nigel Leask calls this 'perhaps [Coleridge's] most successful recuperation of the *Preface*'s egalitarianism', and goes on to comment that 'Coleridge here returns Wordsworth's "good shepherd" to the heavens, preferring a religious to a civic definition of communal parity' (Leask 1988: 63). In the first of these quotations from the *Biographia* the assertion of social equilibrium, the willy-nilly interdependence of the parts (and, presumably, the subjects) of a state seems to allow the individual space only for the private activities of reflection, and thus far we have to agree with Leask's description of Coleridge's career as compact with a migration of 'virtue' from the political to the private sphere. However, we do not need to be ambitious of recuperating Coleridge to find 'hints and insinuations' in his own discourse that he is at least conscious of such a movement. Even in the second of these quotations the vision of religious harmony, like that of social equality, is momentary, and not obviously capable of 'continuance in *real life*'. Furthermore, as even a sketch of his response to Kant suggests, limits are treated as demarcation lines of past error rather than as setting prospective limits to speculation. It is, though, Schiller rather than Coleridge who demonstrates that Kant can be historicized and politicized, and even the abandonment of a retrospective mode in the *Biographia* can be read as an attempt to displace the awkward recalcitrance of contingency into a scheme which is absolute or which is governed by rigid laws (in the first quotation above, those of fulfilled providence) – whether such a scheme is named as a set of principles, as Reason, or as geometry. We can accord with Michael Fischer's claim that 'when Coleridge chooses metaphysics over politics, he is not choosing between evasion and power but between two kinds of power' (Fischer 1982: 458). We ought to do so though knowing that we thereby accede to Coleridge's idiom – hoping perhaps that distinction is not division (Coleridge 1983: II, 11).

It may be, in other words, that this is another way of demonstrating McGann's argument for the pernicious tenacity of influence of Coleridge's discourse – an idiom of ideological exclusion and retreat whose function then as now is largely to dignify its user. Allowing Coleridge's claim for a consistency of 'principles' in his ethical and political views might only lead us to the inference that as an ethical or political virtue consistency is overrated. For Jon Klancher, in *The Making of English Reading Audiences*, the texts by Coleridge with which I have been concerned represent the culmination or crisis of the relation to an audience (Klancher 1987). (His account also squares with Hamilton's description of Arnold repeating and reifying Coleridge's exemplary failure.) Klancher's book as a whole is an important intervention in the debate over 'the Romantic ideology'. It considers the relation between the individual act of reading and its location within a set of historically collective acts, the relation between the idealized critical construct of 'the reader' and the empirical audience. Coleridge is taken as a figure who attempts to carve out an ideal audience, a 'clerisy' of virtuoso readers distinguished both from the newly self-conscious cultural power of the middle class, dieting at the 'two public *ordinaries* of Literature, the circulating libraries and the periodical press' (Coleridge 1972: 38), and from the nascent mass audience – distinguished, that is, not by class but by its transcendence of class: 'Coleridge sought to construct an audience that was *also* an institution, a body of readers and writers capable of governing the relations between all the emerging audiences of the nineteenth century over whom, individually, no institution could claim control' (Klancher 1987: 151). Coleridge posits an audience for the 1809 *Friend* whose centre is nowhere and whose circumference is bounded on opposite sides by Cobbett's twopenny *Political Register* (which began to appear in the year before *Biographia* was published) and the *Edinburgh Review* (Coleridge 1956–71: III, 143), but which is *outside* the system of 'circulation' of either. As this suggests, the actual acts of reading Coleridge describes – interpretative procedures influenced by the German Higher Criticism and a writing style contradistinguished from the 'Anglo-Gallican styles' of disconnected periods which characterize Thomas Paine and, by inference, 'Kubla Khan' – are themselves contemporary, descriptions of phenomenal process which cancel and contain the past yet which continually defer their meaning to a time when it can be institutionally embodied. Like the Bible, the English constitution can only be 'read' by those equipped to interpret it in the present as 'Idea':

> At the heart of the clerisy lies a text that cannot be written and thus an 'audience' that cannot be touched or seen. To become clerics, certain readers have to be drawn from social audiences. And once abstracted from an audience that existed outside himself, the clerical reader must finally realize, in the power of symbolic interpretation, the audience within himself. . . . What will empower the clerisy in its cultural work is the capability to realize from within what ordinary audiences only fitfully recognize outside themselves, a collective apprehension of an Idea.
>
> (Klancher 1987: 168–9)

Klancher's book, like Hamilton's, seems to remind Coleridge's present readers of something variously flattering or embarrassing to them: that they themselves are the 'cultural workers', the 'clerisy' on whom the burden of these imperatives falls. If Coleridge's own discourse continues to supply many of the terms by which it can itself be criticized, this very reflexiveness has seemed to make it difficult of radical appropriation in the way that occurred for example with the 'anarchic' liberalism of Shelley's political writings.

In retrospect the motto 'Knowledge is Power' from the Prospectus to *The Watchman* has, like the inscription on the pedestal of Ozymandias, become ironic. Coleridge cites it as an instance of youthful folly (Coleridge 1983: I, 179): the truth will not set you free, rather it will allow you to intuit a realm of freedom. The ideal of 'the creative and self-sufficing power of absolute *Genius*' (Coleridge 1983: I, 31) is that it *is* ideal, and thus contradistinguished from being distracted by (or dallying with) materiality and contingency as are those of mere talent and as is France (Coleridge 1969: I, 419–23). Those who display absolute genius 'rest content between thought and reality, as it were in an intermundium of which their own living spirit supplies the *substance*, and their imagination the ever-varying *form*' (Coleridge 1983: I, 31). This 'intermundium' is that 'middle state of mind . . . unfixed and wavering' (Coleridge 1960: II, 103) which defines Imagination. The aesthetic is a realm of truths which are not instrumental or whose political efficacy will need to be asserted as immanent or hegemonic.

This would bring us to questions of subsequent influence (or domestication) for which I have, as they say, no space here; but I can suggest ways in which the question might be posed. It is not the case that Hamilton or Leask construct a 'native' Coleridge in opposition to a transcendental and reactionary one – a construction which I might seem to have nodded at myself before heading for Germany. It is interesting to note that there is a shorthand for German idealism from Peacock (in his satire of Coleridge as Mr Flosky in *Nightmare Abbey*) and Byron through to Marilyn Butler which is repeated from within (or perhaps, apocalyptically, *at the end of*) German philosophy itself:

> to call to mind the enormous influence that 'German philosophy' – I hope you understand its right to quotation marks – has exercised throughout the whole of Europe, there is no doubt that a certain *virtus dormitiva* had a share in it: it was a delight to the noble idlers, the virtuous, the mystics, artists, three-quarter Christians, and political obscurantists of all nations, to find, thanks to German philosophy, an antidote to the still predominant sensualism which overflowed from the last century into this, in short – *sensus assoupire*.
>
> (Nietzsche 1966: 19)

That is not Marx but Nietzsche, in 1886, from those sections of *Beyond Good and Evil* which work fragmentarily, like the *Biographia*, to dispose of generalized untenable philosophical fashions of the previous century.[5] Seventy years earlier Coleridge ends the first volume of *Biographia* by positing this very tradition as a prospect. This prospective ambition is dwelt on less often than is the retrospective mode of the *Biographia*. The critique of Wordsworth in the second volume is read as settling accounts with the turn of the last century while the eventual acknowledgement of a literary culture dominated not by Wordsworth but by Lord Byron is discussed less often. Even those readings which enrol Coleridge in a tradition going from Schelling and Hegel to Kierkegaard and Nietzsche thereby extend the developmental model of the first volume of the *Biographia*, aligning it with a philosophical tradition it recognizably invokes for itself. A means of filling the ostentatious gaps in the text is provided by the text itself. Identifying its reactionary ambitions facilitates a reading which can leave those ambitions uncriticized. I have suggested here that the gap or gaps evident in the *Biographia* function heuristically and that they represent alternatives that are finally to be superseded rather than resolved. Coleridge claims that this idealization can be accomplished without compromise of principles. The alternatives themselves can be variously named – French and German, theory and practice, Kant and Wordsworth, and so on. I would add two suggestions: first, that a gap between conceptions of the state and of civil society as modes for the domestication of power is implicit in the *Biographia*, and second, that this might be correlated with the gap between conceptions of post-Enlightenment discourse as instrumental or as communicative which preoccupies so much of our thinking now.

NOTES

1 See Engell, *The Creative Imagination* (Engell 1981).

2 In a recent essay McGann (1989) has dealt explicitly with the *Biographia*. The first two sections mount an argument that has become familiar: first they redescribe Coleridge's text as an exemplary autobiography (exemplary in its demonstration of fidelity to principles even as the autobiographical mode *discovers* those principles); then they redescribe the stand-off between Coleridge and Wordsworth as a stand-off between an 'idea' which is always consciously mediated, an ideology of which poetry is 'the perfect form', and a poetry which is committed only to details and contingencies, to an 'unmediated vision'. But it is the third section of the essay which makes its own contention, based largely on a letter from Byron to Murray in October 1817 which both attacks Coleridge's attack on the 'Jacobinism' of *Bertram* and announces Byron's completion of what becomes the first canto of *Don Juan*: 'that Byron's *Don Juan* was consciously conceived as a response to the *Biographia*' (McGann 1989: 247).

3 Compare Coleridge's annotation of a passage from Hooker which seems to talk about a kind of Unmoved Mover, and to claim that, by analogy, law depends on a lawgiver who cannot therefore be subject to the law: 'An Idea is a POWER . . . that constitutes its own Reality – and is, in order of Thought, necessarily antecedent to the Things, in which it is, more or less adequately, realized' (Coleridge 1984: 1134).

4 For one example, see Hobbes's employment of the analogy in discussing 'error' in *Leviathan*, part I, chapter IV ('Of speech'). Under the marginal heading 'Necessity of Definitions' Hobbes writes:

> in Geometry (which is the only Science that it hath pleased God hitherto to bestow on mankind,) men begin at settling the significations of their words; which settling of signification, they call *Definitions*; and place them in the beginning of their reckoning.
>
> (Hobbes 1968: 105)

Some would argue that there is a difference in kind rather than just in degree in Kant's attempt to ground transcendental reason in a synthetic *a priori* which is not just exemplified by, but functionally similar to geometry. Coleridge uses the Kantian trope for purposes similar to those of Hobbes. I owe this reference, as well as several of the ideas in this essay, to Paul Kenny. For other kinds of help I am indebted to the co-editors of this volume, and to Deborah Vitai.

5 Section 11. The reference is to Molière, whom Nietzsche has just quoted:

Quia est in eo virtus dormitiva
Cujus est natura sensus assoupire

('Because it contains a sleepy faculty whose nature it is to put the senses to sleep.')

4

SHELLEY'S 'MAGNETIC LADIES': ROMANTIC MESMERISM AND THE POLITICS OF THE BODY

Nigel Leask

Anglo-American literary scholarship has by no means ignored the influence of mesmerism or 'animal magnetism' on writers like Coleridge, Shelley, Dickens, Poe, Hawthorne and Browning, but has tended to be inhibited by a crippling methodological distinction between mesmerism as an 'exploded' pseudo-science and literature as a 'live' discourse located within the jurisdiction of the aesthetic (Levere 1980, Dawson 1986, Kaplan 1975, Falk 1969, Tatar 1978). From the perspective of a Popperian history of science, the proscription of mesmerism from the 'scientific/mechanistic tradition' by the French Royal Commission's inquiry into the practice in 1784 seems with hindsight to be perfectly justifiable: as an empirically unfalsifiable theory, mesmerism belongs to the realm of 'imagination' rather than of science (Weyant 1980: 77–114). And yet the guardians of the cuckoo's nest known as the aesthetic have been no more hospitable to this disciplinary changeling than the heirs of scientific positivism. In the most authoritative current study of Shelley and mesmerism, Paul Dawson endorses the distinction by limiting the literary status of mesmerism, implicitly designated as a 'pseudo-science', to the role of image-repertoire for the metaphors of magnetism which litter Shelley's poetry. According to Dawson, a literal/historical reading of these metaphors risks the methodological bankruptcy of making 'the poet's work hostage to the advancement of scientific inquiry which proceeds by deconstructing the fictions and figures of its precursors. Mesmerism has now been relegated to the prehistory of scientific psychology;

but the progress of research has not superseded *Prometheus Unbound*' (Dawson 1986: 34).

The present essay takes an altogether more relativistic stance inspired by Ludmilla Jordanova's demand that 'Scholars may usefully designate as science anything that came under the term in the past – any attempt to apply modern evaluative criteria in order to separate past activities into genuine science and pseudoscience is profoundly unhistorical' (Jordanova 1986: 30). As a complement to this, I follow Jerome McGann's critical disengagement from a trans-historical faith in the 'Romantic Ideology', that 'uncritical absorption in romanticism's own self-representations', to approach the literary work as a network of interwoven discourses in which the universalizing (and epistemologically irreducible) ideology of the aesthetic is one thread amongst many (McGann 1983: 1). To this end, the present essay brackets both the history of mesmerism and the weighty question of Romantic aesthetics in order to address the broader issue of the relationship of the nervous body to voice and text in the Romantic period. Taking as my starting point Coleridge's suggestive identification of the 'zoomagnetic influx' with the 'active imagination', I argue that the therapeutic prerogative linking poetry with mesmerism in Coleridge's terms should be taken literally as the source of parallel strategies, in the early years of the nineteenth century, to engender power in the nervous fibres of the body and educe the utterance of a primordial or 'lucid' voice transcending both the otherness of the female body and the excess of the written signifier. Because Shelley was unhappy with the Coleridgean paradigm – which he understood as the colonization of the sensitive (female) body by the (male) will – he sought to reorientate both poetry and mesmerism to his own ulterior ends, translating the 'gentle control' of Pygmalion into the terrible gaze of the Medusa.

THE EYES OF THE MEDUSA

At the end of June 1816, Byron, his physician John Polidori, Percy and Mary Shelley and Mary's half-sister Claire Clairmont organized a competition in the Villa Diodati, on the shores of Lake Geneva, to write and narrate the best supernatural story. The competition is famous for having given birth to *Frankenstein* and the tale of vampirism which would be the principal source for Bram

Stoker's *Dracula*; Shelley's 'contribution' tends to be forgotten, not least because it was written down as the case history of a hysterical attack rather than a supernatural narrative. Because of the gap in Mary Shelley's *Journal* for the all-important period between 14 May 1815 and 20 July 1816, Polidori's *Diary* is the only eye-witness account of what happened to Shelley in the small hours of 19 June 1816. The significance of this, which I take to be Shelley's first mesmeric experience, must be stressed in the light of Tom Medwin's later claim that before his own arrival at Pisa in October 1820 'Shelley had never previously heard of mesmerism, and I shewed him a treatise I had composed' (Medwin 1847: II, 49). If Medwin is correct, then mesmeric allusions or images in Shelley's poetry before late 1820 (including *Prometheus Unbound*) must be attributed to the operation of some unconscious *Zeitgeist.* However Paul Dawson rightly disputes Medwin's claim on the grounds that Shelley had read Southey's *Letters from England* (1807) in 1810–11 and again in 1815, and that the work devoted a whole chapter to a detailed account of the mesmeric theory and practice of its foremost early practitioner in England, Dr De Mainauduc (Dawson 1986: 16; see also Porter 1985). Polidori's knowledge of mesmerism provides another powerful refutation of Medwin's claim, particularly as he was no amateur in the mould of Medwin. Graduating in medicine from Edinburgh University at the age of nineteen in 1815, Polidori had published his Latin dissertation on somnambulism, *De Oneirodynia, Disputatio Medica Inauguralis, Quaedam de Morbo, Oneirodymia, Complectens*, the year before his European tour with Byron. He was at home in the cosmopolitan scientific and literary culture of Lake Geneva where mesmerism was very much 'on the agenda' in 1816. The *Diary* tells us that on 5 June Polidori had discussed somnambulism with the Swiss Dr Odier who had given him a manuscript on the subject, and later he dined with Mme de Staël at Coppet, presenting her with a copy of his dissertation. Doubtless their talk on somnambulism led to discussion of a cognate phenomenon, mesmerism, which was enjoying something of a revival in France and Germany after the publication in 1813 of J.P.F. Deleuze's *Histoire critique du magnetism animal* and in 1815 of C.A.F. Kluge's *Versuch einer Darstellung des Animalischen Magnetismus*. Mme de Staël's husband, a 'Swedenborgian friend of Lavater and Saint-Martin, [had] mesmerized with the founders of animal magnetism, including Franz Mesmer himself' (Darnton 1968: 149). The 'Romantic generation' of Puysegur, Deleuze and Kluge had updated Mesmer's mechanistic theories, particularly in the light of Galvani's experiments with animal electricity in the 1790s, and by 1815 the phenomenon was being taken seriously by many of the leading philosophical and scientific lights of Europe, including Schelling, Benjamin Constant and S.T. Coleridge. Mme de Staël, barometer of Franco-German intellectual fashion, was no exception, although she apparently remained sceptical; this didn't prevent her 'ailing mystic mentor', A.G. de Schlegel, being magnetized and converted by Dr D.-F. Koreff during the celebrated Prussian mesmerist's visit to Coppet (Darnton 1968: 149). Polidori's interest in mesmerism would almost certainly have been communicated to Shelley, even in the unlikely case of his never having encountered it in England; on 8 June, for instance, Polidori described a rowing party with Shelley, Mary and Claire in which they 'talked, till the ladies brains whizzed with giddiness, about idealism'. Laid up with a sprained ankle in the days after 15 June, he sought to salve his wounded pride, after the company had pronounced that a play he had begun 'was worth nothing', by displaying his medical knowledge. 'Shelley and I had a conversation about principles – whether man was to be thought merely as an instrument' (Polidori 1911: 121).

Polidori's professional knowledge of somnambulism and mesmerism is an important factor in his account of the genesis of Shelley's 'ghost story', an 'inspiration' which seems to have taken the pathological form of a nervous hallucination. Polidori's account – which I quote in full – troubles the poet's metaphor (in the *Defence of Poetry*) of the mind in creation as 'a fading coal which some invisible influence, like an inconstant wind, awakens to transitory brightness' (Shelley 1988: 294).

> Twelve o'clock really began to talk ghostly. L[ord] B[yron] repeated some verses of Coleridge's Christabel, of the witch's breast;
>
> [The beautiful witch Geraldine, having found her way into Christabel's castle and bed-chamber, has cast a dreaming-spell upon the latter and is undressing in front of her]
>
> Beneath the lamp the lady bowed,
> And slowly rolled her eyes around;
> Then drawing in her breath aloud
> Like one that shuddered, she unbound

> The cincture from beneath her breast;
> Her silken robe, and inner vest
> Dropt to her feet, and in full view,
> Behold! her bosom and half her side –
> Are lean and old and foul of hue.
> O shield her! shield sweet Christabel!

> when silence ensued, and Shelley, suddenly shrieking, and putting his hands to his head, ran out of the room with a candle. Threw water on his face, and after gave him ether. He was looking at Mrs. Shelley [Mary], and suddenly thought of a woman he had heard of who had eyes instead of nipples, which, taking hold of his mind, horrified him.
>
> (Polidori 1911: 128)

Nora Crook and Derek Guiton have recently sought the source for Shelley's hallucination in the episode in Rousseau's *Confessions*, when Jean-Jacques shies away in horror from a Venetian prostitute with a malformed nipple ('teton borgne') (Crook and Guiton 1986: 175). Whilst this fits the *Christabel* passage well, it loses the sense of Shelley's fear of the female *gaze* communicated in Medwin's versions of the story: a beautiful woman 'looking down on him with four eyes, two of which were in the centre of her uncovered breasts' and his 'conjur[ing] up some frightful woman of an acquaintance of his at home, a kind of Medusa, who was suspected of having eyes in her breasts' (Medwin 1847: I, 258; 1824: 149). The disturbing sexual orientation of the image is clear, and we should bear in mind the fact that the reader is no less a figure than Byron, whose very arrival in the drawing-room at Coppet had recently caused a lady to be 'carried out fainting' (Polidori 1966: 259). Despite the sexual ventriloquism which he doubtless deployed in his reading of *Christabel*, Byron's position as reader is performatively male and exemplifies the contemporary reading theory in which, as Peter de Bolla has argued, the reader 'in some measure produces the subject positions available for the individual members of the audience; it is his power as an orator that determines the framework for the experience of subjectivity for his listeners, *his* power that holds them in sway' (de Bolla 1989: 150). This body of theory derives (in significantly modified form) many of its assumptions from the discourse on the sublime, 'a legislative discourse that openly excludes the feminine from the experience it describes, the sublime, through its absolute distinction between a masculine sublimity and feminine beauty' (ibid.: 257). Precisely because the reading scene which we are discussing exists at the level of anecdote, analysis of the affective circuits at work can only be conjectural.

Shelley's nervous 'transport' may not have been as unusual as it seems to the modern reader. Medwin describes how Shelley himself could achieve an effect 'almost electric' with his recitation of *The Witch of Atlas* (Holmes 1974: 621) and in an Italian review of his friend, the *improvvisatore* Tommaseo Sgricci, Shelley described how he 'ellettrizzava il Teatro' (Dawson 1981: 25). In 1821 Shelley translated the *Ion*, Plato's dialogue on the transport of the poetic rhapsodist, a work from which he had drawn while composing the *Defence of Poetry* the previous year (Dawson 1981: 22). Shelley here emphasizes the spontaneous, involuntary ('feminine') nature of poetic inspiration, a magnetic virtue running from the poet through his rhapsodist to the auditors (and through successive civilizations) and is very reluctant to admit that the poet has any conscious or willed control over his language. *Epipsychidion* imitated the verbal, unwritten rhapsody of the *improvvisatore* and Shelley described his play *Hellas* as 'written at the suggestion of the events of the moment . . . a mere improvise' (Shelley 1970: 446). A paradigmatic case for Shelley would have been Mme de Staël's Corinne, heroine of her eponymous novel, an *improvvisatrice* who 'electrified the imagination of [the hero] Oswald' and represented 'the image of our beloved country Italy' (de Staël 1807: I, 61, 73). Shelley's remarks on the art of the Italian *improvvisatore* – possibly following de Staël – deploy a dichotomy between British reason and Italian imagination, and it is significant that he identifies himself with the latter; 'the most distinctive character of Italy', he wrote, is that 'among us the imagination performs in an instant the work which the reason accomplishes among others in a long period of time, or after many attempts' (Dawson 1981: 29). Shelley's remarks are important for his development of the figure of the 'Magnetic Lady' which I will argue is prevalent in his later Italian work.

Shelley's 'spontaneous' theory of inspiration is in clear contrast to Byron's *control* of what is in Coleridge's poem a scene of feminine seduction, the 'mastering' of Christabel by the sinister Geraldine. When *Christabel* was published – I will come back to the significance of the fact that it was, in 1816, *un*published – its author gave instructions for the 'vocalisation' of its 'new principle' of metre based on the counting of accents rather than syllables, and on the variation of the number of the latter as a means of controlling 'transition[s] in the nature of the imagery or passion' (Coleridge 1912: I, 215). Coleridge, unlike Shelley, insisted that poetry in general and metre in particular is a marriage of a *female* principle of spontaneous excitement and a *male* principle of will: 'these elements are formed into metre *artificially*, by a *voluntary* act . . . the traces of present *volition* should throughout the metrical language be proportionally discernible. . . . There must not only be a partnership, but a union; an interpenetration of passion and will, of *spontaneous* impulse and of *voluntary* purpose' (Coleridge 1983: II, 65). Possibly taking direct issue with Coleridge's theory in the *Biographia*, Shelley would argue, in the *Defence of Poetry*, that 'Poetry is not subject to the control of the active powers of the mind, and that its birth and recurrence have no necessary connection with consciousness or will' (Shelley 1988: 296). Claire Clairmont wrote in her diary, shortly after seeing Sgricci perform for the first time, 'A great Poet resembles Nature – he is a Creator and Destroyer . . . the torrent of his sentiments should flow like one wave after the other, each distinctly formed and visible yet linked between its predecessor and its follower as to form between them both by beauty and necessity an indissoluble connection' (Clairmont 1968: 195). I suggest that Shelley's poetics sought to privilege a spontaneous, vocalized word based on the model of the *improvvisatore* as a feminized, 'sensitive' alternative to a Coleridgean poetics of the will in which the body of the reciter/poet was a transparent *symbol* for the written text it produced or articulated.

In the Diodati episode Shelley identifies Byron's voice with an evil and seductive will in the persona of the uncanny Geraldine and himself with the (entranced) Christabel, an identification which announces a disturbing transgression of sexual roles. The stable economy of male/female, beauty/sublimity is disrupted and his discovery of the male sublime in the feminine body – a mesmeric effect – transports Shelley with the force of shock. Hence the symmetry between Geraldine's seductive unveiling, to reveal the sublime of terror – shapeless and discoloured – in the place of a shapely breast; in the eighteenth-century tradition of Hogarth and Erasmus Darwin the female breast, the sine-curve, was the archetype of the 'line of beauty'. Shelley's hysteria is caused by his startled apprehension of the commanding and seducing male eye – the will or phallus – in the place of that absent signifier of passive feminine beauty. I want to read this episode – Byron's 'vocalisation' of Geraldine – as an instance of the 'Medusa effect' (following Medwin's account), which Shelley described in his 1819 poem 'On the Medusa of Leonardo Da Vinci': 'it is less the horror than the grace / Which turns the gazer's spirit into stone' (Shelley 1943: 582, lines 9–10). The passage does of course invite psychoanalytical interpretation, and the force of Shelley's horrified perception of the 'female sublime' seems to be strikingly reiterated by Freud's fragment entitled 'Medusa's Head' in the *Standard Works*. For Freud, the sight of the Medusa's head betokens castration, and 'makes the spectator stiff with terror, turns him to stone . . . becoming stiff means an erection. Thus in the original situation it offers consolation to the spectator; he is still in possession of a penis, and the stiffening reassures him of the fact' (Freud 1955: XVIII, 273). Shelley's 'Medusa effect' intends an inversion of the controlling power of the male will, what I will describe as the 'Pygmalion effect' of Coleridge's theory, so that the female gaze turns a man into stone in the place of the male gaze turning a statue into fleshly woman. But Freud's account of the Medusa highlights the *displaced* phallocentrism of Shelley's version; the ambiguity of Freud's 'stiffening' signals a moment of phallic return which – in the case of Shelley – normally marks the collapse of his bid to unbind the Promethean male will. I will argue that the only poem in which he partially succeeded – *The Witch of Atlas* – involves bringing the Medusa's petrified man back to life as a hermaphrodite with *both* male and female genitals. Shelley's disturbance at the Diodati was surely not in the nature of an initiation into the 'horror and the grace' of what might be termed the feminine sublime, but I suggest that the gaze of the Medusa served him in many of his subsequent writings as the model for powerful transport in an intended opposition to that form of masculine voluntarism – exemplified by the Coleridgean paradigm – which regulated conventional accounts of the poetic and mesmeric affect.

I want at this point to consider Shelley's hysterical response to *Christabel* in the light of an interesting comment on the poem's reception made by Coleridge in *Biographia Literaria*. The text of *Christabel* from which Byron read was a manuscript in the hand of Sara Hutchinson which Coleridge had sent him in October 1815: the poem was actually published (in a slightly different version) in May/June 1816 and savaged by the *Edinburgh Review* (XXVII [1816], 58–67). Coleridge, probably incorrectly, considered the attack was Hazlitt's, and in the 'Conclusion' to the *Biographia* (written – and published – in 1817) sought to account for the discrepancy between the 'disproportionate' praise his recitals of the poem had received *before* its publication, and the 'malignity and personal hatred' that it had encountered in printed form. The most palpable reason which Coleridge gives for the discrepancy between recitation and publication is highly significant for my present argument, and I quote it in full.

> [It is] chiefly, for the excitement and temporary sympathy of feeling, which the recitation of the poem by an admirer, especially if he be at once a warm admirer and a man of acknowledged celebrity [such as Walter Scott or Lord Byron], calls forth in the audience. For this is really a species of Animal Magnetism, in which the enkindling Reciter, by perpetual comment of looks and tones, lends his own will and apprehensive faculty to his Auditors. They *live* for the time within the dilated sphere of his intellectual Being. It is equally possible, though not equally common, that a reader left to himself should sink below the poem, as that the poem left to itself should flag beneath the feelings of the reader.
> (Coleridge 1983: II, 239–40)

Coleridge's peevish phonocentrism invites a reading of the Derridean kind which would seek an explanation in terms of the privileging of voice over writing which for Derrida is constitutive of 'western metaphysics'. Peter de Bolla's more localized account of the way in which late eighteenth-century theories of rhetoric prescribe a specific body language for the orator or reciter, from a fear that 'the body may say something else' (de Bolla 1989: 161), evincing a distrust of the excessive signification produced by the solitary, asocial subjectivity of the (female) reader, is of greater relevance to my case here. 'Reading theory claims for the man the aural reality of the public reading scene, whereas it attempts to inhibit the silent perusal of texts, construing such activity as outside the law' (ibid.: 277). The 'aural reality' betokens the transparency of the orator's body: 'it should merely reflect and represent the passion and sentiments contained within the text, be it a text which has been memorised or one that is read from' (ibid.: 151). Behind the translucence of the Coleridgean symbol is the Book, the revealed and *written* word of God which controls and inspires the spoken word, like the male *will* balancing spontaneous effusions in the poetics of the *Biographia* or stimulating female utterance in the conventional mesmeric scene. Shelley's strategy of opposition to this is quite distinct from the deconstructionist's 'play of the signifier', the unleashing of a proliferation of supplementary ('female') interpretations from the written word. He seeks a word which is logocentric without being *phall*ogocentric, the pure voice whose only writing is that of the utterance of the sensitive 'feminized' (because not necessarily female) body. The heroine of his friend Horace Smith's novel *Mesmerism: A Mystery* (published long after Shelley's death in 1845) exemplifies the transport of the sensitive body: 'She seemed to be sensation all over . . . her blood spoke, and every muscle, every fibre was eloquent, even before the tongue could express the emotion that had made them so tremulous and declamatory' (Smith 1845: III, 57). The body is no longer transparent but stiffened, opaque, expressive of its autonomous eloquence – in short it is the body of the *improvvisatore* who recites with no text but that of the immediacy of inspiration. As Mary Shelley wrote in her review of *The English in Italy* the improvised performance as text disappears, 'reaches the ocean of oblivion, leaving no trace behind' (Clairmont 1968: 451). The *improvvisatore* – or often *improvvisatrice* (de Staël's 'Corinne' was only the prototype of numerous female performers heard by the Shelley circle in Pisa) – could not transcribe their inspiration, and when they did, the effect was often wooden and cliché-ridden. Writing seems to have caused them physical disturbance, as when Sgricci was 'overcome by a violent nausea . . . when he tried to perform with a pen what he had been accustomed to improvise on stage' (Clairmont 1968: 473).

Coleridge's account of recitation and Shelley's competing theory of improvisation both construct the social vocalization of Romantic poetry as 'species', albeit distinctive ones, of animal magnetism. The text-centred approach to poetry of modern scholars and silent readers has perhaps blinded the twentieth-century critic to the performative context of much Romantic poetry. Bearing in mind my foregoing discussion of the reading scene, it seems permissible – in a converse movement – to describe animal magnetism as itself a species of poetry, the therapeutic production, in the body, of the vocalized poetic text by means of a form of *dumb oratory*. The magnetizer operated by means of manual 'passes' over the body of the subject, or by the fixity of the gaze, both familiar elements of body language in the gestural lexicon of reading theory. In one near-contemporary work, Gilbert Austin's *Chironomia* of 1806, the author quotes Lavater's description of the eye as 'the tongue of the understanding' and Cresellius' account of the hand as 'a second tongue, because nature has adapted it by the most wonderful contrivance for illustrating the art of persuasion' (Austin 1806: 116, 324). After all, if the French Royal Commission of 1784 had referred the phenomenon of mesmerism 'solely to the imagination of the parties magnetised', it was quite logical to rejoin, with Coleridge, that 'if the zoo-magnetic influx be only the influence of the Imagination, the active Imagination may be a form of the zoo-magnetic Influence' (Levere 1980: 187).

Coleridge's account of poetic recitation as 'really a species of Animal Magnetism' in which the will of the reciter lives in the being of his auditors develops his earlier notion of poetry as the stimulation of torpid nerves based on the medical doctrine of the eighteenth-century Scottish physician John Brown, whose theories anticipated some of those of the mesmerists. Brown defined life as the synthesis of external stimulus on the excitability of the nervous system, attributing all diseases either to a deficiency or excess of stimulation. 'Asthenic' diseases of under-stimulation could be treated by stimulants such as violent exercise, opium or alcohol (Risse 1970: 45–51, Neubauer 1967: 369–82). In a notebook entry of May 1810 which anticipates the theory of metre in chapter 18 of the *Biographia*, Coleridge tentatively added poetry to the Brunonian pharmacopoeia: 'I wish, I dared use the Brunonian phrase – & define Poetry – the Art of representing Objects in relation to the *excitability* of the human mind' (Coleridge 1957–73: III, 3827). Mesmerism, like the Brunonian system so popular amongst English and German Romantics, rejected the complex nosologies and (to use Michel Foucault's term) 'noso-politics' of the medical establishments (Foucault 1980: 167; 1973: 22–37), positing that 'There is but one health, one disease, and one remedy' based essentially on the condition of the nervous system (Coloquhoun 1833: 61–2).

The early history of mesmerism has been authoritatively treated by Robert Darnton and others, and I will only refer to it in passing in order to stress its radical and reformist affiliations in the last decades of the eighteenth century. Mesmerism challenged the hegemony of a centralized medical police; an early proselyte, Nicolas Bergasse, wrote 'the corps of doctors is a political body, whose destiny is linked with that of the state . . . the distributors of drugs and diseases influence the habits of a nation perhaps as much as do the guardians of the law' (Darnton 1968: 84). Mesmerists championed the family as the 'natural' healthful unit of civil society, a mutually beneficial interpenetration of male will and female sensibility. As the Girondin leader Brissot put it

> I, a father who fears doctors, I love mesmerism because it identifies me with my children. How sweet it is to me . . . when I see them obey my inner voice, bend over, fall into my arms and enjoy sleep! The state of a nursing mother is a state of perpetual mesmerism. We unfortunate fathers, caught up in our business affairs, we are practically nothing to our children. By mesmerism, we become fathers once again.
>
> (Darnton 1968: 96)

The Romantic revision of mesmerism (more precisely dubbed 'artificial somnambulism' after the practice of the Marquis Chastenet de Puysegur) did away with much of the theatrical paraphernalia and hermeticism of Mesmer, returning the therapeutic practice to a Rousseauesque simplicity: in Coleridge's words 'Mesmer and Mystery are now gone by forever – so far from any secret being made, the cases are published at present [1817] in all the respectable foreign Journals' (Coleridge 1951: 49). Of central importance to Romantic mesmerists was the operation of the magnetizer's will in the therapeutic operation, revealingly described by the Scots mesmerist J.C. Coloquhoun as 'a determined, despotic volition' (Coloquhoun 1833: 80). Valcourt, mesmerizing hero of Charles de Villers's 1787 novel *Le Magnetiseur amoureux*, proclaimed 'I *will* it, and diseases will vanish in the face of this word pronounced internally with irresistible force' (de Villers 1986: 91; my own translation). The will operated through the dumb oratory of hands and the gaze; Puysegur had discovered the means of artificially inducing a somnambulic sleep by force of will in which the patient had an acute insight – often a literal perception of the internal organs – into her pathology and potential cure. The words pronounced in the condition of 'lucidity' – often uttered in response to intensive interrogation by the magnetizer – had a revelatory and sometimes even prophetic character anticipatory of the 'clairvoyance' of the nineteenth-century spiritualist movement. Puysegur did away with the manual manipulation of the patient's body which had drawn charges of sexual impropriety from the 1784 Commission; in so far as it gave for the first time an oracular voice to the woman subject which compelled the attention of the male magnetizer (in contrast to the analytical gaze of the medical profession fixed upon the silent body) it was certainly reformist in relation to Mesmer's practice. And yet the 'lucid' voice of unrestricted sensibility was still produced and policed by the male will in an analogon of the sexual division of labour constitutive of the power relations of the bourgeois marriage contract (Gallini 1983: 74). As Clara Gallini has written in *La Somnambula meravigliosa*, 'the formerly unheeded female body – daily object of social control – became the object of care, protagonist of a salvific project. But it could never become a liberated body existing in full self-knowledge. In the model of the somnambulic patient one rather finds an image of a freedom impossible in real life, a dream of escape from the burden of the flesh, of flying ever further away in voyages which become increasingly metaphysical. . . . The magnetic cabinet contains the solitude of a woman whose desires are excited in order to be immediately displaced according to the economy of the couple in which the male and female never achieve equilibrium' (Gallini 1983: 75; my own translation).

SHELLEY, COLERIDGE AND MESMERISM

Shelley first underwent mesmeric therapy in Pisa in December 1820 to alleviate the spasms from his kidney stones as an alternative to the terrible, and often fatal, operation known as lithotomy. This supports Dawson's suggestion that Shelley was familiar with De Mainauduc's treatise on mesmerism in Southey's *Letters from England*, which described how 'instead of lithotomy the stone may be cured without danger or pain' by animal magnetism. The magnetizer would direct the 'invisible fluid' through his fingertips to the 'juices' surrounding the stones, the corrosive powers of which it would concentrate and dissolve (Southey 1951: 314). Shelley may have been justifiably sceptical of this claim; his cryptic statement whilst 'under the influence' of Jane Williams that 'what would cure that would kill me' (recorded in the 1822 poem 'The Magnetic Lady to her Patient') refers at least on one level to lithotomy, as Medwin first suggested (Medwin 1847: II, 49). In De Mainauduc's bizarre treatise we also find a notion that 'every form is surrounded by an atmosphere peculiar to itself, composed of those particles of circulating fluids, and analogous to the general atmosphere of the earth' (Southey 1951: 305). Circulation is regulated by the nervous system, 'innumerable conductors . . . adapted by their extreme sensibility to convey information to the sensorium'. Like Brown's definition of health as an equilibrium between excitability and external stimuli, De Mainauduc (here following Mesmer) argued that 'The free circulation of healthy atoms through the whole form is necessary, and . . . obstruction of its porosity, or stoppage of its circulating particles, must occasion derangement in the system and be followed by disease' (Southey 1951: 306). Healthy nerves can unblock 'naturally' without the assistance of another's will, an agency analogous to that of Burke's laxative sublime 'tranquillity tinged with terror' in the 1756 essay on the *Sublime and Beautiful*. The sublime calls forth a transport which as it 'clear[s] the parts, whether fine, or gross, of a troublesome incumbrance . . . [is] capable of producing delight' (Burke 1958: 136). The imposition of the magnetizer's will is an 'artificial' *substitute* for the sublime of nature or art and the ecstatic transport of somnambulic 'lucidity' is very close to the somatic display of the sublime (I hinted above that mesmerism modified the traditional gendered economy of the sublime in its concern with female transport, the imposition of the male will stimulating female lucidity and auto-diagnosis).

The granting to the female subject of an (albeit qualified) access to the sublime is another instance of the reformist tendency of mesmerism in relation to more mainstream discourses of sexuality, although arguably the very notion of the sublime is categorically phallogocentric. For when the regulating nerves are vitiated and unable to perform their function, they can be 'artificially' supplemented by the nervous vitality of another. Given that contemporary theory, exemplified by Cabanis in *Rapports du physique et du moral de l'homme*, presumed that the nervous, as well as muscular, fibre of women was weaker than that of men, artificial supplementation was generally unidirectional (Jordanova 1986: 98–100, Staum 1980: 211–17). De Mainauduc's practice of mesmeric 'treating' had the aim of 'assist[ing] nature by imitating and re-establishing her own law, when she is become inadequate to the task' (Southey 1951: 312). Although mesmerism claimed to cure both sexes, the fact that the magnetizer had to be in robust health and strong-willed usually determined that he be a man, working on the delicate, debilitous and often morbid female nervous system. It is this rule, however, that we find strikingly reversed in the case of Shelley.

Medwin described his cousin as a veritable mimosa – a poet 'so sensitive to external impressions, so magnetic, that I have seen him, after threading through the carnival crowd in the Lung-'arno Corso, throw himself half-fainting into a chair, over-powered by the atmosphere of evil passions . . . in that sensual and unintellectual crowd' (Medwin 1847: II, 46). 'When anything particularly interested him, . . . [Shelley] felt a tremendous shivering of the nerves pass over him, an electric shock, a magnetism of the imagination' (ibid.: II, 191). Two years after he had begun mesmeric therapy, Shelley wrote 'The Magnetic Lady to her Patient' which described his 'magnetization' by Jane Williams, a reversal of the normal gender relations of mesmerism. In this short poem the mesmerized Shelley figures as a 'withered flower' upon whom the soul of Jane weeps 'healing rain', possessing his being 'to its deep' (Shelley 1970: 667). The imagery alludes to an earlier poem, *The Sensitive Plant* of 1820, which as Robert Maniquis has indicated highlights the importance of the mimosa – a problem plant for eighteenth-century botanists and naturalists – in Shelley's thought in general (Maniquis 1969: 129–55). The poem reaches beyond the sensationalism of an eighteenth-century materialist tradition to suggest that feeling – the 'feminine' principle – must yield to a higher form of idealism in an *unfeeling* world. The Lady who tends the garden is a version of the Magnetic Lady of 1822, another representative of the 'female sublime' which I have described as Shelley's 'Medusa effect'. The Sensitive Plant withers and dies without the husbandry of the Lady; unable to blossom and cross-fertilize with the other flowers in the garden, it is condemned to a solitary end surrounded by the rank weeds which have polluted its environment. In the *volte face* of the poem's conclusion Shelley confirms the Lady's transcendence in a moment of aesthetic absolutism which would have been unthinkable in his poetry before 1818; it is not the Lady or the spontaneous poetic voice which passes away, but rather our sensual and contingent lives. The poem reneges on its sensationalist premise that feeling is all-sufficient.

> For love, and beauty, and delight,
> There is no death nor change: their might
> Exceeds our organs, which endure
> No light, being themselves obscure.
>
> (Shelley 1970: 596, lines 134–7)

As in all the later poetry Shelley is torn between a materialistic naturalism positing the self-sufficiency of sensibility as an existential and ethical norm and a Platonizing imperative towards a transcendent ideal which will reinforce and stimulate the diseased mimosa. He is forced to reinscribe the power of the masculine signifier, the phallus, in a disguised, feminine role to supplement disordered nature: this is articulated as the figure of the Magnetic *Lady*, a disturbance of the normal sexual hierarchy of the mesmeric scene.

Enlightenment theories of sensibility offered an immediate communication between subjects, particularly those of different sexes formerly divided by discursive protocols, despite the differing rigidity of male and female nervous fibre. This permitted the 'feminine principle' an increased prestige in cultural and social circuits, although as I have suggested one increasingly policed by male rationality and will, a change exemplified by the reaction to the 'literature of sensibility' in the late eighteenth century (Todd 1986; Mullan 1988). According to De Mainauduc the nervous systems of sentient beings are interconnected by means of 'atmospherical nerves' in relation to which individuals are like mushrooms linked to their rhizome networks; 'the auditory and optic nerves of one man are the auditory and optic nerves of every animated being in the universe, because all are branches sent off from the same great tree in the parent earth and atmosphere' (Southey 1951: 307). Physical distance between bodies, particularly those of different gender, is overcome. Shelley frequently employs a notion of a trans-subjective 'atmosphere' similar to De Mainauduc's, as in the 1819 poem 'Love's Tender Atmosphere' in which the 'warm and gentle atmosphere / About the form of one we love' is 'the health of life's own life'. Other instances are Panthea's account of her 'magnetisation' by Prometheus 'an atmosphere / Which wrapped me in its all-dissolving power' or the 'young lovers' in *The Sensitive Plant* 'Wrapped and filled by their mutual atmosphere' (Shelley 1970: 584, 228, 590). Sensibility is the basis of a necessitarian and monistic world-view in which desire takes the place of will, although in his later writing Shelley was increasingly driven to supplement his 'feminised' cosmology by means of a higher idealism which he struggled (and ultimately failed) to distinguish from the gendered will.

For Coleridge in contrast, the phenomenology of mesmerism supported Schelling and Steffens's postulation of a transcendental will grounded upon the absolute, the basis of his own version of the Germans' *Naturphilosophie* (Coleridge 1956–71: IV, 731). The only cognizable organ for the operation of 'Thought, Passion, Volition' was 'the whole nervous system' and the crux of the mesmerist's claim was whether 'the nervous system of one body, can, under certain circumstances, act physically on the nervous system of another living body' (Coleridge 1969: I, 59, note). After a sceptical inquiry into the available evidence, Coleridge concluded that 'the will or (if you prefer it as even less theoric) the *vis vitae* of Man is not confined in its operations to the Organic Body, in which it appears to be seated; but . . . is capable of producing certain pre-defined Effects on the living human bodies external to it', like the Torpedo and other electric fish (Coleridge 1951: 47). After reading Kluge, Coleridge refined his account of the 'pre-defined Effects' as 'a morbid sleep, from which the Brain awakes, while the organs of sense remain in sleep' (ibid.: 51). Typically, however, Coleridge's hypothetical voluntarism was limited by his valetudinarian condition, which, he felt after reading Deleuze's strictures, would prevent him from actively magnetizing (Coleridge 1956–71: IV, 731). De Quincey, author of a sympathetic essay on animal magnetism, dubbed Coleridge 'the sublime old somnambulist' and publicized his bondage, not to the magnetic will, but to opium; 'a slave he was to this potent drug not less abject than Caliban to Prospero' (De Quincey 1833–4: 456–74; 1970: 220; 1889–90: III, 230).

If Coleridge's drug-addiction undermined his belief in free will on an existential level, Shelley's overwrought and diseased nervous system cut him off from anything but a fantastical participation in the play of what he called 'free love' (Shelley 1970: 426). In his 1821 poem *Epipsychidion* (Shelley 1970: 411–24) he implied that his pathological condition was the result of the prohibitive institution of marriage, arguing for a healthful sexual pluralism. 'Love is like understanding, that grows bright, / Gazing on many truths' (lines 162–3). Projecting a situation in which he is the earth regulated by *both* the sun (Emilia Viviani) and the moon (his wife Mary) he drew upon the language of *female* magnetism to fantasize his liberation from the deleterious 'code of modern morals' (lines 153–4):

> Twin Spheres of light who rule this passive Earth,
> This world of love, this *me*; and into birth
> Awaken all its fruits and flowers, and dart
> Magnetic might into its central heart
>
> (lines 345–8)

Of course the paradox of the ending of *Epipsychidion* is its collapse back into the conventional dualism of an exclusive 'matrimonial' love in which Emily takes the place of Mary, although significantly Shelley has her disguised in a cancelled passage as a hermaphrodite, or, in the second cancelled *Preface*, as 'an effeminate looking youth, to whom he [the 'young Englishman' bound for the Levantine island] shewed . . . so excessive an attachment as to give rise to the suspicion, that she was a woman' (Shelley 1970: 425). Once again Shelley's 'feminine sublime' reinscribes the phallus in a moment of transvestite identification with woman: but his ambivalence with regard to mesmerism is more obvious in 'The Magnetic Lady to her Patient' in which it is clearly a *substitute* rather than a supplement for the 'free love' underpinning his necessitarian ethics. Mesmerism is a form of *willed* love or 'pity' in Rousseau's sense of a primary social sympathy, when natural or 'free' love is impossible in the polluted garden of patriarchal society. Jane Williams, the Magnetic Lady, as wife (or more accurately mistress) of Shelley's friend Edward Williams, can pour the 'power of life' into the sick poet but cannot love him because already committed to a healthful monogamy.

> Sleep, Sleep on! I love thee not!
> But when I think that he
> Who made and makes my lot
> As full of flowers as thine of weeds,
> Might have been lost like thee;
> And that a hand which was not mine
> Might then have charmed his agony
> As I another's – my heart bleeds for thine.
>
> (Shelley 1970: 667)

Shelley is here being forced into admitting the limits of sensibility and desire as natural principles of society and ethics; without the Magnetic Lady, the Sensitive Plant will wither and die in the rank garden. He is unhappy about admitting the principle of control essential to mesmerism, a power to which, in a fragmentary essay possibly written in 1822, he attributed the miracles of Christianity so exploitative of human credulity (Shelley 1988: 142, Dawson 1986: 32); none the less it offers the only balm to a sensibility afflicted with the disease of existence in a corrupted environment. Shelley is brought closer to a Coleridgean Absolute than he would care to admit in his recourse to mesmeric therapy from late 1820, the analogue of which is his (contemporaneous) adoption of a rhetoric of Platonic idealism in his poetry and prose. Only by disguising the gendered power relations of the mesmeric session (the familiar 'Medusa effect' by which the male gaze is transferred to the female) can this concession be mitigated, just as he attempts to feminize transcendence in his late writings. As the poet utters in his somnambulic trance, in response to Jane's inquiry as to what would cure him:

> What would cure, that would kill me, Jane:
> And as I must on earth abide
> Awhile, yet tempt me not to break
> My chain.
>
> (lines 42–5)

PYGMALION, PROMETHEUS AND THE MAGNETIC LADIES

Two days before Shelley's first magnetic session in December 1820, Claire Clairmont noted in her journal that she had been reading Rousseau's 'scène lyrique', *Pygmalion*, translated in Leigh Hunt's *Indicator* for 10 May 1820. Hunt prefaced Rousseau's rendering of the Ovidian story of Pygmalion by describing its author as 'a kind of Pygmalion himself, disgusted with the world, and perpetually yet hopelessly endeavouring to realise the dreams of his imagination' (*Indicator* 1820: XXXI, 241). Hunt articulates a common criticism of Rousseau, and one which had been trenchantly put forward by Mary Wollstonecraft in the *Vindication of the Rights of Woman*: 'I war only with the sensibility that led him to degrade woman by making her the slave of love' (Wollstonecraft 1989: V, 161). Shelley, following his mother-in-law's lead, had already treated Rousseau's visionary erotics in the poem *Alastor* of 1815 and would return to the issue in *The Triumph of Life* in 1822. In fact *Pygmalion* well exemplifies this aspect of Rousseau's thought; given the date of its reading by Shelley's circle, it also offers a framework for understanding some possible connotations of the mesmeric experiments which began in mid-December. Written in 1762 well before the mesmeric fad arrived in Paris from Vienna, Rousseau's *Pygmalion* anticipated many of the themes of that movement which the Shelley circle would almost certainly have regarded in a critical light: the healing, redistributive male will can be seen, through the lens of Rousseau's *scène lyrique*, as a form of (narcissistic) will-to-power.

Pygmalion, a sculptor in love with a statue of his creation, the beautiful Galatea, laments an inequality in the distribution of vital force (the 'sublime essence', 'sacred fire') between Galatea and himself: 'I perish by the excess of life which this figure wants' (*Indicator* 1820: XXXI, 245). He prays that Venus will 'Divide between them that devouring ardour which consumes the one without animating the other' (ibid.). Here is a notable similarity with the redistributive dialectics of mesmerism, the robust male will invigorating a debilitated female sensibility to the end of 'lucid' utterance. Pygmalion's love for Galatea is really a form of self-love or will-to-power: 'I have surpassed the work of the Gods. . . . If I were she, I should no longer see her; I should not be that which loves her' (*Indicator*: XXXI, 243). Pygmalion wants Galatea to have her own voice, but she must pitch her replies in the same tone as her animator. Describing Shelley 'under the influence' on 14 December, Medwin remembered how the somnambulist's replies to his questions were 'pitched in the same tone of voice as my own', and that he improvised some 'faultless' Italian verses (Medwin 1847: II, 49). When Pygmalion's statue comes alive, she 'touches herself, and says "Me!"' Pygmalion is transported and repeats 'Me!' Galatea 'touches herself again' and says 'It is myself' (*Indicator* 1820: XXXI, 245). Woman is no longer a simulacrum of herself, yet another silent and beautiful object in the world, but a subject possessed with a vital force and the power of voice. Yet her 'animation' is the product of male narcissism, as Wollstonecraft had complained in her analysis of Rousseau's Sophie, the degraded 'slave of love'. Perhaps here lies the clue to why Shelley, troubled by his early experiences of being mesmerized by Medwin, would over the next year prefer to be mesmerized by women, either Mary or Jane Williams, 'The Magnetic Lady'.

Shelley's deployment of mesmeric influence in *Prometheus Unbound* (Shelley 1970: 204–74) reworks and inverts the sexual power relations of the Pygmalion or mesmeric norm according to the oppositional logic of what I have termed the 'Medusa' effect. Prometheus clearly represents the principle of male reason punished for overreaching; his defiant assertion of will, the curse against the tyrannical Jupiter is figured at the beginning of Act I as a disease of the heart, daily tormented by 'Heaven's winged hound' (I, 34). But his resolution to forgive his antagonist and revoke the curse is tantamount to a desire to be cured; not until he is mesmerized by Earth, an exemplary Magnetic Lady, is he able to realize his desire, by a species of mesmeric homeopathy which raises the phantasm of Jupiter to repeat a curse otherwise forgotten or unspeakable. The Prometheus/Jupiter relationship is a male agon, spoken and then forgotten, as a curse: in contrast Earth, Prometheus's 'mother', speaks with an 'inorganic voice' which resembles the magnetic influence working on the diseased nervous system. ''Tis scarce like sound; it tingles through the frame / As lightning tingles, hovering ere it strikes' (I, 133–4). Like Jane Williams's 'sympathetic' rather than sexual love, Earth's influence is '*like* . . . entwining love; Yet 'tis not pleasure' (I, 148–9; my italics). Echoing de Staël's *improvvisatrice* Corinne, possessed with the power of giving the audience of her 'improvise' a 'double existence' (de Staël 1807: I, 72), Earth has knowledge of 'two worlds of life and death' and it is her power of imaginatively transporting the chained Prometheus by natural magic that liberates him from his mind-forged manacles. Shelley exploits the full range of mesmeric paraphernalia in this scene, the cryptic nature of which has attracted more critical comment than almost any other in the Shelley oeuvre.

A possible key to its interpretation is Prometheus's address to the phantasm of his antagonist Jupiter ('Tremendous Image, as thou art must be / He whom thou shadowest forth' – I, 246) in which the 'lucid' Titan diagnoses the nature of his own disease. Jupiter is the creation of his own will-to-power, the 'sceptred curse' (IV, iv, 338) and has no more concrete existence than the phantasm evoked by Earth. Another clue to clarifying the scene, noted by Dawson in passing (Dawson 1986: 25, note), lies in a comparison with an analogous scene in *Hellas* in which the Jewish Sage Ahasuerus summons up the phantom of Mahomet II in the mind of the Sultan Mahmud to predict the end of Islamic power in Europe. As Shelley explained in a footnote, Ahasuerus's power is far from being supernatural but is rather 'a sort of natural magic' deployable by anyone 'who has made himself master of the secret associations of another's thoughts'. The Jew creates in the Sultan a 'state of mind in which ideas . . . assume the force of sensations through the confusion of thought with the objects of thought, and the excess of passion animating the creations of the imagination' (Shelley 1943: 479). Shelley's use of the term 'natural magic' here is cognate with that of Sir David Brewster in his 1832 *Letters on Natural Magic*, a work which discusses spectres and other 'supernatural' phenomena as forms of legerdemain employed by 'the prince, the priest, and the sage . . . leagued in a dark conspiracy to deceive and enslave their species' (Brewster 1832: 2). Despite Shelley's assiduous and characteristic avoidance of the term 'will' the note does concede that 'natural magic', whether its name be mesmerism or poetry, *is* an effective mastery of another's thoughts, a position which Shelley can only with difficulty allow in the particular political context of

Hellas. Shelley's unusual use of the male magnetizer Ahasuerus demands the sceptical footnote demystifying the apparently supernatural power of the magnetic male will, which 'anyone' can use if properly informed to expose the temporal limits of the power of tyrants. No such explanation is needed in the mythic context of *Prometheus*; *natural* magic is befittingly employed by Earth as the condition for the Titan's 'unsaying' of the curse, itself a product of belief in the '*super*natural magic' of religion.

In a complementary movement in Act II, scene iv, the male equivalent of Earth, Demogorgon, educes a parallel insight from Prometheus's lover Asia, that only 'eternal Love' transcends necessity. The role of Earth as the magnetic healer of Prometheus has been greatly underestimated by critics, for the 'natural magic' of her *female* mastery of the Titan's thoughts initiates a chain of magnetic influence which reunites Prometheus and Asia and replaces the rule of patriarchal will (religion) with that of a feminized love. Prometheus's transport by Earth, and the communication of that transport to Panthea, Asia and beyond her to the whole cosmos, echoes the effect of the 'natural sublime' described by Shelley in an 1816 letter to Peacock from Mont Blanc. 'All was as much our own as if we had been the creators of such impressions in the minds of others, as now occupied our own – Nature was the poet whose harmony held our spirits more breathless than that of the divinest' (Shelley 1964: I, 497). When Prometheus magnetizes the dreaming Panthea in Act II, scene i, the language of mesmerism is blended with Shelley's rhetoric of love-making familiar from *Alastor* and *Laon and Cythna*; Panthea describes the 'love; which, from his soft and flowing limbs, / And passion-parted lips, and keen, faint eyes, / Steamed forth like vaporous fire; an atmosphere / Which wrapped me in its all-dissolving power' (II, i, 73–6). Prometheus, unlike Pygmalion, transmits the matriarchal Earth's 'natural magic' rather than mobilizing the transcendental (for Shelley, *supernatural*) will of the Coleridgeans. The exiled Asia's 'reading' of the dream of Prometheus in Panthea's eyes is the condition for the arrival of the 'rude haired' Shape of Diotiman love who leads the Oceanides to the cave of Demogorgon, and thence to reunification with the unbound Titan.

Shelley explicitly uses the language of magnetism once again in *Prometheus Unbound* in Act IV (lines 464–6), and like the Prometheus–Panthea/Asia scenario discussed above, it describes the (male) Spirit of the Earth working on the female Moon. But this time the mesmeric transmission of a feminized energy is less convincing and the scene, like Act IV in general, risks collapsing back into phallocentrism. In the last two scenes of Act II Shelley has represented, in the union of Prometheus and Asia, the recovery of a healthful and 'feminized' (in Shelleyan terms) sexual principle and the dethronement of Jupiter. The lovers have renounced any claims upon the empty throne and have retreated into the cavern in the bowels of mother Earth. The infant male Spirit of the Earth is encouraged by Asia to reanimate his 'chaste sister' the Moon when he has grown old enough to love, an aspiration which is realized in Act IV. The power of the Earth on the Moon, the power now of a brother rather than a mother is 'like the polar Paradise, / Magnet-like of lover's eyes' (IV, 465–7). Shelley's attempt to imagine a cosmic 'republic' in Act IV is marred by an excessive anthropocentrism, of which the regendering of Earth as 'brother' is perhaps symptomatic (see Mellor 1988: 7–8). Whereas Act III had been content to leave the centre vacant, Act IV restores the phallus in evoking a feminine sublime, a republican autarchy, a sensitive rather than a domineering will subjected to a domineering rather than a sensitive love. Shelley's utopia is subverted by its phallocentric metaphors of power;

> Man, oh, not men! a chain of linkèd thought,
> Of love and might to be divided not,
> Compelling the elements with adamantine stress;
> As the sun rules, even with a tyrant's gaze,
> The unquiet republic of the maze
> Of planets, struggling fierce towards heaven's
>   free wilderness.
>
> His will, with all mean passions, bad delights,
> And selfish cares, its trembling satellites,
> A spirit ill to guide, but mighty to obey,
> Is as a tempest-wingèd ship, whose helm
> Love rules, through waves which dare not overwhelm,
> Forcing life's wildest shores to own its sovereign
>   sway.
>
> (Shelley 1970: 263–4, lines 394–9, 406–11)

I have already intimated that an analogous shortcoming afflicts *Epipsychidion*, where Shelley's idealization of 'free love' fails to construct a genuinely pluralistic space for itself outside conventional sexual structures. Writing to Gisborne in June 1822, Shelley feared that the Emilia of that poem was 'a cloud instead of a Juno' and regretted his error of 'seeing in a mortal image the likeness of what is perhaps eternal' (Shelley 1964: I, 497). In 'The Magnetic Lady to her Patient' of 1822 Jane Williams's mesmeric power is the product of sympathetic or 'Uranian' rather than solely erotic or 'Pandemic' love, more like the power of Earth over Prometheus than the power of Emilia Viviani over Shelley (Holmes 1974: 435). But between the figures of Earth and Jane Williams appears the most successful of Shelley's Magnetic Ladies, the Witch of Atlas, in the 1820 poem of the same name. Without becoming entangled in the poem's complex mythographic allusions, I suggest that *The Witch* (Shelley 1970: 372–88) excludes the 'Pygmalion principle' by refusing the sexual binarism which mars the project of so many of Shelley's other poems. Like Jane Williams's ministration of magnetic love, the Witch's power and freedom lies in the fact that she is *not* a sexual agent but 'like a sexless bee / Tasting all blossoms, and confined to none' she passes freely amongst mortals (stanza LXVIII).

Shelley's attempt to feminize the magnetic scene idealizes a 'suprasexual' love which, like the Witch of Atlas's 'wizard skill', can overcome 'man's imperial will' (lines 195, 197). *The Witch* is an effusion of poetic spontaneity, an 'improvised' three-day wonder, clad in 'a light vest of flowing metre' in contrast to Wordsworth's overwrought bauble *Peter Bell*, nineteen years in the making. To unveil the Witch – a penetrative quest for text beneath voice, for meaning beneath the veil of improvised, spontaneous beauty – is to commit a sin 'that no priest nor primate / Can shrive you of . . . – if sin there be / In love, when it becomes idolatory' (stanza VI). The figure of the Witch represents a development of Queen Mab, the Medusa-like 'awful LOVELINESS' of Intellectual Beauty, or the 'Cave of the Witch Poesy' in *Mont Blanc*. Like all these feminine figures – as well as the Lady of *The Sensitive Plant* or Urania in *Adonais* – she represents a transcendent, ideal power which dwells in 'the bright bowers [where] immortal forms abide / Beneath the weltering of the restless tide' (lines 551–2). But Shelley's poem works by means of comedy rather than by the Medusan 'transport'; abandoning for once the terrain of a 'feminine sublime' the poem does without the stiffening effect of the Gorgon's gaze. Reworking Mary's tragic creation myth *Frankenstein* in a comic femininized idiom, the Witch's beautiful hermaphrodite, product of her 'natural magic', takes the place of Mary's ugly male monster or Pygmalion's 'slave of love'. The hermaphrodite in *The Witch* represents *both* the petrification of the male induced by the Medusan gaze and the animation of Galatea, stone turned to flesh in a softening of the phallic affect. Richard Holmes suggests that the prototype for Shelley's hermaphrodite was a statue – a Hellenistic copy reworked by Andrea Bergondi – he had seen in the Palazzo Borghese in Rome (Holmes 1974: 605). This seems to be confirmed by the 'connected passages' of *Epipsychidion*: 'others swear you're a Hermaphrodite; / Like that sweet marble monster of both sexes, / Which looks so sweet and gentle that it vexes / The very soul that the soul is gone / Which lifted from her limbs the veils of stone' (Shelley 1970: 427). In *The Witch* Shelley turns stone into flesh marked exclusively by neither male nor female signifiers but by *both*, far surpassing, he stresses at line 326, the 'living image' which 'drew the heart out of Pygmalion' (Shelley 1970: 379):

> A sexless thing it was, and in its growth
> It seemed to have developed no defect
> Of either sex, yet all the grace of both, –
> In gentleness and strength its limbs were decked;
> The bosom swelled lightly with its full youth,
> The countenance was such as might select
> Some artist that his skill should never die,
> Imaging forth such perfect purity.
>
> (stanza XXXVI)

The hermaphrodite is the Witch's somnambulist, upon whose pinions she flies south to a 'windless haven' in the 'Austral Lake', a love journey analogous to that of *Epipsychidion*. But whereas the sexual passion which consumes the poet's language in *Epipsychidion* undermines its intended pluralism, the Witch's retreat is the condition for her somnambulic power of realizing the desires of the dreaming world or subverting the ends of evil men; the soldiers beat their swords to ploughshares. The poem succeeds in projecting a utopianism more successful than Act IV of *Prometheus Unbound* and one which owes a great deal to Shelley's mesmeric experiences. Like the magnetic sleep into which Jane Williams casts him and which tempts the poet to 'break my chain' of life in 'The Magnetic Lady', somnambulism becomes in *The Witch of Atlas* a 'strange panacea' to mortality, the vehicle of an idealism which transcends all binary oppositions of male and female, spirit and matter, life and death. Mary disliked the poem, feeling it reflected a morbid refusal to treat 'the common feelings of men' (Shelley 1970: 388) and her scruples are understandable given the Witch's power to transform death into a lucid sleep;

> And there the body lay, age after age,
> Mute, breathing, beating, warm, and undecaying,
> Like one asleep in a green hermitage,
> With gentle smiles about its eyelids playing,
> And living in its dreams beyond the rage
> Of death or life;
>
> (stanza LXXI)

This is surely the ultimate fantasy of the poetry of voice, as of the mesmeric power which can see beyond the purview of the present, pure self-presence and imagination sustaining the materiality of the body as a kind of somatic writing. The most startling of Edgar Allen Poe's mesmeric stories, 'The Facts in the Case of M. Valdemar', must have the last word here – in the most literal sense – in representing the Romantic somnambule not as a living statue or an imperishable phonetic word but as a corpse in suspended animation. The date of Poe's story – 1845 – is redolent of a very late Romanticism, from the purview of which the vocalized body of Romantic youth has aged and decayed. As Doris Falk points out, the 'voice, after all, is a bodily instrument and reflects the actual state of Valdemar's body' (Falk 1969: 539). After seven months of magnetic trance, the dead Valdemar utters the impossible words: 'For God's sake! – quick! – quick! – put me to sleep – or, quick! – waken me! – quick! – *I say to you that I am dead!*' (Poe 1978: III, 1242). Upon being awoken by the narrator, he liquefies into a 'mass of loathesome – of detestable putridity'. It is a cruel epitaph to the mesmeric and Romantic project of making the body speak and turning the word to flesh – the project of the zoo-magnetic imagination – that Valdemar's voice, a terrible somatic vibration, begs for textuality, for separation from his fast-decaying corpse.

NOTE

I wish to thank Simon Schaffer, Alison Winter, Pete de Bolla, John Barrell and Danny Pick for their generosity in discussion, in sharing work and suggesting sources during the preparation of what turned out to be a somewhat cross-disciplinary article. Its shortcomings are mine, not theirs. Thanks also go to the editors for their comments, which were extremely helpful in writing the final draft.

5

JERUSALEM AND NATIONALISM

Susan Matthews

One of Blake's many roles in contemporary popular culture is as the author of a nationalist hymn. Long the anthem of the Women's Institute, the lyric 'Jerusalem' has recently been claimed in competing political contexts. Played before Tory Party press conferences in the run-up to the post-Falklands election, 'Jerusalem' became a national hymn alongside 'Land of hope and glory' and 'Rule Britannia'. In 1990 the Labour Party conference for the first time ended with a rendering of Blake's 'Jerusalem' by a soprano, an innovation which might signal alternatively a change in Labour or in the politics of nationalism. The myth of England as a chosen land which seems to provide some part of the emotive power of the lyric 'Jerusalem' reappears in Blake's last epic, *Jerusalem*. The elaborate edifice of the poem not only tells and retells stories of the Fall but uses Albion as the figure of the British people. The myth of *Jerusalem* seems on many levels to have the makings of a myth of national supremacy. Yet the cultural meaning of 'Blake' today is not only that of the author of a nationalist hymn but also that of Erdman's 'Prophet against Empire', according to Eagleton, one of the three canonical poets who will 'Smash the ruling class yet' (Eagleton 1986: 185). Moreover any attempt to re-insert *Jerusalem* into the nationalist language of the early years of the nineteenth century is fraught with difficulty.[1] This essay sets out to suggest both the continuities between Blake's writings and contemporary discourses of nationalism and ways in which nationalist languages, particularly within the poetry, are distorted, changed in meaning and finally rejected.

Whereas nationalism has in recent times seemed the preserve of right-wing politics, some versions of the Left now seek to reclaim it. Academic discourse is simultaneously rediscovering forms of popular nationalism in the crucial period following the French Revolution. E.H. Hobsbawm's *Nations and Nationalism* (1990) traces the association of nationalism with socialism. And whereas Britain's confrontation with Napoleonic France was seen by Tom Nairn as a counter-revolutionary war which used patriotism to strengthen the conservative social structure (Nairn 1981), Linda Colley argues that the period saw a rise of popular nationalism: 'Between 1750 and 1830 a wide spectrum of aspiring social groups and sectional interests throughout Britain found patriotic and nationalist language invaluable' (Colley 1986: 117). She suggests that 'it was the dominant landed class which most turned its back on the nation and sought and found refuge in the language of class' (ibid.: 117).

I

The absence of national monuments of the period celebrating British heroes or victories in the Napoleonic wars is taken by Linda Colley as evidence of the wariness of the state towards the potentially subversive force of nationalist discourse. As she points out, nationalist rhetoric is often adopted by radical causes in the period, as in *The Radical Reformers' New Song Book: Being a Choice Collection of Patriotic Songs* dating from the Peterloo era (ibid.: 116). This account might be seen as being confirmed by Blake's involvement in one of the most notable projects for a public monument. In 1799 he engraved three designs by Flaxman for *A Letter to the Committee for Raising the Naval Pillar or Monument* which proposed the erection of a monumental statue at Greenwich. The *Letter* takes as model the public art of ancient Athens:

> A statue might be raised like the Minerva in the Athenian citadel, whose aspect and size should represent the Genius of the Empire: its magnitude should equal the Colossus of Rhodes; its character should be Britannia Triumphant.
>
> (Flaxman 1799: 7–8)

It is not just nation but empire that the monument celebrates:

> We may state, then, that Great Britain having increased its dominion by sea and land, taken together, to as great an extent as the Roman Empire at its utmost height; possessing a proportionate commerce, having conquered all enemies at

> sea in a series of unequalled victories, and controuling the fate of great part of the globe by its power, is desirous to raise a National Monument of such extraordinary success, prosperity, and favour of Divine Providence.
>
> (ibid.: 9)

Whereas the statue is modelled on the 'Minerva in the Athenian citadel', the power of Great Britain is compared to that of the Roman Empire. The personification of Britannia, established in the 1750s, represents nation and empire rather than any single national hero, and it is interesting that it is both military and commercial power that is celebrated.[2] But the clearest indication that it is not just Britain's nationhood, but Britain's dominant role in the world that is being claimed is the argument offered for the choice of the site at Greenwich. This is suggested on the grounds that it is appropriate to Great Britain's position in the centre of the world:

> It is also to be remembered, that the port of the Metropolis is the great port of the whole kingdome; that the Kent road is the ingress to London from Europe, Asia, and Africa; and that, as Greenwich Hill is the place from whence the longitude is taken, the Monument would, like the first Mile-stone in the city of Rome, be the point from which the world would be measured.
>
> (ibid.: 13)

To engrave something is not necessarily to endorse its content. But letters written in the 1790s show that Blake shares the enthusiasm of friends such as George Cumberland and John Flaxman for the art and culture of the ancient Greeks. In sharp contrast to the belief of the late pamphlet that 'Rome & Greece swept Art into their maw & destroyd it' (Blake 1982: 270), ancient Greece provides Blake in the 1790s with an image of a society in which art, the artist and the imagination are rightly honoured. On hearing that Cumberland's plans for a National Gallery show signs of succeeding, Blake predicts that 'the immense flood of Grecian light & glory which is coming on Europe will more than realise our warmest wishes' (Blake 1980: 16–17).

The naval pillar was never built, but in 1801 James Barry added a naval pillar to the background of his painting *Commerce or the Triumph of the Thames* in his series of large paintings in the Royal Society of Arts, London, in response to the competition for a monument to honour England's maritime victories. In Barry's painting, 'the Thames disperses the manufactures of the Midlands carried by the trailing nereids to the four principal trading continents. Europe offers in return grapes and wine, Asia silks and cotton, America furs, and Africa slaves' (Pressly 1981: 101). Blake is outspoken in defence of Barry in his annotations to Reynolds's *Discourses* and in his reference (later deleted) in his *Public Address* of about 1810 to 'the really Industrious, Virtuous & Independent Barry' (Blake 1982: 576).[3] In these images of London as the centre of the world, Europe, Asia, America and Africa return to London as commercial centre. An unlikely parallel, or parody, is provided in the production of Blake's Lambeth books of the 1790s as *America* is followed by *Europe* and *The Song of Los* containing 'Africa' and 'Asia'. The four continents are produced from a house near the Thames. The epic, as Bakhtin (1981) has told us, is a form which strives for inclusiveness and for mastery. In *Jerusalem*, London and Golgonooza become the place of creation from which the nations of the world emanate:

> All these Center in London & in Golgonooza, from whence
> They are Created continually, East & West & North & South,
> And from them are Created all the Nations of the Earth,
> Europe & Asia & Africa & America, in fury Fourfold!
>
> (Blake 1982: 227)

Blake's myth, like the visual imagery of nationalist art of his time, continually moves out from nation to world in a process which disturbingly echoes not only the revolutionary universalism of the 1790s but also the language of empire.

Blake's most explicit language of nation and of empire occurs in two prose works which date from the years in which *Jerusalem* was being written and in which Britain was at war with France: the *Descriptive Catalogue* provided for his unsuccessful exhibition of 1809 and the notebook draft of about 1810 known as the *Public Address*. In the *Public Address* Blake takes on the role of patriot striving for the regeneration of his country:

> Resentment for Personal Injuries has had some share in this Public Address But Love to My Art & Zeal for my Country a much Greater.
>
> (Blake 1982: 574)

His concern, he claims, is for the state of the public arts in England, represented particularly in the debased public taste in engraving:

> Whoever looks at any of the Great & Expensive Works <of Engraving> that have been Publishd by English Traders must feel a Loathing & Disgust & accordingly most Englishmen have a Contempt for Art which is the Greatest Curse that can fall upon a Nation.
>
> (ibid.: 577)

As in *Jerusalem*, the language hesitates between the national and the universal. Blake writes:

> To recover Art has been the business of my life to the Florentine Original & if possible to go beyond that Original <this> I thought the only pursuit worthy of [*an Englishman*] <a Man>.
>
> (ibid.: 580)

'[A]n Englishman' is written, deleted and replaced by 'a Man'. Art in England is seen as both deriving from that of Italy and as rivalling Italy: 'England will never rival Italy while we servilely copy' (ibid.: 578). For Blake works within at least three different models: one which belongs with the syncretic mythographers and leaps national boundaries, seeing Britain as the true heir to Hebrew religion and Italian art; another which belongs within the contemporary world of competing emergent nations and empires, and a third which borrows the sophisticated cosmopolitanism of the liberal elite. Blake is thus concerned with the concept of English character, typical of the emergent nationalism in its emphasis on the blunt, honest, sincere man. Here Hogarth figures as an image of English originality:

> Englishmen rouze yourselves from the fatal Slumber into which Booksellers & Trading Dealers have thrown you Under the artfully propagated pretence that a Translation or a Copy of any kind can be as honourable to a Nation as An Original [Belying] Be-lying the English Character in that well known Saying Englishmen Improve what others Invent[.] This Even Hogarths Works Prove a detestable Falshood.
>
> (ibid.: 576)

But he is also, along with Hayley, Flaxman and Cumberland, aware of European culture. Indeed a letter from Flaxman to Hayley in 1784 shows that at this date there was a plan to complete Blake's education by sending him to Rome (Blake 1980: 3). Perhaps most surprisingly, Blake uses the language of competing nation states in the challenge he offers to Buonaparte:

> let it no more be said that Empires Encourage Arts for it is Arts that Encourage Empires Arts & Artists are Spiritual & laugh at Mortal Contingencies. . . .
>
> Let us teach Buonaparte & whomsoever else it may concern That it is not Arts that follow & attend upon Empire[s] but Empire[s] that attends upon & follows [wherever Art leads] The Arts.
>
> (Blake 1982: 577)

The opening statement does not seem to fit with the second: 'Arts & Artists are Spiritual & laugh at Mortal Contingencies'. It might be that the empire which 'attends upon & follows The Arts' is thereby translated into something which is not empire. But the apparent meaning is that the arts have a public function in time of war, not just as a propagandist means to defeat an enemy, but as a tool for building empires. Napoleon, who is said to have drawn up a shortlist of works of art to be transported back to France on the successful conquest of England, of course did use art explicitly as a symbol of military conquest.[4] The process of high-minded looting, however, began earlier in the postrevolutionary period in France; its politics, from the point of view of English sympathizers, may therefore have been more complex. As Francis Haskell and Nicholas Penny describe, it was in 1794 that 'the Revolutionary administration in Paris first proclaimed the principle that the Louvre, newly established as a public museum, was the rightful home for such masterpieces of art as could be seized from conquered territory' (Haskell and Penny 1981: 108). In 1798, at the request of the French Minister of the Interior, the authors of a popular vaudeville wrote a song to celebrate the capture of masterpieces of art, whose refrain was:

> Rome n'est plus dans Rome
> Elle est tout à Paris.
>
> (ibid.)

This almost seems to be what Blake imagines in the *Descriptive Catalogue* where he argues that his invention of portable fresco would have made it possible to transfer the greatest works of art to England:

> If the Frescos of APELLES, of PROTOGENES, of RAPHAEL, or MICHAEL ANGELO could have been removed, we might, perhaps, have them now in England.
>
> (Blake 1982: 527)

The civic-humanist call for the encouragement of public art becomes part of the nation's sense of cultural superiority.

II

Yet another form of nationalism appears in the *Descriptive Catalogue*. Here Blake offers that traditional function of epic poetry – the mythic account of the nation's origins:

> The British Antiquities are now in the Artist's hands; all his visionary contemplations, relating to his own country and its ancient glory, when it was as it again shall be, the source of learning and inspiration. . . . Mr. B. has in his hands poems of the highest antiquity. . . . The Artist has written it under inspiration, and will, if God please, publish it; it is voluminous, and contains the ancient history of Britain, and the world of Satan and of Adam.
>
> (Blake 1982: 542–8)

Exactly what Blake is proposing to offer to his public is unclear. At first he seems to be offering the lost epic literature of the primitive nation – just as Macpherson did in publishing his 'translation' of the poems of Ossian. But 'the British Antiquities' are also 'all his visionary contemplations'. Later it seems as if the ancient poems have acted as source material for a new 'voluminous' work, for Blake says: 'The artist has written it.' Blake of course is on record in the annotations to Wordsworth's *Poems* as accepting Macpherson's claims (Blake 1982: 665). But his defence may not have quite the meaning it seems to have: inspiration makes nonsense of arguments about the date of poems, and makes it quite possible for a modern poet to write poems of the 'highest antiquity'. What is interesting about the remarks from A *Descriptive Catalogue* is the attempt to present to the public a poem of inspiration in nationalist terms, as 'the ancient history of Britain'.

But what are the British antiquities that Blake uses in *Jerusalem*? There are several ways in which the poem could be seen as using national mythology. The Preface to chapter 1 of *Jerusalem* offers to the public a poem about giants and fairies:

> After my three years slumber on the banks of the Ocean, I again display my Giant forms to the Public. My former Giants & Fairies having reciev'd the highest reward possible, the [*love*] and [*friendship*] of those with whom to be connected is to be [*blessed*], I cannot doubt that this more consolidated & extended Work will be as kindly recieved.
>
> (Blake 1982: 145)

The references to giants and fairies could be seen as an attempt by Blake to evolve a distinctively British and popular machinery for his poem. *Jerusalem* is the only one of Blake's long poems in which giants and fairies are a significant presence; they appear only once each in *Milton* and *The Four Zoas*. Richard Hurd in *Letters on Chivalry and Romance* argued for an association between Gothic elements and English literature. He claims that the 'religious machinery' of Gothic legend has a greater popular appeal than that of Greek legend, having 'in it something more amusing, as well as more awakening to the imagination' (Hurd 1762: 48). He also discusses the 'current popular tales of Elves and Fairies' as 'even fitter to take the credulous mind, and charm it into a willing admiration of the *specious miracles*, which wayward fancy delights in, than those of the old traditionary rabble of pagan divinities' (ibid.: 48). Perhaps most important is that he finds Gothic elements in both Spenser and Milton, particularly in Milton's Satan:

> when Milton wanted to paint the horrors of that night (one of the noblest parts of his *Paradise Regained*) which the Devil himself is feigned to conjure up in the wilderness, the Gothic language and ideas helped him to work up his tempest with such terror.
>
> (ibid.: 52)

But whereas Hurd writes of superstitions fit 'to take the credulous mind', Blake in *A Descriptive Catalogue* describes Shakespeare's use of witches and fairies as poetic metaphors, introducing the examples from Shakespeare in order to support his argument for the seriousness of Chaucer's characterization: 'Shakespeare's Fairies also are the rulers of the vegetable world, and so are Chaucer's; let them be so considered, and then the poet will be understood, and not else' (Blake 1982: 535).

In *Jerusalem*, Blake seems to create supernatural machinery with a limited or subsidiary role, associated with the vegetable world, and by implication with femininity. It is the *daughters* of Albion who are described as:

> Names anciently rememberd, but now contemn'd as fictions!
> Although in every bosom they controll our Vegetative powers.
> (Blake 1982: 148)

Genii, gnomes, nymphs and fairies (sixty-four thousand of each) provide the guards for the gates of Golgonooza, acting like Los's spectre in chapter 1 as servants. But in chapter 2, the transformation of the zoas into elements and then into these creatures follows the negative step of the separation and division of Albion's emanation:

> Albion groans, he sees the Elements divide before his face.
> And England who is Brittannia divided into Jerusalem & Vala
> (ibid.: 178)

The Gothic supernatural is used to represent a narrow and distorted image of the true spiritual forces:

> And the Four Zoa's who are the Four Eternal Senses of Man
> Become Four Elements separating from the Limbs of Albion
> These are their names in the Vegetative Generation:
> [*West Weighing East & North dividing Generation South bounding*]
> And Accident & Chance were found hidden in Length, Bredth & Highth
> And they divided into Four ravening deathlike Forms,
> Fairies & Genii & Nymphs & Gnomes of the Elements.
> (ibid.: 178)

In the following chapter, giants, witches, ghosts and fairies reappear in the company of druids, and of the northern gods Thor and Friga. There is already a suggestion of mischievous energy in the fairy who introduces *Europe*, but the Gothic supernatural in *Jerusalem* is associated with a more sinister kind of cruelty through the image of sacrifice:

> The Giants & the Witches & the Ghosts of Albion dance with
> Thor & Friga, & the Fairies lead the Moon along the Valley of Cherubim

> Bleeding in torrents from Mountain to Mountain, a lovely
> Victim
>
> (ibid.: 214)

Blake draws on contemporary ideas of the Gothic supernatural in *Jerusalem* but suggests that they are not the true British antiquities. They are debased forms which result from the loss and division of Albion's emanation, England or Britannia, into the two opposed forms of Jerusalem and Vala. Vala therefore becomes associated with a negative form of femininity.

The feminization of the Gothic supernatural may be in part the result of Pope's use of a comparable machinery in *The Rape of the Lock*, based, according to the Preface on 'the Rosicrucian Doctrine of Spirits': 'According to these Gentlemen, the four Elements are inhabited by Spirits, which they call *Sylphs, Gnomes*, *Nymphs*, and *Salamanders*' (Pope 1963: 217). The passage from canto II in which Ariel gives orders to his 'Sylphs and Sylphids . . . / Fays, Fairies, Genii, Elves and Daemons' provides a parallel to the account of the work of Los's sons in *Milton* while using a machinery which is more like that of parts of *Jerusalem*. Pope's new machinery is specifically associated with femininity, an association which Blake carries over to Hayley in his role as reader of Pope's Homer:

> Thus Hayley on his Toilette seeing the Sope
> Cries Homer is very much improvd by Pope.
>
> (Blake 1982: 505)

The British antiquities have become part of feminized, middle-class polite culture. To these, Blake opposes biblical myth, seen more as a part of an oppositional British culture, a culture which included the figures of Richard Brothers, the self-styled 'Prince of the Hebrews' who planned to establish a kingdom with its seat in Jerusalem, and Joseph Bichero who predicted the restoration of the Jews to Jerusalem.[5]

Blake's nationalism could be seen as part of the change which results in his turning away from the classics, for which he displays considerable enthusiasm in the 1790s, and yet the national myth he finds available is coloured by its association with middle-class polite culture. The address 'To the Public' is filled with irony.[6] Not only have Blake's earlier works failed to receive 'the highest reward possible' but, if this is envisaged as the love and friendship of the select group of Blake's patrons and friends, then the public must be redefined as the few rather than the many. The 1809 Advertisement for Blake's exhibition quotes '"Fit Audience find tho' few"' MILTON' (Blake 1982: 527). *Jerusalem* addresses 'The Public', a unifying term, and yet splits the public into 'Sheep' and 'Goats', implicitly admitting Blake's loss of the public as audience for his national epic. The defacement of the plate addressed 'To the Public' often seems to display Blake's estrangement from his audience. He removes, for instance, the words which ask for acceptance of author by audience: 'Therefore [*Dear*] Reader, [*forgive*] what you do not approve, & [*love*] me for this energetic exertion of my talent' (Blake 1982: 145). As a writer and artist, Blake oddly spans different classes, associated not only with London's radical underground but also with liberal middle-class society centred on figures such as his patrons William Hayley and B.H. Malkin. The public are in danger of becoming the few of Hayley's circle. The search for the British antiquities is therefore more complex than the adoption of the Gothic supernatural, and depends on the restoration of Hebrew myth as a challenge both to the middle-class use of classical and of British myth.

The choice of Albion as the central figure of the national epic immediately sets up a contrast with the mythology of the national epic of the type espoused by William Hayley. The project of the national epic had already been taken up by the liberal establishment. William Hayley, in the 1782 *Essay on Epic Poetry*, called on poets to create national epics using British legend, attacking those who deny the suitability of 'the annals of our martial isle' (Hayley 1968: 110). National epic poets, in his account, respond to the appeal of Liberty:

> 'Here,' cries the Goddess, 'raise thy fabric here,
> Build on these rocks, that to my reign belong,
> The noblest basis of Heroic Song!'
>
> (ibid.: 111)

National sentiment is here seen as in France as a liberal force, belonging within the discourse of civic humanism. Many of the long poems of the period could be seen as belonging within this project for a national epic. *The Prelude* of course discusses plans for a national epic. John Ogilvie's *Britannia: A National Epic Poem in Twenty Books* appeared in 1801 with a preface which refers to Hayley's views on epic, and Joseph Cottle published *Alfred* (1800) and *The Fall of Cambria* (1808). Perhaps the most suggestive parallel to Blake's attempts is provided by the epic ambitions of John Thelwall who in 1801 announced plans for a 'National and . . . Constitutional Epic' *The Hope of Albion, or Edwin of Northumbria.* The poem was never completed, but the fragments published in 1801 show Thelwall using patriotic and nationalist themes. The Argument to Book 1 of *The Hope of Albion* contains an 'Invocation to the tutelary Angel of Patriotism'. But it also contains an account of a negative form of nationalism, 'sullen passions' raised 'in the popular mind':

> scorn, and deadly hate
> Of alien tribes, and national pride that steels
> The obdurate heart, presumptuous, and confounds
> Reason and right; moulding the infatuate herd
> (Their own worst foes!) to the pernicious views
> Of crafty politicians: whence the woes
> That thin the human race – oppressions, wars,
> Famine, and fire, and pestilence; whate'er
> The Good with horror view, the Great with pride.
> (Thelwall 1801: 195)

In the preface to the collection which contains the fragment of Thelwall's patriotic epic, he explains that by the time he came to work on the poem he found 'the press teeming, and, perhaps, the public already satiated with NATIONAL HEROICS, which, when his principal work was first projected, was *a desideratum* in English poesy' (Thelwall 1801: xlvi). The project seems to show that the national epic was not necessarily a conservative form, though it may have been one of a writer retired from active politics. The late 1790s see Blake, like Thelwall and Wordsworth, contemplating long poems from a place of retirement.

In most attempts to provide a British mythology, the name of Britain is traced back to a Roman conqueror, Brutus, who seizes the island from giants descended from Albion. Not only did Pope write a fragment of a British national epic on Brutus in 1743, but Ogilvie's 1801 'national epic' *Britannia* also uses the story of Brutus which derives from Geoffrey of Monmouth and appears in Milton's history. Although Blake describes himself as 'believing with Milton the ancient British History' (Blake 1982: 543), he in fact makes a very different use of British myth, rejecting the figure of Brutus as liberator. In Ogilvie's poem, as in Milton's history, liberation can only come to the oppressed natives through the intervention and rule of a Roman soldier. Ogilvie's muse predicts the arrival of a foreign liberator:

> She saw the day
> Approaching near, by Heaven ordain'd, to free
> From thrall the natives, by a foreign host,
> From orient climes, beneath a Chief renown'd
> That spread the sail for Albion: doom'd to crush
> The tyrants of the land.
>
> (Ogilvie 1801: 57)

Blake's Advertisement for his 1809 exhibition describes his painting *The Ancient Britons*: 'Three Ancient Britons overthrowing the Army of armed Romans; the Figures full as large as Life – From the Welch Triades' (Blake 1982: 526). Here Blake presents the Romans as opponents rather than liberators of the Ancient Britons:

> The most Beautiful, the Roman Warriors trembled before and worshipped:
> The most Strong, they melted before him and dissolved in his presence:
> The most Ugly, they fled with outcries and contortion of their Limbs,
>
> (ibid.: 526)

By choosing Albion, Blake places his myth in an age of giants before the arrival of Brutus, the Roman, or Hercules, the Greek. He thus strengthens the nationalist force of his myth.

But Blake also places the mythic figure of Albion before the events of Hebrew myth. In doing so, he constructs a very different form of Hebraism from that of Richard Brothers or Joseph Bichero. Blake's notebook commentary on *A Vision of the Last Judgment* describes what seems to be an earlier version of the mythology of *Jerusalem* in which 'our Ancestor' is clearly placed before Hebrew history:

> an Aged patriarch is awakd by his aged wife <He is Albion our Ancestor <patriarch of the Atlantic Continent> whose History Preceded that of the Hebrews <& in whose Sleep <or Chaos> Creation began, [*his Emanation or Wife is Jerusalem <who is about to be recievd like the Bride of the*>], at their head> <the Aged Woman is Brittannia, the Wife of Albion Jerusalem is their daughter>>.
>
> (Blake 1982: 558)

In *The Marriage of Heaven and Hell* in the early 1790s Blake used the figure of Ezekiel to suggest that the authority accorded to the Hebrew scriptures creates a form of oppression, one which denies to the religions and myths of other nations an equal validity and produces an ideology which supports empire:

> and we so loved our God, that we cursed in his name all the deities of surrounding nations, and asserted that they had rebelled; from these opinions the vulgar came to think that all nations would at last be subject to the jews.
>
> This said he, like all firm perswasions, is come to pass, for all nations believe the jews god, and what greater subjection can be.
>
> (Blake 1982: 39)

The passage from the *Vision of the Last Judgment* might be seen as creating exactly the same scope for misunderstanding as is described in the 'Memorable Fancy'. Instead of the Hebrew scriptures being granted priority as they were by the mythographer Jacob Bryant (who saw all other bodies of myth as derived indirectly and incorrectly from them, the Egyptian from the Hebrew and the Greek from the Egyptian), Blake seems here instead to give priority to British myth. In the *Descriptive Catalogue* Blake asserts the value of British myth but does not appear to rank the myths of various nations:

> The antiquities of every Nation under Heaven, is no less sacred than that of the Jews. They are the same thing as Jacob Bryant, and all antiquaries have proved. How other antiquities came to be neglected and disbelieved, while those of the Jews are collected and arranged, is an enquiry, worthy of both the Antiquarian and the divine.
>
> (Blake 1982: 543)

But when in the Preface to chapter II of *Jerusalem*, addressed 'To the Jews', Blake returns yet again to this issue something rather strange seems to happen:

> Jerusalem the Emanation of the Giant Albion! Can it be? Is it a Truth that the Learned have explored? Was Britain the Primitive Seat of the Patriarchal Religion? If it is true: my title-page is also True, that Jerusalem was & is the Emanation of the Giant Albion. It is True, and cannot be controverted. . . .
>
> Albion was the Parent of the Druids; & in his Chaotic State

> of Sleep, Satan & Adam & the whole World Was Created by the Elohim.
>
> (Blake 1982: 171)

This passage alters the mythic relationships of the passage from *A Vision of the Last Judgment* in a way which modifies the nationalist focus of the myth. In *A Vision of the Last Judgment*, Jerusalem is Albion's daughter and Britannia his wife. In the Preface to *Jerusalem*, it is Jerusalem rather than Britannia who is Albion's wife or emanation. The change might be a result of unease about using the figures of British national myth. Britannia appears only four times in the poem, mostly towards the end, at the stage at which figures who have been misappropriated begin to be cleansed of false associations. The form of Blake's argument in the Preface to *Jerusalem* adopts and then parodies the method of a mythographer such as Jacob Bryant. He sets up a proof of his account, marking the steps of his demonstration in a way which dismisses logic: 'Is it a Truth that the Learned have explored? . . . If it is true, my title-page is also True. . . . It is True and cannot be controverted' (ibid.). The theories developed by Bryant have the effect of creating a hierarchy of groups of myth. Blake's use of his kind of argument about priority could be seen as parodically undoing his logic, mocking the attempt to establish an order of myths. The figure of Albion may be intended in part to avoid the kind of ranking necessary to Bryant, for Albion is placed before creation, before the appearance of such figures as Adam, Satan, Noah or Arthur (with whom he is equated in *A Descriptive Catalogue*). Each of these later figures can be associated with him, since each is a point of origin, the father of a nation; all men are descended from Adam, but all are also descended from Noah. In the sense that the fallen world can be seen as an image of hell, all are also descended from Satan. Spenser in *The Faerie Queene* uses Arthur as an origin in a more limited sense, since he derives Queen, realm and race from him. But in attempting to pre-empt all other myths by using Albion as the name of the eternal man, the way is opened to a reading which turns the poem into a myth of national supremacy. Albion, dying, at the end of chapter I remembers a time when 'Albion coverd the whole Earth, England encompassd the Nations' (Blake 1982: 170).

The narrator, whose voice introduces chapter I, is given the power to restore to the nation the national memories that are lost:

> Names anciently rememberd! but now contemn'd as fictions!

Although in every bosom they controll our Vegetative powers.
(ibid.: 148)

Yet the degree of power and authority which is to be accorded to the rediscovered figures of British myth remains unclear.

III

Blake's unfinished *The French Revolution* seems to create an image of popular nationalism in the replacement of the king of France with a figure of the French people. In *Jerusalem*, the figure of the British people, Albion, takes on an odd dual role as both national and universal figure. Yet the case for *Jerusalem* as a nationalist epic does not seem hard to make; its concern with themes of national identity and regeneration is obvious. The question is rather what kind of nationalism, or whose nationalism, the poem represents. Is its nationalism always ironic – an attempt perhaps to use and manipulate the nationalism of the nation at war – or is it an oppositional nationalism, one which creates an image of the nation as utopia? The superimposition of the figure of Albion as nation on Albion as universal man is surely open to two readings, one of which dissolves the national identity in the universal, but the other of which becomes an image of empire.

In many places, *Jerusalem* does seem to be a straightforward epic of national identity. As Los works at his furnaces in the fourth and final chapter he sees an image which is taken by commentators such as Stevenson as a sign of the imminent reawakening of Albion, a clearly positive development.[7] Los cries out:

What do I see? The Briton Saxon Roman Norman
amalgamating
In my Furnaces into One Nation the English: & taking refuge
In the Loins of Albion.
(Blake 1982: 252)

Yet this straightforward image of the nation formed from diverse ethnic strands is immediately complicated by the superimposition of biblical myth:

The Canaanite united with the fugitive
Hebrew, whom she divided into Twelve, & sold into Egypt
Then scattered the Egyptian & Hebrew to the four Winds!
This sinful Nation Created in our Furnaces & Looms is Albion
(ibid.: 252)

This parallel implicitly questions the image of national unity: the joining of Canaanite and Hebrew leads to division, betrayal and scattering. The joining of 'Briton Saxon Roman Norman' produces a 'sinful Nation': national strength and unity are not necessarily seen positively here. But if Albion is a 'sinful nation', it is also, according to the Voice Divine, a chosen nation:

> I elected Albion for my glory; I gave to him the Nations,
> Of the whole Earth. He was the Angel of my Presence: and all
> The sons of God were Albions sons: and Jerusalem was
> my joy.
>
> (ibid.: 191)

Albion given 'the Nations / Of the whole Earth' could be read as an image of empire. Albion's despairing words at the end of the first chapter lament the loss of a time in which England as a commercial power was the centre of the world, just as in the proposal for the naval pillar at Greenwich:

> In the Exchanges of London every Nation walkd
> And London walkd in every Nation mutual in love &
> harmony
> Albion coverd the whole Earth, England encompassd the
> Nations,
> Mutual each within others bosom in Visions of Regeneration;
>
> (ibid.: 170)

The same words are echoed in Jerusalem's lament in the fourth chapter (ibid.: 234). This apparent celebration of Britain's commercial power is perhaps only surprising in view of the outspoken criticism of the debilitating power of commerce in the *Public Address*:

> <Commerce is so far from being beneficial to Arts or to Empire that it is destructive of both <as all their History shews> for the above Reason of Individual Merit being its Great hatred. Empires flourish till they become Commercial & then they are scattered abroad to the four winds>.
>
> (Blake 1982: 574)

As so often (and so perplexingly) in Blake's writing similar images reappear in both positive and negative guises. The image of Albion covering 'the whole earth' reappears as a fear of a lost unity, a scattered identity. The fear of a British diaspora runs through *Jerusalem*. Los at work at his furnaces cries, 'O when shall the Saxon return with the English his redeemed brother!' (Blake 1982:

241). Here the German Saxon is imagined as part of the English people, parted from the Anglo-Saxon by history and the North Sea.[8] Los is answered by Albion's daughters speaking from the Euphrates, exiled like the daughters of Jerusalem in Psalms and Lamentations. Los laments that 'The English are scattered over the face of the nations'. The English, unlike the Jews or the Africans, would not seem to be 'scattered over the face of the nations' unless war, empire, trade or the loss of America are imagined as the scattering of the nation.

The nationalist language of *Jerusalem* then seems to be highly complex, and to work in ways which are distinctly different from that of other contemporary nationalist literature. If nationalism rests on organic notions of identity, then Blake's organicism is so radical that it tends to unify not only the disparate parts of the nation but the world: in the myth underlying *Jerusalem* a time is imagined in which Britain is not an island but is joined to America and in which Canaan and England are the same place. There are also indications that the nationalism of *Jerusalem* parodies and rejects some aspects of the contemporary discourse of nationalism, even that with which Blake in other contexts seems to be associated. The Thames is equally important in the iconography of *Jerusalem* and in Barry's painting for the Royal Society of Arts, yet the figure of the Thames takes on a different identity. Los calls out to Albion:

> Found ye London! enormous City! weeps thy River?
> Upon his parent bosom lay thy little ones O land
> Forsaken.
>
> (Blake 1982: 241)

The Thames is envisaged as comforting parent to England's children rather than as receiving slaves from Africa, but also, further upstream, as a youthful river, the place of pleasure:

> Separate Albions Sons gently from their Emanations,
> Weaving bowers of delight on the current of infant Thames
> Where the old Parent still retains his youth.
>
> (ibid.: 242)

Blake imagines a young figure of the Thames, just as in *Milton* he imagines a youthful figure of Time. There are also indications that in *Jerusalem* the project for the naval pillar appears in a negative form. The spectre

reads the Voids
Between the Stars; among the arches of Albions Tomb sublime
Rolling the Sea in rocky paths: forming Leviathan
And Behemoth: the War by Sea enormous, & the War
By Land astounding: erecting pillars in the deepest Hell
To reach the heavenly arches.

(ibid.: 251)

Leviathan and Behemoth have already been associated in Blake's *Descriptive Catalogue* with Pit and Nelson and in the paintings described there become the focus for a parodic account of the heroes of national myth. The pillars erected 'in the deepest hell' are not only versions of Pandemonium but more specifically forms of the naval pillar. Los's work is to destroy such images of national heroics: Los beheld undaunted, furious

His heavd Hammer; he swung it round & at one blow,
In unpitying ruin driving down the pyramids of pride
Smiting the Spectre on his Anvil.

(ibid.: 252)

Not only the pillars but the 'pyramids of pride', which might be seen as versions of the Napoleonic obelisk, are destroyed.

If the myth of Albion is potentially a nationalist myth, however, *Jerusalem* also contains an implicit model which focuses again on the theme of national identity in a way which is far more subtle than that of the prose works. The model is signalled in the number of chapters planned for the poem, and in the decision to label them as chapters rather than books. Although *Jerusalem* is a poem in four chapters, the title page once announced that it was a poem 'In XXVIII Chapters'. The division of the final poem into four chapters has been taken as evidence that the intended model is Milton's brief epic, the four book *Paradise Regained*. But if 'twenty-eight' is the significant number, and 'Chapter' the important word, then it suggests instead the model of Acts of the Apostles, one of the two books of the Bible with this number. The four chapters of *Jerusalem* are each prefaced by an address to one of the groups which make up the nation, or the potential audience for Blake's epic. And whereas the poem as a whole takes Acts as its model, these are versions of the Pauline epistles. Blake writes 'To the Christians', 'To the Jews', 'To the Deists' and 'To the Public' instead of 'To the Romans' or 'To the Hebrews'. Like the Pauline epistles, the prefaces rebuke as well as praise. In the Preface 'To the Christians', Blake defines Christianity as 'liberty both of body & mind to exercise the Divine Arts of Imagination' and uses the apostles as his authority: 'The Apostles knew of no other Gospel.' He uses the opposition of flesh or body to spirit which is central to Paul's epistle to the Galatians:

> What is Mortality but the things relating to the Body, which Dies? What is Immortality but the things relating to the Spirit, which lives Eternally! What is the Joy of Heaven but Improvement in the things of the Spirit? What are the Pains of Hell but Ignorance, Bodily Lust, Idleness & devastation of the things of the Spirit[?]
>
> (Blake 1982: 232)

This plate is headed by a reference to the conversion of St Paul which is a quotation from Acts: 'Devils are / False Religions / "Saul Saul" / "Why persecutest thou me".' Acts begins with the instructions given to the apostles by Jesus before the Resurrection, and the first is 'that they should not depart from Jerusalem, but wait for the promise of the Father' (Acts 1: 4). *Jerusalem*, Blake's poem, tells of Albion's desertion of his true bride, Jerusalem, for Vala, the figure associated with war and the female will. Moreover, *Jerusalem* tells of the witness of the poet Los (Urthona's spectre) in 'time of trouble':

> Therefore the Sons of Eden praise Urthonas Spectre in Songs
> Because he kept the Divine Vision in time of trouble.
>
> (Blake 1982: 193)

Keeping the divine vision in time of trouble is the subject of Acts of the Apostles, of *Jerusalem*, and is also the predicament of the radical artist in the time of a nationalist war. One of the central preoccupations of Acts of the Apostles, as of *Jerusalem*, is the question of identity, of an identity of belief or of custom, nation or race. Acts tells of the opposition of Jewish believers to the mission to the Gentiles, an opposition which is focused on the debate over circumcision. The decision is 'that we trouble not them, which from among the Gentiles are turned to God' (Acts 15: 19). In *Jerusalem*, national identity is discovered in the process of recognizing a likeness with another nation, as the map of Britain is superimposed on the map of Israel: identity and otherness become the same. As Golgonooza is built, Los is able to see Palestine in London:

is that
Mild Zions hills most ancient promontory; near mournful
Ever weeping Paddington? is that Calvary and Golgotha
Becoming a building of pity and compassion?
(Blake 1982: 155)

Within the context of *Jerusalem* identities are continually redefined. Babylon, Jerusalem and Albion become the names of places only on one level of meaning. As Morton Paley points out, Brothers' 'intention was to establish a kingdom with its seat in Jerusalem' whereas 'Blake's Jerusalem is to be built in England's green and pleasant land' (Paley 1983: 132). And once 'Jerusalem' has ceased to refer to a geographically real place, it is surely just as possible for England to be generalized by means of the double national and universal reference of the word Albion in a way which takes it beyond national myth. Yet to deny Blake's writing any historical reference seems equally unsatisfactory. The complex politics of nationalism are present in the nationalist discourses used and transformed within his writings in such a way that it is not possible to extract a single Blakean view on nationalism from the prose and poetry. The voice of the patriot from the *Public Address* is not that of *Jerusalem* or even of any of the voices which go to make up that many voiced poem. The potentially nationalist discourse of the *Descriptive Catalogue* is undercut by the paintings it accompanies. Yet the language of Blake's poetry cannot entirely redefine its own terms. The shifts in identity and the shifts in meaning characteristic of it do not reduce the likelihood that the Eternal Man will seem to be male and that Albion will be read as a figure of the nation. Whilst *Jerusalem* works towards a point at which national identities merge, it nevertheless does so through the form of a national epic poem.

NOTES

1 The most helpful discussion of Blake's nationalism is by Marilyn Butler (Butler 1988: 49).
2 The iconographic establishment of the figure of Britannia is described in Newman 1987: 77–9.
3 John Barrell argues that 'the influence of Barry upon Blake – sometimes as mediated, perhaps, by John Opie – is very apparent' (Barrell 1986: 227).
4 See Haskell and Penny 1981: 67.
5 Richard Brothers and Joseph Bichero are discussed by Morton D. Paley (Paley 1983: 131–2).

6 See John Barrell's interesting discussion of Blake's use of the concept 'the public' (Barrell 1986: 253–7).
7 W.H. Stevenson comments: 'This is one of the first signs of hope; Albion, hitherto shattered and disintegrated, is seen to display in the course of history the power of brotherhood in uniting nations in himself' (Blake 1971: 829).
8 W.H. Stevenson's suggestion. See Blake 1971: 808.

6

'THE VOICE WHICH IS CONTAGION TO THE WORLD': THE BACCHIC IN SHELLEY

Michael Rossington

The spirit of Bacchus, which signifies both liberation and joy, is a consistent dimension of Shelley's mature poetry. In the politically charged work of his *annus mirabilis*, 1819, Bacchus, the maenads, and the fauns and nymphs associated with them, suggest not simply orgiastic excess and sexual licence but also the disruption of social order. Implicit in adherence to the cult of Bacchus is a non-hierarchical society in which each living organism, however insignificant, has its place. Bacchus is therefore allied with the god Pan, and the spirit of nature which he represents; democratic and collective as opposed to hierarchical and authoritarian, a culture for the masses rather than the divinely appointed. The Bacchic is also associated with Shelley's version of an ideal, originary moment of history, whose geographical and cultural basis is the Orient. Bacchus's journey to India is followed loosely in the poetic locations of *Alastor* and *Prometheus Unbound* and in the myth of an undifferentiated society, where 'the Celt knew the Indian' (*Prometheus Unbound*, II. iv. 94).[1]

While some critics, influenced by Nietzsche's *Birth of Tragedy*, have sought to discover a central principle in these multiple connotations, the Bacchic is not a singular 'key to all mythologies' in Shelley's work. Rather, it serves as a way of questioning and deconstructing the authority and power which reside in political orders, gender divisions and national identity as well as mythology. Its context is the allegorical significance of Bacchus manifest in the work of Percy Shelley's contemporaries at this time, especially

Mary Shelley, Thomas Love Peacock and Horace Smith, where the Bacchic embodies an ideal state of political flux and challenges the dominant aesthetic categories and often explicitly Christian readings of Greek myths by contemporary critics including Lockhart and A.W. Schlegel. If the Bacchic is a way to disperse and fragment political order in society, it also disturbs more recent notions of 'Romantic Hellenism' and the idealist aesthetic which that collocation invokes.

I

The idealist aesthetic of ancient Greece delineated by Marx in his *Critique of Political Economy* has been a source of continual unease to those searching for a materialist and fully historicized explanation of the apparently transcendent power of classical cultural forms. Many readings of myth in Romantic poetry, fuelled by the tradition of German aesthetic criticism beginning with Winckelmann (which Marx sustains), have assumed that Romantic Hellenism is simply the concentrated aesthetic product of the fusion between poetry and myth. This dehistoricizing manoeuvre effectively perpetuates the criticism of Shelley's mythological poetry and that of his contemporaries in *Blackwood's* and the *Quarterly* by which any subversive ideological import in the use of myth can be converted into a channel for the universal claims of an alien religious and social morality. Likewise, the category of 'Romantic Hellenism', put simply, is the means by which a prescriptive definition of what constitutes good taste in the use of classical mythology is endorsed. The Bacchic challenges the universal claims of such taste and sensibility.

In a post-Freudian, and post-Nietzschean, era we are accustomed to the use of myth for purposes other than the purely aesthetic, as bids for universality and authority. Harold Bloom's brilliant mythopoeic Shelley is strung between the Old Testament and Freud and sounded for lyrical power. The Hebraic poet of *Shelley's Mythmaking* challenges the Hellenic tradition by which Victorian culture could neutralize Shelley, denying or negating the sense of struggle which Bloom insists upon (Bloom 1959). What a Bloomian, Romantic criticism fails to recognize, however, in both *Prometheus Unbound* and *Hyperion* is the bid, in one case successful and in the other abortive, to transcend the aesthetic rewards of such a struggle, and to arrive on the other side, so to speak; that is, to overcome the issue of authority itself. Mythology is paradoxically used in both these poems to question the pre-eminence of the male individual artist and reformer, be he Prometheus or Apollo.

Even recent deconstructionist criticism has transformed Romantic myth-making into a reflexive trope. In an early essay, de Man applies his view that Hölderlin's use of poetic imagery expresses a nostalgia for 'the intrinsic ontological primacy of the natural object' (de Man 1984a: 7) to the Romantic poets' recourse to myth generally. According to de Man's hypothesis, Romantic versions of Hellenic myths would be expressive of a wider representational problem: 'the tension and duality inherent in the mythological situation would be found to reflect the inherent tension that resides in the metaphorical language itself' (de Man 1984a: 7). De Man's interrogation of the category of the aesthetic enables us to question the allegorical status assigned to mythology in Romantic poetry but only in such a way as to negate its significance as a mode of political critique. His argument draws on the manifest self-consciousness of the Romantic poets towards language and, in the case of Keats's 'Hyperion' poems, is bolstered by the transparent tension that exists in the poems between the struggle within the Greek Pantheon and a language that is adequate to articulate it. In another deconstruction of Keats's encounter with ancient Greece, influenced by Bloom and Derrida, Martin Aske reinforces the Romantic myth of the artist's struggle as much as he offers to explain it: 'Keats appeals to antiquity as a supreme fiction, that is, an ideal space of possibility, whose imaginative rehabilitation might guarantee the authority of modern poetry' (Aske 1985: 1). Such a construction of classical authority remains aesthetic, treating mythology on its own terms, and overlooking the ideological freight with which it is burdened.

Marjorie Levinson (1988) and Paul Hamilton (1989), on the other hand, have shown that the linguistic embarrassments and overreaching ambition of Keats's mythological poetry arise less from the inherent duality ascribed to language itself by de Man than from the context of Keats's revisionary aesthetic and his bourgeois, 'vulgar' ambition to extend a new language of poetry into domains of art which had hitherto been the preserve of a defensive culture. Keats's poetry paradoxically imitates that version of early nineteenth-century political economy which informed the criticism that was so fatal to his career. Levinson and Hamilton thereby expose the limitations of a purely aesthetic explanation of Keats's self-conscious fictionalizing. Their exemplary critiques can help to explain the paradox of the disproportionate opprobrium wreaked by reviewers on Keats's and Hunt's ostensibly innocent use of Greek mythology in comparison with the contemporary critical response to Shelley's far more explicitly political renditions.

Romantic critics, including Lockhart and Schlegel, underpinned their understanding of the aesthetic powers of Greek drama and mythology with an emphasis on authority. Thus in Schlegel's Christian reading, Aeschylus's tragedy is 'an image of human nature itself' because the struggle between man and God is suitably unresolved (Schlegel 1815: I, 112). In his review of *Prometheus Unbound* in *Blackwood's*, Lockhart reinforces his earlier condemnation of Keats and the Cockney School, but rejects the charge that his dismissal of Keats was grounded in class prejudice. Although he condemns the immorality of Shelley's volume, Lockhart ends up in the paradoxical position of defending Shelley, despite his association with Hunt and Keats, as a poet who is 'altogether out of their sphere' (Lockhart 1820: 687), his greatness assured because of the quality of his poetic style. In the Preface to *Adonais*, Shelley implicitly exposes Lockhart's suspect motivations for doing this by pointing to the superiority of *Endymion* to the work of 'a long list of the illustrious obscure' (Shelley 1970: 431). A few months earlier, in January 1821, Shelley had received the copy of Ollier's *Literary Miscellany* containing *The Four Ages of Poetry* by Peacock in which the uses of mythology are cited as representative of the debasement of contemporary poetry: 'We know too that there are no Dryads in Hyde-park nor Naiads in the Regent's-canal' (Peacock 1924–34: VIII, 19). Though Shelley expresses his desire to rebut Peacock's essay, 'very clever, but, I think, very false' (Shelley 1964: II, 258), he concurs with Peacock's mockery of poets like 'Barry Cornwall': 'The world is pale with the sickness of such stuff' (ibid.: II, 261). Yet the weakness of the mythological as a mode of poetry was not merely confined to Peacock's essay. Francis Jeffrey, reviewing Keats's *Endymion* and *Lamia* volumes in the *Edinburgh Review*, claims that his subject 'has the disadvantage of being mythological' (Jeffrey 1820: 204), despite compensating features:

> We have more than doubts of the fitness of such personages to maintain a permanent interest with the modern public; – but the way in which they are here managed, certainly gives them the best chance that now remains for them; and, at

all events, it cannot be denied that the effect is striking and graceful.

(ibid.: 207)

Hartley Coleridge, on the other hand, is more certain of the culpable indulgence of fantasy employed in mythological writing: 'The Grecian Age was hot fantastic youth. . . . We are grown up to serious manhood, and are wedded to reality' (H. Coleridge 1822: 119). The consensus amongst both liberal and conservative critics appears to have been that the use of classical mythology epitomized the weakness, and symptomatically the 'effeminacy', of contemporary poetry. In a letter to William Gifford, Shelley entreats that he give due notice to *Hyperion* but at the same time suggests his own detachment, 'for the canons of taste to which Keats has conformed in his other compositions are the very reverse of my own' (Shelley 1964: II, 253).

Shelley's strategic use of mythology is, then, distinguished from that of the Cockneys, Keats and Leigh Hunt, both by the reviewers and by himself. Hunt's may seem a markedly anodyne way of announcing an oppositional journal: 'The INDICATOR will attend to no subject whatsoever of immediate or temporary interest. His business is with the honey in the old woods' (Hunt 1820b: I, 1), but his good cheer conceals a secular critique which elsewhere he directs implicitly against Wordsworth:

> The depreciators of this world, – the involuntary blasphemers of Nature's goodness, – have tried melancholy and partial systems enough, and talked enough of their own humility. It is high time for them, and for all of us, to look after health and sociality; and to believe, that although we cannot alter the world with an ipse dixit, we need not become desponding, or mistake a disappointed egotism for humility.
>
> (Hunt 1818: 15–16)

In his Preface to *Foliage* (1818), he emphasizes a set of values directly contrary to those of the more established reviews, 'The main features of the book are a love of sociality, of the country, and of the fine imagination of the Greeks' (Hunt 1818: 18). Yet even as Hunt attacked a contemporary literary culture based on the power of metropolitan reviewers ('The notions about poetry can no longer be controuled, like the fashions, by a coterie of town gentlemen' (ibid.: 12)) his work and that of Keats was written off by the likes of Lockhart as an uneducated misappropriation of a cultural heritage. Shelley, perhaps recognizing Hunt's tentative and oblique methods, encouraged him to more directly creative ventures, and reprimanded him for the inappropriate mere translation of mythology in *Foliage*:

> I am sorry to hear that you have employed yourself in translating the 'Aminta' [of Tasso], though I doubt not it will be a just and beautiful translation. You ought to write Amintas. You ought to exercise your fancy in the perpetual creation of new forms of gentleness and beauty. You are formed to be a living fountain and not a canal however clear.
>
> (Shelley 1964: II, 152)

Shelley's desire to do more than translate mythology is evident in *A Defence of Poetry* when he seizes the opportunity to develop and synthesize the sentiments of his Preface to *Prometheus Unbound* and his essay, 'On the devil and devils'. In both, Milton embodies the duty of the poet to mediate a historical consciousness and becomes the paradigm of being able to write from within a tradition at the same time as criticizing it: 'Milton's poem contains within itself a philosophical refutation of that system of which, by a strange and natural antithesis, it has been a chief popular support' (Shelley 1988: 290). That Milton has refuted 'that system' does not invalidate the opposition between good and evil through which he works the contrary readings of *Paradise Lost*:

> The *Divina Commedia* and *Paradise Lost* have conferred upon modern mythology a systematic form; and when change and time shall have added one more superstition to the mass of those which have arisen and decayed upon the earth, commentators will be learnedly employed in elucidating the religion of ancestral Europe, only not utterly forgotten because it will have been stamped with the eternity of genius.
>
> (Shelley 1988: 290)[2]

The 'systematic form' of good and evil in religion is undermined by the possibility, indeed necessity, of reading the poem in more than one way. This is effectively what Shelley puts into practice in relation to Aeschylus's *Prometheus Bound*.

Yet the word 'system' has an ambivalent and usually negative connotation in Shelley's vocabulary in the discussion of mythological poetry. In his criticism of Keats's work, he uses the word to suggest the authority of an existing canon of Greek classical myth towards which he finds Keats overly respectful. Of Keats's *Poems* (1817), he remarks, 'He has a fine imagination and ought to become something excellent; but he is at present entangled in the cold vanity of systems' (Shelley 1964: II, 31). Having read *Endymion*, not uncritically, he informs Keats that he will have him sent copies of *Prometheus* and *The Cenci*, and remarks, 'In poetry *I* have sought to avoid system & mannerism; I wish those who excel me in genius, would pursue the same plan' (Shelley 1964: II, 221). Although he most likely has Byron in mind here, the radicalization of form and genre is clearly an ambition which is intended to undermine the claims to authority of classical myth in the eyes of the contemporary critical establishment. For Shelley such authority resides not only in the idealized fictions bequeathed by Greek mythology but in the material evidence of ancient Greek society: 'What the Greeks were, was a reality, not a promise' (Shelley 1949: 407). Shelley's definition of Greek culture and myth is thus quite distinct from Keats's projection of, and investment in, classical authority. As such, we can see that it is not only the fragmentary state of much Romantic poetry which contributes to a historicized critique of traditional forms; the forms of mythological poetry too, as displayed in the use of the Bacchic, break with 'system' to inform new myths, aware of, yet openly distanced from, the classical as expressed by A.W. Schlegel and Lockhart.

II

The period of study and discussion of Greek and Roman comic writers such as Lucian and Apuleius in the Shelley circle extends back to the summer of 1817 at Marlow, and was, as Marilyn Butler has demonstrated, profoundly important in shaping the poetry of the circle in the subsequent four years: 'The crucial fact about the classicism of Shelley and Peacock is that it does evolve into paganism – not so much an aesthetic as an ideological cult' (Butler 1981: 131).[3] Through its singular projection of gender, populism and sexuality the Bacchic disrupts and subverts the authority, asceticism and masculinity of the kind of Christianity projected by Lockhart and Schlegel. Yet the Bacchic is not only a strategic threat to the critical establishment: it is also related to the development of a self-transforming aesthetic of the kind that Shelley realizes most effectively in the final act of *Prometheus Unbound* but which is evident also in apparently innocuous lyrics like 'The Cloud' which were often unthinkingly admired by those who condemned the morality of his longer poems. The Bacchic has the ideological advantage, in terms of the contemporary view of mythology and Shelley's own scepticism about 'system' in poetry, of permitting an ever-shifting and elusive aesthetic, one that in *Prometheus Unbound* indeed 'was never intended for more than 5 or 6 persons' (Shelley 1964: II, 388). That Shelley was pushing the bounds of taste but also that his popular poetry could engage the Bacchic in a different, most disturbing and recognizable sense show the sophistication of its uses.

For Shelley the Bacchic assumes a new significance in the volume of poems published in 1820, *Prometheus Unbound: A Lyrical Drama in Four Acts with Other Poems*, as well as those composed in 1820, and merits consideration as an urgent and confident poetic response to the circumstances of political unrest in both England and Europe in the autumn of 1819 and 1820. His formulation of the ambiguities of the Bacchic is realized in part in response to the sculptures depicting Bacchus and associated gods in the Uffizi, which he visited in the autumn of 1819.

Euripides' *Bacchae* serves as a convenient distillation of the tensions which the Bacchic expressed for Shelley in his remarks on these statues. According to its commentators the play incorporates many of the ambiguities of the figure of Dionysus/Bacchus, and dramatizes them in terms of the conflict between the tragedy of Pentheus and the divine comedy which Dionysus releases. The play can be interpreted as a series of dramatic binary oppositions. Dionysus, as a deity, demands respect and obedience within his religious cult; hence the rites and mysteries are exclusive and remain shrouded in fear for the uninitiated. However, his cult appeals to the disempowered and marginalized elements of Theban society – women and the populace (even slaves). In *Bacchae*, Dionysus sees himself as the heroic defender of the people against Pentheus, who is depicted as tyrannical. But the release through *orgia* and *mania* associated with dance and physical ecstasy also leads to the mass hysteria and violence which destroys Pentheus. Possession by the Dionysian spirit bequeathes an oracular power, making humans divine and therefore prophetic. But such oracular power comes only through destruction (tearing humans or animals limb from limb). Dionysus is a conqueror, who travels to India and converts the populace to his cult, but he is also referred to as a 'foreigner' who threatens Hellenic society. Finally, Dionysus has magical powers which enable him to transform himself and others, but he can also convince his adherents that they are responsible for the destructive consequences of his influence.

In Shelley's work, this double bind, whereby the radical and subversive aspects of the Bacchic are countered by the dangers of religious excess and collective fervour, suggests a political situation for which the nearest correlative was the French Revolution and the Terror. Euripides' play represents the tragedy of a familiar political impasse in which tyranny is compounded by mass violence. A.W. Schlegel singled out *Bacchae* for particular praise in his *Lectures* (Schlegel 1815: I, 181–2), which Shelley read and reflected upon throughout his period in Italy, perhaps because of the way in which divine will rebukes human folly. But *Bacchae* can be seen to offer a vision of the consequences of tyranny which releases unharnessed, collective *orgia*. Once removed from a ritual context, revolution functions to dislodge all order in society. Bacchic and maenadic fervour thus symbolizes both the teleology of revolution and its dangers.

Shelley's view of the conflict between morality and aesthetics in maenadism is, in part, documented in his 'Note' on an altar engraved with the reliefs of four maenads (one of whom appears to be Euripides' Agave, with the head of Pentheus) seen in the Uffizi. Here the investment in an idealized notion of classical Greece is used to outweigh the terrors of the rituals depicted:

> This was indeed a monstrous superstition only capable of existing in Greece because there alone capable of combining ideal beauty and poetical and abstract enthusiasm with the wild errors from which it sprung. In Rome it had a more familiar, wicked, and dry appearance – it was not suited to the severe and exact apprehensions of the Romans, and their strict morals once violated by it sustained a deep injury little analogous to its effects upon the Greeks who turned all things – superstition, prejudice, murder, madness – to Beauty.
>
> (Shelley 1988: 349)

It is not simply that the compensations of Greek art are allowed to prevail over the dubious morality of what is represented, but that Greek society is perceived to transform moral excess into aesthetic form. Indeed the very endurance of Greek art is predicated here upon a morality which in any other age or society would corrupt it. Within artistic form, this 'monstrous' cult and its 'wild errors' are offset, such that they can seem quite natural:

> Nothing can be imagined more wild and terrible than their gestures, touching as they do upon the verge of distortion, in which their fine limbs and lovely forms are thrown. There is nothing however that exceeds the possibility of Nature, although it borders on its utmost line.
>
> (Shelley 1988: 349)

The paradox of an aesthetic of classical sculpture associated conventionally with restraint and beauty, which is made to represent a state of excess as 'natural', is part of Shelley's attempt to legitimate a form of art in which heightened physical release symbolizes political freedom. Under the sign of Greece, an exemplary culture and society, Shelley is tempted to license a sublime violence which is at odds with his condemnation of the Terror elsewhere.

Shelley's 'Notes on Sculptures' develop his study of Greek society begun in earnest with the translations of Plato and his reading of Herodotus in the summer of 1818 at Bagni di Lucca.[4] They bear the marks of Winckelmann's influence in their preoccupation with drapery and contour, and the influential aesthetic description of Greek sculpture as embodying 'noble simplicity and tranquil grandeur' (Nisbet 1985: 42). Yet they disrupt the German aesthetic by incorporating into its sublime language an ideal character for Bacchus in an idiom usually reserved for the more established deities in the Greek Pantheon typified by Apollo. Shelley's comment on the statue in the royal collection at Naples, 'a Bacchus more sublime than any living being' (Shelley 1964: II, 63), and his view of the figures of Bacchus and Ampelus in the Uffizi, 'Less beautiful than that in the royal collection of Naples and yet infinitely lovely' (Shelley 1988: 347), elevate Bacchus into an ideal deity:

> The countenance of Bacchus is sublimely sweet and lovely. . . . It has a divine and supernatural beauty, as one who walks through the world untouched by its corruptions, its corrupting cares; it looks like one who unconsciously yet with delight confers pleasure and peace.
>
> (Shelley 1988: 347–8)

Here the emphasis is less on Bacchus's irrational or even sensual character than on his divine immunity to corruption and the universal pleasure he disseminates. Bacchus is then a symbolic projection of Greek art itself.

> Like some fine strain of harmony which flows round the soul and enfolds it and leaves it in the soft astonishment of a satisfaction, like the pleasure of love with one whom we most love, which having taken away desire, leaves pleasure, sweet pleasure.
>
> (Shelley 1988: 348)

If, to Shelley, Bacchus is a paradigm of the power of Greek art, then he is also a symbol of resistance against a Christian morality which condemns his subversive immorality. Shelley's hostility to Michelangelo – 'I cannot but think the genius of this artist highly overrated' (Shelley 1964: II, 80) – is based on his view that the artist displays 'no sense of moral dignity & loveliness' (ibid.: II, 112), and he attacks Michelangelo's statue of Bacchus for pandering to vulgar prejudice:

> The countenance of this figure is the most revolting mistake of the spirit and meaning of Bacchus. It looks drunken, brutal, and narrow-minded, and has an expression of dissoluteness the most revolting. . . . It wants as a work of art unity and simplicity; as a representation of the Greek Deity of Bacchus it wants everything.
>
> (Shelley 1988: 352)

Michelangelo depicts Bacchus through an ethic which is opposed to the ideal of freedom he represents for Shelley: 'It is altogether without unity, as was the idea of the Deity of Bacchus in the conception of a Catholic' (Shelley 1988: 352).

The incorporation of the Bacchic qualities of pleasure and the unconscious are key dimensions of *Prometheus Unbound*, and Shelley associates them with his sense of the ideal vocation of the poet. In a letter to Peacock in which he refers to another version of Bacchic release, nympholepsy, he suggests that the 'poetical and abstract enthusiasm' of the Bacchic is close to his own sense of the impetus to write:

> What a wonderful passage there is in *Phaedrus* – the beginning, I think, of one of the speeches of Socrates – in praise of poetic madness, and in definition of what poetry is, and how a man becomes a poet. Every man who lives in this age and

> desires to write poetry, ought, as a preservative against the false and narrow systems of criticism which every poetical empiric vents, to impress himself with this sentence, if he would be numbered among those to whom may apply this proud, though sublime, expression of Tasso: *Non c'è in mondo chi merita nome di creatore, che Dio ed il Poeta.*
>
> (Shelley 1964: II, 29–30)

The definition of writing poetry in his own age is set against the constrictions of the prevailing models of criticism. Divine frenzy is, in a sense, an appropriate metaphor for the kind of freedom sought in *Prometheus Unbound*, which eludes the 'false and narrow systems of criticism which every poetical empiric vents'.

It is perhaps no accident therefore that many contemporary reviewers of *Prometheus Unbound* were not simply dissatisfied with poetry which seeks 'to act upon the passions without consulting the reason' (*Lonsdale Magazine* 1820: 498), but condemned the poet as simply mad:

> To our apprehensions, Prometheus is little else but absolute raving; and were we not assured to the contrary, we should take it for granted that the author was lunatic – as his principles are ludicrously wicked, and his poetry a mélange of nonsense, cockneyism, poverty, and pedantry.
>
> (*Literary Gazette* 1820: 580)

To condemn Shelley to 'the white-washed walls of St Lukes or Hoxton' (mental hospitals in London) (ibid.: 582) is the kind of misreading which aims to marginalize the work more effectively than the reviews by Lockhart in *Blackwood's* (Lockhart 1820) and Walker in the *Quarterly* (Walker 1821), which engage with the implications of Shelley's interpretation of the Bacchic.

Lockhart's review begins by arguing that the allegorical meaning of Aeschylus's *Prometheus Bound* is fully compatible with the Christian faith:

> No one, however, who compares the mythological systems of different races and countries, can fail to observe the frequent occurrence of certain great leading Ideas and Symbolisations of ideas too – which Christians are taught to contemplate with a knowledge that is the knowledge of reverence.
>
> (Lockhart 1820: 679–80)

According to Lockhart, Shelley has seized the allegory and 'grossly and miserably . . . tried to pervert its purpose and meaning' (ibid.: 680), substituting for it a critique of contemporary institutions:

> Mr Shelly [*sic*] looks forward to an unusual relaxation of all moral *rules* – or rather, indeed, to the extinction of all moral feelings, except that of a certain mysterious indefinable *kindliness*, as the natural and necessary result of the overthrow of all civil government and religious belief.
>
> (ibid.: 680)

The major part of Lockhart's review is a continuation of his articles on Greek tragedy in the early numbers of *Blackwood's*. He expresses approval of the austerity of the opening act but condemns the important speech of the Spirit of the Hour in Act III, as evil. Lockhart attempts to 'separate the poet from the allegorist' (ibid.: 681), praising the former and condemning the latter. Not all reviewers took exception to this creative allegorizing. One of the few positive reviews saw the deliverance of Prometheus as 'a symbol of the peaceful triumph of goodness over power; of the subjection of might to right; and the restoration of love to the full exercise of its benign and all-penetrating sympathies' ([Gold's] *London Magazine* 1820: 382). According to this view a revolutionary mythology is entirely legitimate:

> It presents us with the oldest forms of Greek mythology, informed with the spirit of fresh enthusiasm and of youngest hope; and mingles with these the creatures of a new mythology, in which earth, and the hosts of heaven, spirits of time and of eternity, are embodied and vivified, to unite in the rapturous celebration of the reign of Love over the universe.
>
> (ibid.: 382)

This 'new mythology' obviously challenges the absolute and authoritative status of the kind of mythology supported by Lockhart with his authoritative allegorical meanings. By undermining Lockhart's bridge between classical drama and mythology and the twin forces of church and state in early nineteenth-century Britain, *Prometheus Unbound* asserts a radical instability which upsets Greek classicism and the aesthetic taste it bequeathes.

The Bacchic influence in *Prometheus Unbound* is most marked after the austere Aeschylean Act I is over. Panthea's dream of the liberation of Prometheus, at the opening of Act II, suggests how the Bacchic is fused with the liberating spirit of Pan, manifest in her own name. In her description, Panthea's prophetic, sexual dream transforms herself, Ione and Asia: Prometheus's voice 'fell / Like music which makes giddy the dim brain / Faint with intoxication of keen joy' (II. i. 65–7), then his love 'Steam'd forth like vaporous fire; an atmosphere / Which wrapt me in its all-dissolving power' (II. i. 75–6). The spirit by which Panthea 'felt / His presence flow and mingle through my blood / Till it became his life and his grew mine / And I was thus absorbed' (II. i. 79–82) is transferred to Ione: 'I felt within thy parted lips / The sweet air that sustained me' (II. i. 103–4). Thus a chain of oracular prophecy is woven within the poem, which becomes essential to its conclusion. By locating the revolution against Jupiter in the natural world, populated by spirits, Shelley distinguishes the way that the poem is resolved through Demogorgon from the priestly connotations of the more familiar Delphic oracle.

The transforming properties of Bacchus are emphasized in the fauns' discussion of Silenus's songs which will foretell Prometheus's freedom in Act II, scene ii, and Asia's description of Prometheus's reign in terms of Bacchic joy to Demogorgon:

> and the harmonious mind
> Poured itself forth in all-prophetic song,
> And music lifted up the listening spirit
> Until it walked, exempt from mortal care,
> Godlike, o'er the clear billows of sweet sound;
>
> (II. iv. 75–9)

Yet even the invisible and beneficent spirits of nature in Act II, which symbolize the revolution from below, can be used to image impending political crisis. Thus the Semichorus's words ('those who saw / Say from the breathing Earth behind / There steams a plume-uplifting wind / Which drives them on their path' – II. ii. 51–4) foreshadow the more threatening image of long-awaited political change in the 'Ode to the West Wind' where the clouds heralding the storm of social unrest:

> Like the bright hair uplifted from the head
>
> Of some fierce Maenad, even from the dim verge
> Of the horizon to the zenith's height,
> The locks of the approaching storm . . .
>
> (Shelley 1970: 578, lines 20–3)

Yet Bacchic fervour does not simply suggest a political apocalypse; there are hints, as with the 'Notes' on the Uffizi statues, of alternative connotations. The character of Panthea articulates a melancholic and sceptical view of the oracular fervour associated with Demogorgon's haunt:

> Hither the sound has borne us – to the realm
> Of Demogorgon, and the mighty portal,
> Like a volcano's meteor-breathing chasm,
> Whence the oracular vapour is hurled up
> Which lonely men drink wandering in their youth,
> And call truth, virtue, love, genius, or joy, –
> That maddening wine of life, whose dregs they drain
> To deep intoxication, and uplift
> Like Maenads who cry loud, Evoe! Evoe!
> The voice which is contagion to the world.
>
> (II. iii. 1–10)

This 'contagion' appears to signify the consequence of tearing aside what the Spirit of the Hour later calls 'the painted veil, by those were, called life' (III. iv. 190) and of inflaming the world with a powerful, disruptive energy. But the 'maddening wine of life' also looks forward to the draught of Nepenthe in 'The Triumph of Life' (Shelley 1970: 516, lines 358–9), the consumption of which erases both pain and memory and which is given to Rousseau by the 'shape all light'. Its function is to counteract the despair which corrupted those idealistic radicals ('lonely men . . . wandering in their youth'), whom Shelley associates with postrevolutionary politics, with forgetfulness. It is this despair which the Earth confesses to having spread:

> There is a Cavern where my spirit
> Was panted forth in anguish whilst thy pain
> Made my heart mad, and those who did inhale it
> Became mad too, and built a Temple there,
> And spoke, and were oracular, and lured
> The erring nations round to mutual war,
> And faithless faith, such as Jove kept with thee;
>
> (III. iii. 124–30)

This negative prophecy, reflected by the Earth's earlier self, induces violence and destruction and its parallel is later incorporated into the image of the French Revolution in the 'Ode to Liberty': 'How like Bacchanals of blood / Round France, the ghastly vintage, stood / Destruction's sceptred slaves, and Folly's mitred brood!' (Shelley 1970: 607, lines 171–3). But in *Prometheus Unbound*, the Bacchic theme is finally associated with poetic resolution when the principal characters retire to the cavern described by Earth in the passage above; the Spirit is to conduct Prometheus and Asia 'beyond the peak / Of Bacchic Nysa, Maenad-haunted mountain, / And beyond Indus and its tribute rivers' (III. iii. 153–5). The source of the Bacchic in *Prometheus Unbound* is located finally in the Indian Caucasus, removed both from an unspecified, timeless mythological realm and from the western centre of Hellenic culture with which modern critics like Schlegel and Lockhart attempted to associate the Greek tragedians. The sense of Bacchic play in the final act shows the emergence of the cosmological, populist and feminine elements present in symbolic form elsewhere in the poem, combined with the disappearance of the principal protagonists. The Bacchic thus erases those differences implicit in gender and history without having to resolve them.

III

For Shelley, the incorporation of the Bacchic and the realm of Pan into his poetry becomes a way of challenging the interpretation of Greek mythology as the preserve of a neoclassical, gentlemanly audience, and yet at the same time has the advantage of distancing his poetry from the dangers of a populism implied by the grosser aspects of the Bacchic, and to that extent fulfilling his cautiously optimistic politics of the period 1819–20.

The implications of the Bacchic in Shelley's poetry extend beyond nature and prophecy in *Prometheus Unbound* to the representation of the uncontrollable forces of change. As already noted, the success of Shelley's indirect strategy conceals from critics the political motivation of poems like 'The Cloud', and more obviously, 'Ode to the West Wind'. But Shelley's politics, as evidenced in *A Philosophical View of Reform*, written between the autumn of 1819 and 1820, become increasingly cautious and distanced from the populism of Cobbett as the political situation in England and Europe seems to augur well for hopes of radical change. Thus 'The Masque of Anarchy', despite its radical tenor, represents a disciplined and formal, literary image of the people as a force totally distinct from the wild and uncontrollable aspects of nature, the clouds, volcanoes and wind, which symbolize revolutionary change in the poems published in 1820.[5] It is the soldiers, like the Furies who taunt Prometheus, who are shown to be crazed and bloodthirsty. Likewise, the wild maenadic dance in 'The Triumph of Life' presents the futility of life itself, and seems to condemn the sensuality of Rousseau's life. The Bacchic, while mediated through nature, is a form of prophecy; its human form threatens the revolution towards which that prophecy aspires.

NOTES

1 All references to Shelley's poetry are to the text of Shelley 1970.
2 A version of this passage is present in 'On the devil and devils' (Shelley 1988: 267–8), along with an elaboration of Shelley's reading of *Paradise Lost*. For an argument for dating 'On the devil and devils' to 1820, see Butler 1989; for a suggested dating of 1819, see Curran and Wittreich 1972.
3 Contemporary works which should be read in the context of Shelley's use of the Bacchic are Horace Smith (1821), Mary Shelley (1922) and Peacock's 'Rhododaphne' (Peacock 1924–34: vii, 1–94).
4 For details of Shelley's reading at this time, see Holmes 1974: 424–38, and Cameron and Reiman 1961–86: VI, 618–33.
5 See Matthews 1957; this celebrated article shows the political implications of Shelley's nature imagery, another version of which is the disruptive force of the Bacchic.

7

THE WANTON MUSE: POLITICS AND GENDER IN GOTHIC THEORY AFTER 1760

Harriet Guest

I

The Gothic revival of the 1760s and 1770s, prolific in glooms, grottos and gardens, in architecture and furniture design, in fantasies and histories, painting and poetry, represented in this paraphernalia the pleasures of privacy and sensuality, seduction and superstition. In 1765 Horace Walpole wrote in a letter to a friend of the composition of his novel, *The Castle of Otranto* (1764), that:

> In the evening I sat down and began to write, without knowing in the least what I intended to say or relate. The work grew on my hands, and I grew fond of it – add that I was very glad to think about anything rather than politics – In short I was . . . engrossed in my tale.
>
> (Walpole 1937: I, 88)

The account is striking in its insistence on what this activity negates, or is excluded from: this writing goes on after hours, without self-conscious knowledge or intention, and it affords a pleasure that is to do with not thinking about politics. The work itself flourishes like an organism in these exclusive, negatively defined conditions, and the engrossment of the writer, growing fond of his tale, suggests an analogous and almost sensuous absorption. Thomas Warton, who wrote extensively about the Gothic in his prose and poetry, emphasized its sensuality and femininity, writing that his fondness for the 'bliss' of Gothic's 'ravish'd pleasures' demonstrated 'the weakness of a lover's heart', in playing truant from the 'chaste design' of classical and rational truth (Warton 1802: I, 57–8, lines 35, 36, 45).

For these writers, the pleasure of Gothic is bound up with its furtive and feminine opposition to the social and fraternal virtues of public life, and what they allude to, in that notion of pleasure, is a definition of Gothic that is by no means limited to the novels which are now its most familiar manifestation. Their conception of the Gothic, I think, illuminates the ambivalently repressive and subversive status of those novels, but it is a site that extends beyond that genre to embrace much of what is excluded from the classical and public, and, in the 1760s at least, from the commercial sphere. Richard Hurd, whose writings provided the revival with its theoretical basis, described it as the 'world of fiction', in which the muse 'had wantoned it so long' (Hurd 1811: IV, 349), before she was constrained to stoop to truth, and this feminine, fantastic and lascivious characterization indicates an indiscriminate formlessness and elasticity of identity that is as open to diverse appropriations and redefinitions as are the discursive interconnections of the public, commercial and political.

The Gothic in these decades seems to be a heterogeneous or barbaric assemblage of ornament and furniture, of detail, without substantial qualities. It is defined by its lack of classical unity, of a visible plan of action, and thus by its proliferation of occasional detail, circumscribed by specificity of place and historical time. Eighteenth-century critics disagree about which times and which places give it this specificity, but they usually agree in locating it in opposition to any classical or republican ideal, in societies – often feudal or catholic – governed by arbitrary power. For Gothic fictions, they argue, are the means by which the popular imagination apprehends the mystified operations of arbitrary power, and by which popular subjection to that power is maintained, through the manipulation of prejudices and superstitions. They trace the fabulous extravagances of the Gothic back to its origins in oriental despotism, though they disagree about whether the northern imagination first became captivated and enraptured by the fantastic myths of the feminized Orient before or after the Crusades. Warton, for example, advanced the theory that the gods of the Norsemen were chieftains of the Asiatic Goths. There are then two critical ingredients in Gothic culture – a benighted and powerless populace, and superstitious fictions which are fabulous but not necessarily supernatural. And for these critics the distinction between popular prejudice and the fantasies it endorses is important, because the pleasure of the eighteenth-century reader involves the capacity to displace from one to the other those qualities – of gender, of political implication – that are incompatible with their pleasure.[1]

Later in the century, that sense of Gothic as the source of an irresponsible and extrapolitical pleasure becomes charged with a specific political significance. Gothic comes to be identified with a fondness for the traditions of the past that invests them with prescriptive force. It seems to describe a past that cannot be examined, that is obscured by the dark barbarism of the ages that produced it, but which nevertheless claims the authority of custom or prejudice. In her *Vindication of the Rights of Men* (1790), for example, Mary Wollstonecraft repeatedly attacks the Gothicism of Burke's *Reflections on the French Revolution* (1790). She traces in Burke's arguments 'gothic notions of beauty', which admire the ivy more than the trunk it supports, and demand that 'our *feelings* should lead us to excuse, with blind love, or unprincipled filial affection, the venerable vestiges of ancient days' (Wollstonecraft 1989: V, 10). She argues that he expresses a sentimental affection for the institutions of Gothic feudalism, for its gallantry and inequality, for its privileging of sensual and physical power, of materialism and hereditary property. In contrast, her own position, and that of the French Assembly, are defended for the rational use of the visible evidence of recent experience. Her hostility seems to indicate that the Gothic has been firmly appropriated to Burkean conservatism, and her own radicalism is marked by its extrusion of the Gothic as a manifestation of sentimental nationalism, and of that 'infantine sensibility' (Wollstonecraft 1989: V, 58) that makes personal property and feminine chastity the indistinguishable objects of gallantry.

The earlier theories of Gothic that I want to discuss, however, describe the territory of its pleasure in terms that do not readily yield their political affiliation. For theorists locate the pleasure of Gothic in its feminine privacy, excluded from the masculine and political concerns of public life, and in its fantastic opposition to that public reality, as well as to the pragmatic acquisitiveness of the market place. Gothic, in these decades, allows the reader to enjoy what Walpole described as the 'emptiness' of dreams and visions, and the meaningless 'babble of old people' (Walpole 1941: II, 192). That negative definition of the Gothic in the 1760s and 1770s means that it is a space in which the complex of shadowed relations between the extrapolitical and the feminine, the trivial and the illicit, the corrupting and the pleasurable, are renegotiated and recast. For the processes of privatization and evacuation that define the Gothic might confine it to celebrating its own fictionalization, and thus maintaining and enforcing the values of the commercial and public spheres that extrude it. Or it may constitute a region of extrapolitical activity that can reflect upon and inform, perhaps reform, the nature of what it is excluded from; a negative image that marks the positive imprint with traces of its own processes of development. The Gothic might not only be defined in terms of its opposition to the real world of politics, on the one hand, and the hard-headed materialism of commerce, on the other. It might disclose and articulate the significances of its exclusion, and 'the gesture or moment of [its] differentiation' (Isaak 1987: 12) from those, with implications that I suggest are most clearly brought into focus by its changing construction in terms of gender difference.[2]

In the theoretical discussions I am referring to, there is a clear if problematic division of critical opinion between men and women. It is striking that both Warton and Richard Hurd allude to Gothic, as I have already suggested, as an unchaste or prostituted pleasure: for them, it is ravished and wanton. In the criticism of Elizabeth Montagu, or of Clara Reeve, these sorts of terms are conspicuous by their absence. Gothic fable and romance are feminine, in their writings, but the Gothic is nevertheless understood to exercise a 'potent agency' (Montagu 1777: 149) that is neither corrupt nor unambiguously trivial. In their criticism that difference has complex implications for the readers, and perhaps writers, of feminine fiction, and for the definition in exclusive terms of the public and political sphere. Though Wollstonecraft condemned Burke's veneration for the Gothic, her Gothic novel, *The Wrongs of Woman: or, Maria* (1798), indicated that the category was not exclusively identified with his position. Earlier theories of Gothic, I think, articulate most clearly the distinctions within the notion of the Gothic that enabled later radical positions to be identified both by their distance from and closeness to it.[3]

II

I want to look at the treatment of these issues in Richard Hurd's *Moral and Political Dialogues* (1760) and *Letters on Chivalry and Romance* (1762), and then to discuss the relation between his arguments and those of Elizabeth Montagu. Montagu explicitly acknowledges her debt to Hurd's theories, and I want to explore the ways in which her arguments both adopt his theories and diverge significantly from them, and finally to consider in more general terms the implications of the gendering of Gothic. The combination of the popular and the fantastic that I have suggested characterizes Gothic theory describes a model for government through prejudice, a model reminiscent of the arguments for the prescriptive authority of custom advanced by Burke and Samuel Johnson. But in Hurd's discussions this combination is represented as a means of celebrating the private and extrapolitical pleasure of the literary critic. Hurd argues that most of the more fantastic improbabilities of Gothic fiction are grounded in the specific cultural and material nature of feudal society, in historical circumstances which very few eighteenth-century scholars had researched. But he is not concerned to argue that readers of Gothic should become acquainted with the particular details of that history, so that they can understand their representation in fantasy. The reader's pleasure is augmented by the knowledge that this basis exists, rather than by the 'ungrateful task' (Hurd 1811: IV, 261) of uncovering it, for what the reader needs to believe, in order to become engrossed in Gothic fantasy, is only that someone somewhere did once find these visions plausible. Thus he writes that 'A legend, a tale, a tradition, a rumour, a superstition; in short, any thing is enough to be the basis of [the Gothic writer's] air-formed *visions*' (ibid.: IV, 321). The masculine reader enters into the popular superstition, he recognizes in it the mystification of a historically specific truth, but at the same time he preserves his capacity to view it with sceptical detachment, his perception of its truths as superstitious fantasies. Hurd explains that:

> We must distinguish between the *popular belief*, and *that of the reader*. The fictions of poetry do, in some degree at least, require the *first* (they would, otherwise, deservedly pass for *dreams* indeed): but when the poet has this advantage on his side, and his fancies have, or may be supposed to have, a countenance from the current superstitions of the age in which he writes, he dispenses with the *last*, and gives his reader leave to be as sceptical, and as incredulous, as he pleases.
>
> (ibid.: IV, 322)

The reader, then, enters into the fantasy, but in the same movement he withdraws and distances himself from it, establishing his rational, sceptical superiority to popular credulity. Hurd writes, about the Gothic poets:

> Does any capable reader trouble himself about the truth, or even the credibility of their fancies? Alas, no; he is best pleased when he is made to conceive (he minds not by what magic) the existence of such things as his reason tells him did not, and were never likely to, exist.
>
> (ibid.: IV, 321–2)

The reader's doubled perspective, his capacity on the one hand to be made to conceive things, and on the other to reject and dismiss them, is similar to that of Henry in *Northanger Abbey*, who found it amusing that reading Radcliffe's *Mysteries of Udolpho* made his hair stand on end for two days (Austen 1971: 95–6), though in Hurd's account the combination of engrossment and differentiation, absorption and amused scepticism, is more immediate. It is a position which enters into the implicitly politicized, and therefore true or real, nature of popular superstition. But the popular or political implications of those beliefs are apprehended as pleasurable fantasies, which seduce the imagination, and flatter the reason, but leave the heart, Hurd argues, indifferent and untouched.

The sense in which Gothic literature might both manifest and repress political discontents dissipated, evacuated, in fantasy is, in Hurd's letters, represented as a result of its characteristic historical specificity. For that fantasy is dissipating or wanton because it is only true and real in relation to specific historical moments and circumstances. It therefore treats truths with feminine abandon, proliferating them in a mass of occasional detail, and representing them as pluralized fictions. Hurd argues that Gothic, chivalric manners appear singular because they are intimately related to the political constitution that produced them, and to the particular stage of feudalism from which he believes they sprang. But because those manners, in his words, 'never did subsist but once, and are never likely to subsist again', they appear 'romantic, and unnatural' (Hurd 1811: IV, 343). Classical manners, in contrast, appear customary and archetypal, although they are equally unfamiliar. And because they are customary, readers are prepared to believe that they may exist, somewhere beyond their experience, and therefore, 'we readily agree to call them *natural*, and even take a fond pleasure in the survey of them' (ibid.: IV, 343). Gothic is therefore opposed to the unity of classical and public truth, for it seems to lack universal or political reality. And that lack is manifested in its antipathy to the classical and political ideal of unity of action.

The Gothic represents actions or truths which are historically diverse and discrete, and it is therefore characterized by an apparent formlessness, a negation of public unity. Hurd describes this negative form, this coincidence of fantasy and pluralized truth, through an extended analogy between literature and garden-design. The 'truest taste in gardening' (ibid.: IV, 302), he argues, is:

> that which *Kent and Nature* have brought us acquainted with; where the supreme art of the designer consists in disposing his grounds and objects into an *entire landskip*; and grouping them . . . in so easy a manner, that the careless observer, though he be taken with the symmetry of the whole, discovers no art in the combination.
>
> (ibid.: IV, 301)

The observer agrees to call the unified symmetry of this landscape natural, although he is taken with it because it is the product of the self-effacing hand of art. But in the Gothic garden the more conspicuous hand of art produces an apparent diverse formlessness that contrasts with this 'natural' unity.

The design of this classical landscape, Hurd suggests, is analogous to dramatic unity of action as a result of its relation to the spectator, for it is to the careless observer that the landscape presents itself as a unified whole, through the controlling focus granted him by the designer. Hurd writes of the Gothic garden, in contrast, that:

> A wood or grove cut out into many separate avenues or glades was among the most favourite of the works of art, which our fathers attempted. . . . These walks were distinct from each other, had each their several destination, and terminated on their own proper objects. Yet the whole was brought together and considered under one view, by the relation which these various openings had, not to each other, but to their common and concurrent center.
>
> (ibid.: IV, 301)

The design of this garden does not present its symmetry to the careless observer, its several destinations or bounds are not disposed so that he can easily 'take a fond pleasure in the survey of them'. The distinct walks of the garden indicate a plurality of proper objects which have no relation to each other even though they can be brought under one view. What that one view can disclose is their common point of departure, as it were their common motive or design, but not their unity of action. Their severalness therefore seems to manifest a kind of self-conscious spontaneity that offers a tantalizingly ambivalent denial and confirmation of the unity natural to the controlling survey.

This implies a notion of composition which may inform Richard Wilson's paintings of Gothic subjects. *The White Monk*, for example, which was frequently reproduced after its first exhibition in the early 1760s, represents a pleasurably ambivalent relation between unity and dissolution that is strongly reminiscent of Hurd's account. The spectator's position before the image affords 'one view' of the whole landscape, but it does not disclose the relation between the discrete elements that make up the composition, which each seem to have their own proper objects, to be actions which do not find their unifying focus in the observer's careless eye. David Solkin has argued that 'all parts of the view remain subject to a strict formal pattern', but that it is a view of 'formal divisions and typological contrasts' (Solkin 1982: 66, 68). There is, for example, no apparent narrative link between the lovers in the foreground and the monk on the cliff, and their distinctness may best be understood in terms of the Gothic aesthetic of pleasurable separateness.

In the design of Gothic the fantastic proliferation of proper objects, of truths specific to discrete historical circumstances, seems to reveal the inadequacy of the one view, and thus to impoverish the idea of unity, to identify it with what is easy, fond and careless, rather than commanding or imperious. The paths of the Gothic garden are trodden by knights animated by a militant spirit of enterprise. Their errant but deluded zeal points up the negligence with which the careless and perhaps indolent tourist overlooks the unity of the classical landscape. But it is the doubled perspective characteristic of the Gothic, the sense in which it affords both a common centre and a plurality of distinct truths, that makes it so pleasurable to Hurd's critical reader. For it is that sense of at once entering into the dissipating diversity of the Gothic, of being occluded, subjected, within its design, and yet achieving a position of detachment from which the whole appears to be brought together, that allows the reader to feel both ravished and godlike, both dissipated and transcendent. The reader can enjoy the pleasures of fantasy and pluralized truth, but his scepticism

The White Monk, by Richard Wilson, *c.* 1760. Reproduced by kind permission of the National Museum of Wales.

nevertheless confirms in him the presence of those masculine and public attributes necessary to the recognition and grasp of universal and political reality.

III

That account of Hurd's letters suggests, I think, that the politicization of Gothic might take one of a number of forms. It might involve the manipulation of fantasy as a means of enforcing the subjection of the populace, making fantasy, like custom, the tool of prescriptive authority that it was imagined to have been in the past. Or it might identify fantasy as a medium of popular protest, the means by which the vulgar identify and manifest their discontent. And there is a third set of possibilities, made available by that unstable relation between fiction and truth in Gothic. The dissipating, feminized space of fantasy itself might acquire a public and political charge, destabilizing the definition of that truth. Or, and with different implications, the knights of industry might come to seem heroic in the context of Gothic fantasy, legitimating the claims of both commerce and the Gothic to recognition in the public and political world. These are not possibilities that Hurd's arguments acknowledge: the pleasure of Gothic fictions for him is always supportive, complementary to the public seriousness of classical truth. For him the pleasure of fantasy is the manifestation of its extrapolitical emptiness. But in the Gothic theories of Elizabeth Montagu, I think, fantasy itself does become invested with a political significance.

Montagu discusses Gothic most fully in her 'Essay on the praeternatural beings in Shakespeare' and in the third of her 'Dialogues of the dead' (1769), where Plutarch and a modern bookseller exchange views on literature. Her discussion, particularly in the 'Essay', adopts much of Hurd's theory, but it constructs the distinction between popular superstition and its fictions in significantly different terms. In the first place, her account of the popular basis of Gothic fiction places greater emphasis on the idea that these are national superstitions – it expresses a sort of amused affection for the national tradition they form. This is of course partly because they are being employed by Shakespeare, who, she writes, could touch 'the latent passions of civil rage and discord' with judicious mastery (Montagu 1777: 153). Shakespeare, she implies, could transform popular passions into fantastic superstitions, lovable national traditions. But while she suggests that this conversion of civil rage into harmless custom does augment the pleasure of the spectator and critic, she (perhaps like Hurd) thinks that this construction of the customary should be treated with sceptical caution. These national customs and superstitions are not prescriptive, predictive or exemplary. They are confined to the historical past. She writes of the heroes of Gothic chivalry that to see them as exemplary is 'to be in the condition of superstitious people, who chuse rather to act by intimations they receive in the dreams of the night, than by the sober counsels of morning meditation' (ibid.: 311). The pleasure they give is the pleasure of unreality, of empty dreams of the past. It does not acquire the authority of prescriptive custom, for if affection for it manifested more than nostalgic fondness, this would reduce polite as well as vulgar readers to the subject condition of 'superstitious people'.

So Montagu's argument, like Hurd's, insists on the emptiness of Gothic superstitions. But the implications of its dreamy fictions are different for her, perhaps because she is concerned with different readers and spectators. Montagu argues, like many of her contemporaries, that the effect of literature on women is more significant than its effect on men. The bookseller in her dialogue cynically rehearses the belief that:

> The women have greater obligations to our writers than the men. By the commerce of the world men might learn much of what they get from books; but the poor women, who in their early youth are confined and restrained, if it were not for the friendly assistance of books, would remain long in an insipid purity of mind, with a discouraging reserve of behaviour.
> (ibid.: 308)

And Plutarch, his interlocutor, agrees that women are more likely to be 'betrayed into these dangerous studies', though he implies that what they endanger is precisely a desirable purity of mind and reserve. In her accounts of the pleasures of Gothic fiction, then, it seems to be primarily female readers and spectators that Montagu has in mind, and it is their relation to chaste political reality that is problematic.

I suggested that in Hurd's account the pleasure of reading Gothic arose from the reader's ability to engross himself in popular superstition, to entertain its fantasies, but at the same time to distance himself from them, to regard them with sceptical detachment. He enjoys them because they dissipate truths into proliferating fictions, because their historical specificity opposes them to the universal and unitary truth of the classic. And Montagu's argument is similar, in that the reader enjoys seeing fearful instances of civil rage dissolved in superstitious fantasies. Where she departs from Hurd, however, is in her account of the nature of the pleasure that fantasy offers. In Hurd it is the pleasure of controlled dissipation: the pleasure the masculine reader derives from knowing that he is being made to conceive impossibilities. In his private capacity, the reader enjoys this experience of self-division, this power to participate in popular fiction while preserving his position of superior individual difference. The dissipation of enjoying a fantasy that he knows to be untrue or unnatural constitutes for him a kind of vicarious experience of temporary subjection that is pleasure. In Montagu's account, however, the value, the pleasure, of the popular superstitions out of which Gothic fantasy is formed does not depend on this sense of temporary and vicarious subjection to a mystified source of authority. She argues that Shakespeare's use of national superstitions 'avails him only with critics of deep penetration and true taste, and with whom sentiment has more sway than authority' (ibid.: 160).

In Montagu's argument, then, the critic who derives pleasure from the representation of Gothic superstition, in Shakespeare and in other literature, enjoys through their sentiment a kind of liberation from the sway of authority. Superstitious fictions promote sentimental endorsement for what she identifies as the 'rude spirit of liberty' animating the Gothic muse. In her discussions, sentiment is not the instrument of repression, or the psychic manifestation of subjection that it becomes, for example, in Wollstonecraft's criticisms of Burke. Sentimental approbation, Montagu argues:

> will augment our pleasure; whether we give the reins to our imagination, and, as Spectators, willingly yield ourselves up the pleasing delusion, or, as Critics, examine the merits of the composition.[4]
>
> (ibid.: 165)

The combination of willing submission and critical examination produces in Hurd's reader a pleasure that is licensed and perhaps licentious in its extrapolitical definition, whereas in Montagu's audience it produces sentimental pleasure in the spirit of liberty – a pleasure that may be available to political articulation.

It may be appropriate to perceive the difference between the theories of Hurd and Montagu in terms of gender because the effect of the privileging of sentiment in her arguments is to blur the distinction between classical and public, chaste and unitary truth, and the wanton proliferation of Gothic fictions. In her discussions, Gothic is not represented in terms of indiscriminate and promiscuous femininity, perhaps because for the female critic, reader and spectator the contrast between the plural, fictionalized truths of Gothic, and the chaste and manly truth of public virtue has a different significance. For that audience was anyway denied the governing authority of manly truth, excluded from the fraternity that agrees the definition of the natural and universal; women were not public citizens.

Samuel Johnson did not like Montagu's work on Shakespeare – which is surprising given its debt to his own criticism, and its favourable reception by his friends.[5] He pronounced that there was 'not one sentence of true criticism in her book' (Boswell 1934–50: II, 88), and his judgement may respond to the absence of a sense of public truth in her essay. That absence, however, allows Montagu's argument, briefly, to recognize in or attribute to women's position in the late 1760s a discourse capable of articulation in the public sphere of aesthetic and political judgement – a discourse of sentiment that implies neither the prescriptive Gothicism of Burke nor the radical rejection of sensibility that characterizes Wollstonecraft's *Rights of Men*. Her criticism articulates a feminine position constituted in a socialized pleasure, a sentiment public in its opposition to the authority of the chaste design of universal truth, and which is therefore not defined in terms of the individual difference that Hurd's reader achieves through his pleasure, and which reveals Gothic as the site of a privatized and licensed dissipation. The pleasure that Gothic fantasy makes available to Hurd's reader is bound up with its extrapolitical designation, whereas in Montagu's criticism the ambiguous status of sentiment seems to deflect that designation and to disclose its necessary ambivalence. For in her account the sentimental pleasure of Gothic seems available to those spectators who may know but not necessarily participate or believe in a unified political reality, and it may thus make available to educated middle-class women a kind of liberty from its dominance.

IV

The difference between the ways in which Montagu and Hurd define the pleasures of Gothic might most readily be accounted for in terms of what Terry Eagleton has described as the 'bourgeois "feminization of discourse"' in the mid- to late-eighteenth century. This feminization, he argues, 'prolongs the fetishizing of women at the same time as it lends them a more authoritative voice' (Eagleton 1982: 13). A reading in these terms might point to the appropriation of Gothic to a specifically national history, a powerful myth of the customary that set the parameters for that unwritten and apparently vague, misty, but in fact rigorously exclusive and prescriptive definition of national identity that underpinned and enabled the imperial and commercial development of British power in the second half of the eighteenth century. A schematization of the processes of this appropriation might point, for example, to William Blackstone's use of the fantastic architecture of the Gothic castle as an image for the vagaries of English law (Blackstone 1767–9: III, 268), and to J.H. Pott's argument that if the fictions of Shakespeare were somehow 'consonant to the English character', then the Gothic ruins 'everywhere to be seen' in the English landscape 'must have the same consonance of character, the same congenial beauties' (Pott 1782: 57–8). This manifestation of national identity in architectural fantasy provides in the 1780s and 1790s some basis for the image of the British Empire as the natural conserver of Indian national identity, in, for example, William Hodges's perception of a familial affinity between Gothic and Indian buildings (Hodges 1787: 5). Gothic facilitated the definition of national character in terms that were both wantonly heterogeneous in their embrace of private and diverse individuals, and redeemed in an idealization of chaste and maternal femininity, the sacred power of Britannia.

This notion of the Gothic would seem peculiarly appropriate to the combination of commercial and imperial power because of its capacity to describe as heroic the apparently avaricious private ambitions of entrepreneurs and adventurers thought to have no explicit concern for the public good – those whose aims could seem both individualistic and amoral. Though Hurd had been careful to contrast nostalgic respect for the fantastic aspirations of the Gothic knights of history with admiration for the progressive ambitions of commerce, those errant knights operating in a fabulous and feminine sphere excluded from the real political concerns of the public world came to be perceived as analogous to eighteenth-century commercial adventurers.[6] James Beattie, in his discussion of the Gothic in his essay 'On fable and romance', argues that 'the chastity of a knight errant was to be no less unimpeachable, than the credit of a merchant now is' (Beattie 1783: 548–9), and points to the material basis of both chastity and credit in private property. Clara Reeve, in *The Progress of Romance*, argues in defence of the propriety of Gothic notions of heroism that their example could inspire those 'wholly immersed in low, groveling, effeminate, or mercenary pursuits' with an 'avarice of fame and glory' (Reeve 1785: I, 103, 101). That virtuous avarice, in her arguments, is contrasted and yet paralleled with the greedy desires of the effeminate or mercenary.

In opposition to the ideal of the chaste masculine and paternal or fraternal public, commerce 'begets Avarice, gross Luxury, or effeminate Refinement' (Brown 1757: 153), and its effects are clearly alluded to in Reeve's account of those engaged in mercenary pursuits:

> The thirst of immoderate wealth or pleasure, will engross their attentions and desires; or else they will sink into a state of supine indolence, and become entirely negligent of what they owe to themselves, to their connexions, or to their country.
> (Reeve 1785: I, 102)

The appropriation of notions of Gothic heroism and knightly enterprise to this thirst after pleasure or wealth could enable commercial adventurers to be celebrated as the defenders of the national and imperial faith. At the same time, it acknowledged the uneasy amorality with which that enterprise was perceived to be tinged – the sense that the thirst after wealth, or the extravagant pleasures of egregious heroism, occluded or excluded explicit commitment to the public or national good, and ultimately produced a vain and luxurious decadence that effeminated and corrupted the ideal masculinity of the state. For the Gothic ages were perceived to be both heroic and benighted, indolently barbarous. Beattie warns, in the conclusion to his essay:

> Let not the usefulness of Romance-writing be estimated by the length of my discourse upon it. Romances are a dangerous recreation . . . and tend to corrupt the heart, and stimulate the passions. A habit of reading them breeds a dislike to history, and all the substantial parts of knowledge;

> withdraws the attention from nature, and truth; and fills the mind with extravagant thoughts, and too often with criminal propensities.
>
> (Beattie 1783: 573–4)

Gothic fantasy and romance, Beattie's argument implies, promote both heroic self-denial and a more-than-extravagant criminality, both chaste frugality and promiscuous luxury.[7]

What is at issue in the relation between the appropriation of Gothic heroism to the fantastic ambitions of commercial enterprise and the chaste public fraternity seems to be a kind of mutual incorporation or reciprocal conversion: a process that is illuminated by Joshua Reynolds's comments on the Gothic in his sixth 'Discourse' of 1774. Reynolds is talking about the right of the great painter to select materials from the work of lesser artists, and make them 'his own property'. He argues that:

> the inferior branches of the art, will contribute to furnish the mind and give hints, of which a skilful painter, who is sensible of what he wants, and is in no danger of being infected by the contact of vicious models, will know how to avail himself. He will pick up from dunghills what by a nice chymistry, passing through his own mind, shall be converted into pure gold; and, under the rudeness of Gothick essays, he will find original, rational, and even sublime inventions.
>
> (Reynolds 1975: 107)

Works in 'the inferior branches of the art', Reynolds continues:

> afford a rich mass of genuine materials, which, wrought up and polished to elegance, will add copiousness to what, perhaps, without such aid, could have aspired only to justness and propriety.
>
> (ibid.: 108)

The Gothic here is vicious, infectious, excremental, its femininity implied in the discursive closeness of the notions of physical corruption and prostitution. It is redeemed to purity through some alchemically inverted process of ingestion, which renders its mass pure, if not quite chaste, and discloses in it the matter of 'sublime inventions'. Yet the difficulty of the conversion Reynolds describes seems almost to besmirch the purity and propriety of his prose, while it adds polish to its judgement. The great artist may be 'in no danger' of infection, as masculine virtue is unstained by feminine wantonness, but the process Reynolds describes does not only manifest the superior power of the artist's healing touch, for his aspirations also need the 'aid' that the ornamental excrescence of the Gothic affords. It is because Gothic is excremental, feminine and wanton, because of its recalcitrant materiality, whether that is figured as the 'rich mass' of gold or dung, that it can 'add' to a chaste masculinity austere in its lack.

What Eagleton describes as the bourgeois feminization of discourse is articulated in the texts I have discussed in terms of the complex network of relations between the Gothic, public and political masculinity, and commerce. The uneasy relation between those is manifested in the slippage between apparently opposed terms: between heroic and 'effeminate, or mercenary' avarice, between the private and unimpeachable possession of chastity, and the promiscuous breeding of 'criminal propensities', between the copious elegance of 'genuine materials' and the potentially infectious viciousness of rudeness and ornament. In so far as the fantastic political reality of public and masculine purity is perceived to assimilate or to depend upon the copious elegance and 'effeminate Refinement' attendant on commercial luxury, the discourses that constitute it seem to be subject to bourgeois feminization, producing a tension in the differentiation of gender that theories of the Gothic articulate. For the Gothic is characterized in terms of extravagant fictions imbued with the luxuriant and voluptuous materialism of the feminized Orient. But, in the theories of Gothic published in the 1770s and 1780s, it is also seen to describe a severely chaste and warlike manliness: Beattie, for example, argues that 'Warm and fruitful countries generally produce (unless where a spirit of commerce and manufacture prevails) effeminacy and indolence' (Beattie 1783: 523), and those 'soft' characteristics are contrasted with the physical hardiness of the Gothic knights, and, implicitly, with the rigorous spirit of the early stages of commerce. In the feminized territory of Gothic fantasy, as in the feminized discourses of political embourgeoisification, a more immediately physical manliness is privileged in the place of the chaste masculine definition of the discourses of public power. This emphasis on sexual differences, rather than on the explicit gendering of discourses that define political power and sexuality, is indicated in Clara Reeve's comment that male critics have insidiously confused novels with romances, and:

> having seen a few of the worst or dullest among them [both], have judged of all the rest of them; – just as some men affect to despise our sex, because they have only conversed with the worst part of it.
>
> (Reeve 1785: I, 112)

The immediacy of the transition from genre to sexuality, from judgement in the republic of letters to misogyny, works, in these decades, to articulate the instability of public and political discourses in the anxieties and pleasures of sexual difference, and, more specifically, to focus that ambivalence on the bodies of women.[8] For the blurring of the ideological opposition between the private and the public or political in bourgeois discourse can be seen, as Eagleton's phrase suggests, to be inscribed in bourgeois constructions of feminine sexuality.

Richardson's Clarissa, perhaps the ideal manifestation of that femininity, seems to articulate the conflict this ambivalence creates in her complaint that 'those imputed qualifications which used so lately to gain me applause, [are] now become my crimes'. Clarissa believes that this slippage between the laudable and criminal is the result of the 'disgust and anger' directed at her, which 'alter the property of things' (Richardson 1985: 257). Her comments might be taken to indicate the sense in which the uncertainties attendant on the emergence of bourgeois and commercial hegemony produce conflicted responses of applause, and angry disgust, which are focused and articulated in the criminalization and deification of femininity. And the problematic privileging of gender difference which that identification involves may also be manifested in the way in which the theories of Gothic advanced by the critics I have discussed seem to be distinguished along lines of gender.

There are, however, some problems involved in reading Gothic in the terms suggested by this model of the bourgeois feminization of discourse, difficulties that, I want to suggest, can best be understood in terms of those possibilities for the politicization of the Gothic that I mentioned earlier. I suggested then that the implications of describing the knights of industry in terms of Gothic heroism might be different to those of feminized fantasy itself, in so far as that Gothic space might be conceived to be politicized. I have suggested that Montagu valued the shared pleasures of Gothic fantasy, but did not regard Gothic heroism as exemplary, and the distinction involved may be similar to that between Wollstonecraft's contempt for Burke's Gothic notions of history, and endorsement of the pleasurable fictions of the Gothic novel. If the changes taking place in these decades involve a redefinition of the boundaries between public and private, to describe the opposition between the public and commercial world outside and the domestic sphere it is imagined to enclose, so that the power of private and commercial wealth gains an audible voice in the real, manly world of politics, then what is involved in that transition may be perceived differently by those who write from the position of women. Not because of the unchanging force of any ahistorical conception of sexual difference – though the discourses that constitute the Gothic employ a vocabulary of fetishism that may call into play the 'Psychological consequences of the anatomical distinction between the sexes',[9] in a bourgeois culture which invests a charged significance in chastity and virility, wantonness and emasculation – but because for those writers the boundaries between public and private were differently constituted. The transition involved in articulating their 'private' interests, in increasing the published audibility of these writers, is not identical or smoothly coextensive with the empowerment of a private and commercial bourgeois system of values.

In *The Wrongs of Woman*, Mary Wollstonecraft writes of the moment at which the heroine decides that she is free from the constraints of 'matrimonial obedience':

> How had I panted for liberty – liberty, that I would have purchased at any price, but that of my own esteem! I rose, and shook myself; opened the window. . . . the clouds seemed to flit away obedient to my wishes, to give my soul room to expand. I was all soul, and (wild as it may appear) felt as if I could have dissolved in the soft balmy gale that kissed my cheek, or have glided below the horizon on the glowing, descending beams. A seraphic satisfaction animated, without agitating my spirits; and my imagination collected . . . an immense variety of the endless images, which nature affords, and fancy combines, of the grand and fair.
>
> (Wollstonecraft 1989: I, 152–3)

This is the language of sentimental enlightenment, signalling the heroine's emancipation from those 'delusive prejudices' (ibid.: I, 154) that support 'the institutions of society, which . . . enable men to tyrannize over women' (ibid.: I, 153). In the context of this Gothic novel, it seems strongly reminiscent of the theories of Gothic reading I discussed earlier. The subject is dissolved in an experience of expansive and almost sensual pleasure, a pathetic, superstitious fallacy that is known to be fantastic, yet animated, and in a sense legitimized, by the spirit of liberty. The Preface to the novel suggests that it 'ought rather to be considered, as of woman, than of an individual' (ibid.: I, 83). The passage itself seems accessible to this directive not just through a process in which the intersubjectivity assumed to be common to all women blots out differences of class, race and individual experience, but because the fantasy of liberty, in its privacy and specificity, articulates a gender-specific utopian politics.

Elizabeth Montagu wrote, in a letter to Elizabeth Carter of 1759, that she 'thought it an excellence, a perfection . . . a virtue' that Carter could claim 'a wild and untractable love of liberty, because you want a place where you can enjoy some hours every day uninterrupted' (Montagu 1813: IV, 208). Her comments on the desire for solitude, like Wollstonecraft's representation of Maria's self-emancipation, describe a 'love of liberty' that is virtuous because it is private. But the notion of privacy that is at issue in these passages is distinct from the ideal domestic retirement that Montagu alludes to when she writes that 'The virtues of women are blasted by the breath of public fame, . . . they were ordained to give a silent light, and shed a mild benignant influence on the world' (Montagu 1777: IV, 313–14). Montagu's letter to Carter, and Wollstonecraft's novel, allude to a private space defined in its differentiation from masculine reality, a space which, in its fantastic and feminine formlessness, is opposed to politically powerful truth. Its privacy licenses the articulation of the Gothic 'spirit of liberty' because it is sentimental, emptied of political force. The domestic privacy in which women give a silent light, in contrast, alludes only obliquely to the gendered discourses of political power, and is constituted not by its opposition to that chaste truth, but in terms of sexual difference, as an inversion of the manly world of commercial and political enterprise.

The juxtaposition of these different constructions of privacy tends to throw into relief, as it were, the public and political nature of the discourses that construct the first, and the more obviously sexualized nature of the second. But the contrast between the two does not depend on the notion of political reality displacing or being displaced by fantasies of sexual difference. The contrast is between notions of private femininity as either pleasurably wanton and extrapolitical, or chastely immured from representation in truth or fantasy, in directly or obliquely public terms. For the construction of femininity in terms of its extrapolitical formlessness, rather than in containment within and from masculine realities, may indirectly constitute a feminine utopian fantasy capable of political articulation. The pleasurable spirit of liberty that animates the Gothic muse produces an 'untractable love' incompatible with feminine domesticity, and which, in specific historical moments, manifests the coincidence of fantasy and truth.

NOTES

1 These issues were debated in, for example, Hurd 1811, Warton 1774 and Beattie 1783. For more recent discussions of Gothic fiction, see, for example, Ellis 1989: part 1, Napier 1987: chapter 1, and Punter 1980: chapter 1. See also Walpole's argument that *The Castle of Otranto* 'was fit for nothing but the age in which it was written' (Walpole 1961: 221).

2 Clearly, the extrapolitical status of Gothic in these decades was not apolitical, or without ideological implications, but the notion identified by the critics I discuss is distanced from the specific political implications appropriated to the Gothic in the 1740s, and apparent in, for example, James Thomson's *The Castle of Indolence* (1748). For a broader survey of the status of Gothic, see Madoff 1979: 337–42.

3 Wollstonecraft's perception of Gothic sensibility may have changed in the years that separate the two publications I refer to, as Mary Poovey argues (Poovey 1984: chapters 2–3). What interest me are the terms in which the Gothic can accommodate and articulate those changed and apparently opposed positions.

4 Montagu's argument here does not suggest that the critic and spectator are distinct persons, though she, like Johnson, thought that Shakespeare's power lay in his capacity to speak to the situation of the individual as well as to the audience as a whole (Montagu 1813: IV, 107–8).

5 See for example, Seward 1811: I, 131.

6 See Hurd 1811: III, 176–7, and Dialogues III and IV.

7 For an illuminating discussion of the implications of the criminalization of reading, see de Bolla 1989: chapter 10. On frugality and luxury, see Pocock 1975: 430–1, 444–6.

8 On literary criticism and political discourse in the later eighteenth century, see Hohendahl 1982: 50–4.
9 From the title of Sigmund Freud's paper of 1925, quoted in Tickner 1988: 111.

8

PLAGIARISM WITH A DIFFERENCE: SUBJECTIVITY IN 'KUBLA KHAN' AND *LETTERS WRITTEN DURING A SHORT RESIDENCE IN SWEDEN, NORWAY AND DENMARK*

Jane Moore

In 1927 John Livingston Lowes alleged that parts of Mary Wollstonecraft's *Letters Written during a Short Residence in Sweden, Norway and Denmark*, published in 1796, quietly reappear in Coleridge's 'Kubla Khan', which was written the following year (Lowes 1978: 148, 545).[1] Lowes's suggestion has set the agenda for much later discussion. My own paper, written from the theoretical perspectives of feminist poststructuralism and Lacanian psychoanalysis, places Coleridge's plagiarism within the field of sexual politics and the politics of desire and power as they are played out in Romantic writing. I propose the thesis that the plagiarism of *A Short Residence* can be read as an attempt by the male Romantic subject, Coleridge, to fill in the lack which Lacan argues is the condition of subjectivity, and which other critics have suggested is what causes the Romantic desire for absolute selfhood.[2] I add that desire always operates at the level of specific interests, including those of gender.

My readings of *A Short Residence* and 'Kubla Khan' aim to demonstrate how the desire for oneness and sameness, which in Romantic writing finds expression in the concept of the sublime, is differently inscribed in these respectively female- and male-authored texts. I should add here that I am aware of the problematic nature of the Romantic desire for oneness as experienced by male poets. A letter to John Thelwall on the subject of sublimity, which was written at the same time as 'Kubla Khan', demonstrates something of the characteristic movement of jubilation *and* loss in Romanticism. Caught between success and failure, Coleridge writes to Thelwall,

> I can *at times* feel strongly the beauties, you describe, in themselves, & for themselves – but more frequently *all things* appear little – all the knowledge, that can be acquired, child's play – —the universe itself – what but an immense heap of *little* things? – I can contemplate nothing but parts, & parts are all *little* –! – My mind feels as if it ached to behold & know something *great – something one & indivisible* – and it is only in the faith of this that rocks or waterfalls, mountains or caverns give me the sense of sublimity or majesty!
>
> (Coleridge 1956–71: I, 349)

The desire for 'something *great*', although not altogether abandoned, is at least rendered precarious by Coleridge's recognition of the gap separating the imaginary realm of desire, plenitude, sublimity, from the reality of a world fragmented by difference where the poet is only one of many 'little things'.

Nevertheless, despite the anxieties and hesitations surrounding it, the desire to experience the sublime oneness of a magisterial subjectivity remains within Coleridge's writing. I argue that this desire is especially present in 'Kubla Khan', not in spite of but because of its impossible fulfilment: it is precisely the poet's knowledge that he cannot revive within himself the Abyssinian maid's 'symphony and song' and his corresponding inability to 'build that dome in air' which keeps alive the sublime project in the same moment that it puts its fulfilment into question. I therefore place Coleridge's plagiarism of Wollstonecraft alongside the Abyssinian maid as an example of his desire to erase the signs of sexual and textual difference which threaten the possibility of self-mastery and sublimity.

Before I go on to argue these points in relation to Wollstonecraft's and Coleridge's writing, I want to make some general observations on the relationship between plagiarism and desire, which I theorize in Lacanian terms. The three scenes of desire which follow demonstrate that desire operates in an economy of love and death. The first two, taken respectively from Patrick Suskind's best-selling novel

Perfume, published in translation in 1987, and Anne K. Mellor's anthology *Romanticism and Feminism*, published in 1988, introduce the third, which is the scene of Coleridge's plagiarism.

I

Perfume is subtitled *The Story of a Murderer*. In the fetid fictional world of that novel a perfume-maker is murdered by the masses. But this is no ordinary murder. And the victim, Grenouille, is no ordinary man. Himself a mass murderer of fragrant young women, Grenouille makes a monstrous hero; but it is not for this that he dies. He is killed because he is loved too much. Doused in a perfume made by and for himself, Grenouille's body is devoured by the hungry mouths of the masses, all of them intoxicated by his indescribable scent: 'Each of them wanted to touch him, wanted to have a piece of him. . . . They tore away his clothes, his hair, his skin from his body, they plucked him, they drove their claws and teeth into his flesh, they attacked him like hyenas' (Suskind 1987: 262). When the cannibals have completed their carnage they are afraid to look into one another's eyes. What happens when they pluck up courage to do so is revealed in the novel's concluding sentences: 'When they finally did dare it, at first with stolen glances and then candid ones, they had to smile. They were uncommonly proud. For the first time they had done something out of Love' (ibid.: 263).

Perfume is and is not a love story. Which is to say it is a story about the relationship between desire and death which demonstrates that a lover's discourse and the discourse of desire always, at least at a figural level, involve death. Just as in Lacan's *Four Fundamental Concepts of Psycho-Analysis* where the desiring subject, the analysand, says to the object of its desire, the analyst, '*I love you, but, because inexplicably I love in you something more than you – the* objet petit a *– I mutilate you*' (Lacan 1979: 268), so Grenouille's lovers display their consuming passion for him, which inexplicably is for something more than him, by devouring all of him. In this scenario desire is the 'something more' which breaches love (the crowd act of 'out of Love') and leads to death.

In Lacanian psychoanalytic theory the *objet petit a* is the 'other' who is the site of the subject's desire and the object of its love. In Romanticism the *objet petit a* is frequently figured as feminine. As Anne K. Mellor has observed, the Romantic canon is dominated by male poets who 'have been heralded because they endorsed a concept of the self as a power that gains control over and gives significance to nature, a nature troped in their writings as female' (Mellor 1988: 8). In this reading of Romanticism men are subjects and women are objects, the objects, that is, of male desire and power.

But to describe the relationship between men and women in Romanticism in these predatory terms is arguably to oversimplify the respective subject positions they occupy. Mellor offers a binary model of sexual difference which fixes man in a position of authority and power, and places woman permanently on the underside of power, knowledge and selfhood. In Lacanian theory, however, the acquisition of subject identity for *both* sexes is a *process*, not a fixed or self-conferred given. Furthermore, it is a process surrounded by self-doubt and uncertainty. Lacan argues that a subject's identity, masculine or feminine, is neither absolute nor permanent. This is because subject identity is not constituted in nature or biology but in the order of culture and language. Subject identity is conferred and constantly reshaped in the linguistic exchange between subject and other: 'What I seek in speech', writes Lacan, 'is the response of the other. What constitutes me as subject is my question' (Lacan 1977: 86).

However, the reply from the other which constitutes the subject's identity can induce self-anxiety in the subject as well as self-knowledge. This is because in order to have its identity confirmed the subject has to look beyond itself, to the other. For a male subject to acquire a masculine identity he must recognize the difference of himself from the other, from the *objet petit a*, who is female. But because the *objet petit a* exists in a relation of difference to the subject, because she is precisely other than him, she introduces '"lack" and "gap" into the operations of the subject' (Bowie 1988: 117). His recognition of the difference of woman simultaneously confirms *and* puts into question the possibility of possessing a full or absolute masculine identity: identity is put into question because the lack which is introduced by the other creates a gap between itself and the subject, which 'incapacitates the subject for selfhood, or inwardness, or apperception, or plenitude, or mutuality' (ibid.: 117). In this way the other negates the possibility of absolute subjectivity in the same moment that it keeps the desire for self-unity, for sameness-unto-self, alive.

In Lacanian theory, then, it is the difference of woman which breaches the binarism of sexual difference and which brings into the foreground the instability of male subject-identity, an instability that is always present but not always acknowledged. I argue later that the figure of woman, who is there in 'Kubla Khan' in the traces of Wollstonecraft's text and in the Abyssinian maid, is the *objet petit a* that introduces the lack, the otherness of femininity, which ultimately incapacitates the male poet.

My second scene is an illustration of the way that men in Romanticism have reacted to the increasing influence of feminist literary criticism. In recent years a new school of male critics has arisen in Romantic studies. These 'new men', as opposed to the old Yale men, consciously address the issue of gender in Romanticism.[3] Their concerns are laudable and their prose is persuasive. In an essay entitled 'Romanticism and the colonization of the feminine', which is included in Mellor's *Romanticism and Feminism* and is representative of the 'new man', or 'men in feminism' school, Alan Richardson (1988) argues that male poets in the Age of Feeling revalued a range of activities and emotions, such as tears and breastfeeding, which men had previously belittled as feminine and wholly female attributes, before appropriating them for themselves. In the same essay Richardson suggests that when male poets eulogize their sisters in Romantic poetry, as when Wordsworth in *The Prelude* praises Dorothy 'for all the early tenderness / Which I from thee imbibed' (Wordsworth 1959: 1850, XIV, 493, lines 234–5) and when Manfred mourns Astarte who 'was like me . . . / She had the same lone thoughts and wanderings' (Byron 1986: IV, 74, lines 105, 108–9), they do so not in order to inscribe their sisters as individuals in their own right, but to project 'idealized feminized' versions of their male selves (Richardson 1988: 16–19).

Richardson is at his theoretical best here, but interestingly enough, his argument is made at women's expense. He criticizes feminist re-evaluations of Romanticism for omitting to consider the relevance of Nancy Chodorow's feminist analysis of mothering roles. His own essay makes good that lack, but in doing so it arguably re-enacts the colonizing gesture with which male Romantics are charged. Like Wordsworth and Byron before him, Richardson turns to the figure of woman, which in this instance is feminist criticism, to project an idealized, feminized and feminist version of himself.

Richardson's Romantic involvement with feminism is not unique. Marlon B. Ross also has an essay in *Romanticism and Feminism* (Ross

1988). And the involvement of men in feminism more generally is evident in the volume of essays entitled *Men in Feminism* (Jardine and Smith 1987). The question is whether men in feminism are offering their support for feminism or alternatively supporting women who by implication need men to speak for them. Certainly Richardson's essay pays very little attention to the gender power relations which allow him to speak so unhesitatingly on behalf of feminist literary concerns, and to the extent that his appropriation of feminist criticism unconsciously reproduces the sexual dialectics he finds in Romantic texts, then the appearance of 'men in feminism' is and is not a love scene.

My third illustration, although on the face of it a love scene, is, no less than the previous two, an instance where desire engenders death. Publication of *A Short Residence* in 1796 brought Wollstonecraft a string of male admirers. One of them, William Godwin, famously remarked: 'If ever there was a book calculated to make a man in love with its author, this appears to me to be the book' (Godwin 1987: 249). The text also played Cupid for other contemporary readers, among them Count von Schlabrendorf, who wrote notes in the margins of his copy, half suggesting he had fallen in love with the author (Holmes 1987: 302); and Robert Southey, who wrote excitedly to Joseph Cottle, asking: 'Have you met with Mary Wollstonecraft's [travel book]? She has made me in love with a cold climate, and frost and snow, with a northern moonlight' (ibid.: 17). Yet of all Wollstonecraft's contemporary readers, it was perhaps Coleridge who most completely fell in love with her book. Taking to its extreme the maxim that imitation (by way of assimilation) is the sincerest form of flattery, Coleridge's subsequent plagiarism of that book might be interpreted as an act of love. Or, perhaps more accurately, as an act, like the murderous feast held by Grenouille's worshippers, 'done out of Love' (with all the attendant ambiguity of that phrase).

John Livingston Lowes seems to imply this point, or something like it, when he suggests that Coleridge's interest in Wollstonecraft's writing, which 'bore fruit in something more definite than falling in love with a cold climate and a northern moonlight', was the result of his 'sheer omnivorousness' (Lowes 1978: 148). Jane Gallop theorizes the point when she argues that: 'To represent another text is to assimilate the other's discourse into one's own, to re-establish a single economy' (Gallop 1982: 125–6); and Julia Kristeva endorses it in her statement that psychoanalysis 'has shown us, ever since

Freud, that interpretation necessarily represents appropriation, and thus an act of desire and murder' (Kristeva 1983, cited in Smith and Kerrigan 1983: 33).

II

If Coleridge did indeed read *A Short Residence*, then, as Lowes points out, he almost certainly came across the following passage from Letter 17, which describes the waterfalls at Trollhattan:

> Coming to the conflux of the various cataracts, rushing from different falls, struggling with the *huge* masses of rock, and *rebounding* from the profound cavities, I . . . acknowledg[ed] that it was indeed a grand object. A little island stood in the midst . . . which, by dividing the torrent, rendered it more picturesque; one part appearing to issue from *a dark cavern*, that fancy might easily imagine a *vast fountain, throwing up its waters from the very centre of the earth*.
>
> (Lowes 1978: 545, note 127)

With 'Kubla Khan' in mind, Lowes asks whether this extract perhaps lent 'a word or two, at least to "*Huge* fragments vaulted like *rebounding hail*"?' (ibid.).

Other readers of Wollstonecraft's and Coleridge's texts have certainly thought so. One of them, Richard Holmes (Holmes 1987: 39), detects traces of Letters 17 and 15 in lines 17–21 of 'Kubla Khan':

> And from this chasm, with ceaseless turmoil seething,
> As if this earth in fast thick pants were breathing,
> A mighty fountain momently was forced:
> Amid whose swift half-intermitted burst
> Huge fragments vaulted like rebounding hail,

Another of Wollstonecraft's readers, Claire Tomalin, is convinced that '[s]ome of her phrases were good enough to provide Coleridge with inspiration' (Tomalin 1974: 190). And not only Coleridge but Wordsworth too. Tomalin suggests that Wordsworth's narrative poem 'Ruth', written in 1799, about an English girl wooed and abandoned by her faithless American lover, has passages in it which evoke Mary and Imlay's story (ibid.: 223). Holmes makes the same point (Holmes 1987: 41), adding that Coleridge may also have been evoking Wollstonecraft's loveless predicament resulting from her desertion by Imlay, as well as Scandinavia's haunting moonlight, when he wrote in lines 14–16 of 'Kubla Khan' of

> A savage place! as holy and enchanted
> As e'er beneath a waning moon was haunted
> By woman wailing for her demon-lover!
>
> (Coleridge 1912: I, 297)

One of the questions raised by this plethora of intertextual allusions and possible plagiarisms is how to read them. For Lowes, the significance of the re-inscription of Wollstonecraft's text in Coleridge's poem lies with the poet himself. That is to say, what is at stake is Coleridge's poetic integrity, his originality and genius. Holmes and Tomalin place less emphasis on Coleridge as the source of meaning: instead they are concerned to establish the influence of Wollstonecraft's writing on other texts contemporaneous with hers. Yet although both critics turn to intertextuality to explain the assimilation and appropriation of shared themes and tropes in Romantic writing, they each finally, albeit paradoxically, place Coleridge at the point of meaning. Coleridge is thus made culpable for the crime of plagiarism, which in traditional literary circles is probably the most serious charge that can be brought against a writer.

It is also, from the perspective of poststructuralism, the most difficult to prove, or even to conceptualize. In poststructuralist theory language is a social fact, meanings are public and shared and there is no available knowledge outside culture. This suggests that the author is not the source of meaning but one of its effects, and that reading and writing are irreducibly intertextual activities. As a consequence plagiarism is no longer opposed to the concept of individual Romantic creativity, but is itself a radical condition of the Romantic text. Plagiarism becomes part of the very structure of writing.

In this context it raises issues concerning the intertextual production, circulation and appropriation of knowledge. Michel Foucault's essay on these matters, entitled 'What is an author?' (Foucault 1969), adopts the title of Roland Barthes's famous essay to proclaim 'The death of the author' (Barthes 1968). If the author is dead, Foucault's essay asks, 'What difference does it make who is speaking?' (Foucault 1969: 210). In the light of this question, which alludes to yet another essay title, Mary Jacobus's 'The difference of view' (Jacobus 1979), I want now to turn to 'Kubla Khan' and *A Short Residence.*

III

The concept of the sublime ego is probably Romanticism's most important and simultaneously least attainable ideal. It is unattainable because the sublime ego seeks ultimately to collapse the difference between subject and object, self and other. Initially, however, the poet is hesitant, he is aware of his littleness in relation to nature's vastness. In 'Ode to the West Wind', for example, he (Shelley 1970: 577–9) is overawed by the

> Wild Spirit, which art moving everywhere;
>
> (line 136)

with whom he repeatedly pleads (demands?) to listen to his poem, 'hear, O hear!' Yet towards the end of the 'Ode' the poet begins to appropriate for himself that which initially alienated him:[4]

> Be thou, Spirit fierce,
> My spirit! Be thou me, impetuous one!
>
> (lines 61–2)

In the final lines the desired fusion of subject and object is *almost* realized when the poet imagines the wind to speak his words not only for him but as him:

> Scatter, as from an unextinguished hearth
> Ashes and sparks, my words among mankind!
> Be through my lips to unawakened Earth
>
> (lines 66–8)

I write *almost* because the union that the poet desires with the wind is only imagined. As a consequence, the ego is held in suspension, caught between the possibility of success and failure, fiction and reality. The sublime ego is not achieved.

In theory it never can be. This is because subjectivity is an effect of difference. The collapse of difference, therefore, implies the negation of subjectivity. Yet this negation can never occur within the symbolic order of language, which is a realm of difference. After entry into the symbolic order of difference plenitude of being becomes impossible, except perhaps in imaginary dream-worlds or in death.

Nevertheless both 'Kubla Khan' and *A Short Residence* are texts which promise the possibility of sublimity, and the corresponding attainment of self-unity. But in each case the promise produces different results. When Coleridge contemplates the sublime (which for him, as for Burke, inheres in the 'vastness' and 'infinity' of nature) the rock and the waterfall are elevated to a position of symbolic importance. For Wollstonecraft too, the rock and the waterfall are sublime objects. I will discuss Wollstonecraft first.

Letter 15 of *A Short Residence*, which describes a cascade near Frederikstad that the narrator is eager to visit, is remarkable for the overwhelming sense of lack and loss that contemplation of nature by a woman produces. From the beginning the letter is structured by lack and loss, delay and deferment. It opens with a delay: Wollstonecraft's travel party miss the ferry. It continues with a digression on a barren because fire-damaged forest which, like Wollstonecraft's world-weary self, is starved of the nourishment necessary for life. When the cascade is finally reached, what is found there is in one sense nothing at all. This is in the sense that the description of the cascade comprises nothing more than a string of negative acknowledgements of Wollstonecraft's life and her precarious hold on it:

> I cannot tell why – but death, under every form, appears to me like something getting free – to expand in I know not what element; nay I feel that this conscious being must be as unfettered, have the wings of thought, before it can be happy.
> (Wollstonecraft 1989: VI, 311)

When Wollstonecraft contemplates the sublime, when she looks at the cascade, she ends up thinking about herself, about death, but also rebirth and immortality. In death Wollstonecraft seeks a new life, hoping to find a space free from the present-day social and sexual restraints which delimit her ego. Only in death, then, is it possible for a woman to imagine acquiring the plenitude of being which is the condition of the Lacanian imaginary and the *raison d'être* of the Romantic sublime.

It is difficult not to see the importance of gender in this situation: because Wollstonecraft *is a woman*, and is therefore bound by the legal and social restrictions placed on her sex in the eighteenth century, she can only envisage autonomy of any form after death. Legally, women in the eighteenth century were dispossessed; the heroine of Wollstonecraft's novel *The Wrongs of Woman: or, Maria* had good reason to call women 'the *out-laws* of the world' (Wollstonecraft 1989: I, 146). The obligatory surrender of Maria's economic and social independence to her husband recalls William Blackstone's definition of marriage as a state where women were barely allowed to be subjects at all:

> By marriage, the husband and wife are one person in law; that is the very being or legal existence of the woman is suspended during the marriage, or at least is incorporated and consolidated into that of the husband: under whose wing, protection, and *cover*, she performs every thing.
>
> (Blackstone 1767–9: I, 442)

However, not only women of the period but men too, especially Men of Feeling, conceived of themselves as life's victims. But for these men, tyranny often occurs in the form of feelings, melancholia, even madness, rather than social institutions. Poets of the 1760s, such as William Collins and Edward Young, are disempowered by the very feelings through which they experience life. In *Night Thoughts* Young goes so far as to seek release in death:

> Death,
> Strong Death, alone can heave the massy Bar,
> This gross impediment of Clay remove,
> And make us Embryos of Existence free.
>
> (Young 1989: I, 40, lines 124–7)

Wollstonecraft's letters in *A Short Residence* demonstrate that she too is a Woman of Feeling. Like Collins and Young before her, she feels rather than thinks her thoughts, and her feelings revolve around ideas of death.

The passivity and loss of control experienced by men and women of feeling regarding their own lives also infects their writing. This can be seen in the temporal and spatial discontinuities of Young's *Night Thoughts* and in Collins's apparent inability to shape words into their correct syntactic order. Patricia Meyer Spacks observes that the entire strophe of William Collins's 'Ode on the Poetical Character' is a single, long, impenetrable and syntactically imperfect sentence (Spacks 1967: 72). Loose syntax also marks the spontaneous and emotional style of Wollstonecraft's letters. Letter 15, for example, continues:

> Reaching the cascade, or rather cataract, the roaring of which had a long time announced its vicinity, *my soul was hurried* by the falls into a new train of reflections. The impetuous dashing of the rebounding torrent from the *dark cavities which mocked the exploring eye*, produced an equal activity in my mind: *my thoughts darted from earth to heaven*, and I asked myself *why I was chained to life and its misery*? Still the tumultuous emotions this sublime object excited, were pleasurable; and, viewing it, my soul rose, with renewed dignity, above its cares – *grasping at* immortality – it seemed *as impossible to stop the current of my thoughts*, as of the always varying, still the same, torrent before me – *I stretched out my hand* to eternity, bounding over the dark speck of life to come.
>
> (Wollstonecraft 1989: VI, 311; my emphasis)

This moment of potential sublimity which is also one of sensibility produces disorder in the narrator's thought and vision. A language that is her own, but which she does not in any sense possess, eludes her. Signifiers and syntax slide beyond her control: as punctuated, the syntax of the sentence beginning 'Still the tumultuous emotions . . .' does not hang together. The result is not so much a 'proper' sentence as a string of fragmented unco-ordinated statements which resolve nothing. And it is not only language which the narrator is unable to control. Her vision, too, is disordered by the natural world. The 'impetuous dashing of the rebounding torrent' effects a ceaseless movement which mocks the 'exploring eye' and continually defers the object of its gaze.

Vision, which in these lines is metaphysical, not merely physical, has a particular significance in the philosophy of feeling. As one eighteenth-century critic puts it, 'the eye is the best avenue to the heart' (Kames 1785: II, 351). The gaze is also of central importance in instances of Romantic sublimity; Wollstonecraft's moment of potential sublimity demonstrates the power of vision. Spectacle produces emotion, thus creating the conditions for sublimity; it is her view of the cascade which raises Wollstonecraft's soul 'with renewed dignity, above its cares'.

But this moment of potential sublimity is remarkable for the sense of precariousness and uncertainty which surrounds it. The moment itself follows directly on from the question 'I asked myself why I was chained to life and its misery?' It therefore substitutes for the (absent) answer to the question. But the answer itself is unsatisfactory in the sense that nothing much is concluded here at all. The moment lacks a resolution; on the contrary, the hand stretched out to eternity returns empty. Even the prospect of death, and the freedom it promises, is displaced into the absent future.

Yet still a greater sense of uncertainty surrounds the status of the sublime in Letter 15. The problem is how to categorize a sublime experience where the female subject is not empowered by her experience and is left utterly bereft. A possible solution would be to read Letter 15 as an example of the 'failed sublime', which is the phrase Patricia Yaeger uses to designate the distinctly 'feminine' experience which she identifies in women's writing (Yaeger 1989: 201). Yaeger argues that '[t]he Romantic sublime is a genre that is, historically and psychologically, a masculine mode of writing . . . concerned with empowerment, transport, and the self's strong sense of authority' (ibid.: 192). She goes on to suggest that the key difference between the Romantic (masculine) sublime and the 'failed' (feminine) sublime is the fate of the ego:

> For Shelley and Wordsworth the sublime mode permits a normal retrieval of mythic powers that are initially alienated in order to insure their internalization; this energy is finally reverberated so as to strengthen the ego. But for women, such retrieval is still abnormal or deviant.
>
> (ibid.: 210)

Letter 17 of *A Short Residence*, which describes another sublime moment and another cascade, appears to fall into the pattern of Yaeger's feminine or failed sublime, but the passage begins by repeating the pattern which Yaeger identifies in poems by men, not women.

> I . . . wandered about; and at last coming to the conflux of various cataracts, rushing from different falls, struggling with the huge masses of rock, and rebounding from the profound cavities, *I immediately retracted, acknowledging that it was indeed a grand object.* A little island stood in the midst . . . which, by dividing the torrent, rendered it more picturesque; one half appearing to issue from a dark cavern, that fancy might easily imagine a vast fountain, throwing up its waters from the very centre of the earth.
>
> (Wollstonecraft 1989: VI, 316; my emphasis)

The narrator begins by making a difference between subject and 'grand object'. She acknowledges her inferiority to that object and immediately withdraws from it, as any male poet would. Wordsworth makes a similar movement in *The Prelude* when during the boat-stealing episode 'With trembling oars' he pulls back from the 'huge peak, black and huge' (Wordsworth 1959: 1850, I, 25, lines 378, 385, 386) and returns frustrated to the security of the covert.

Whereas Wordsworth physically removes himself from the grand object, Wollstonecraft stays put. But this is not an assertive gesture. On the contrary, her retraction, which might at first seem more forceful than Wordsworth's retreat, renders her immobile: she retracts into herself, but in doing so she loses her sense of self. As she gazes on the sublime scene, she grows 'giddy', she is 'stunned' by what she sees and is 'scarcely conscious' of her position:

> I gazed *I know not how long, stunned* with the noise; and growing *giddy* with only looking at the never-ceasing tumultuous motion, I listened, *scarcely conscious where I was*, when I observed a boy, half obscured by the sparkling foam, fishing under the impending rock on the other side.
>
> (Wollstonecraft 1989: VI, 316; my emphasis)

The only movement which occurs here on the part of the narrator takes place at the level of sight and thought. It is a moment of potential sublimity but there is no sense here, as there is in Wordsworth's boat-stealing episode, that Wollstonecraft's ego is strengthened by her experience. On a literal reading of the passage her ego is stunned and displaced: she is 'scarcely conscious' and she loses all self-orientation. A less literal, more optimistic reading, would identify here the expansion of Wollstonecraft's ego in what is arguably a pleasurable and probably sublime moment. It is not, however, a scene of empowerment: the little boy re-introduces the domestic patriarchal world Wollstonecraft has fleetingly escaped and brings her firmly back to a world of cares. The moment of sublimity is henceforth forgotten.

To 'rise and then forget', Yaeger suggests, 'is not a gesture typical of the masculine sublime' (Yaeger 1989: 201). The young Wordsworth initially retreats from the 'huge peak, black and huge', and as Yaeger also observes, he remembers the spectacle for many days, his imagination continues working with the 'huge and mighty forms', which in lines 410–11 of *The Prelude* give rise to purified 'feeling and thought' (Wordsworth 1959: 1850, I, 27).

IV

'Kubla Khan' complicates, but does not disprove, Yaeger's thesis that forgetting is not a gesture typical of the masculine sublime. Its preface is an elaborate ruse designed to explain away the *inability* of the poet to *remember* and recapture in the poem the vision of his dream.[5] The interruption of the visitor from Porlock is the means by which he is able to offer a (false) justification of the difference between his dream, which was complete and entire, and his writing, which is incomplete and unfinished. He tells us that 'he could not have composed less than from two to three hundred lines' while asleep (Coleridge 1912: 296, lines 15–19). Running to a mere fifty-four lines, the poem itself is a poor substitute. Not only is the poet unable to supply the missing lines, but within the poem he suffers another, possibly more serious lapse of memory: he fails to revive within himself the Abyssinian maid's 'symphony and song', which would allow him to 'build that dome in air', and to complete his poem.

But despite these acknowledgements of defeat and admissions of lack, the poem operates within an economy of domination and mastery, to which the ruse is central as a means of denying defeat.

To begin with it is, of course, a man, Kubla Khan, who dominates the poem of the same name. Moreover, his dominion, unlike the wild wilderness that Wollstonecraft loses herself in, is perfectly proportioned and painstakingly measured, even down to the last five miles. Xanadu is a closed world with no room for dissent; a nature that threatens to be chaotic is very quickly tamed by the poet's pen which goes on to map the mazy five miles of the river's quietly meandering course through wood and dale. Nature, not man, is in retreat. This is in contrast to *A Short Residence*, where the narrator who retreats from the wildness of nature is compelled to acknowledge its awesome, hypnotic and terrifying power.

Not only is nature tamed and contained within the poem's measured pace, so too is woman. If, as Holmes and other critics have suggested, the 'woman wailing for her demon-lover!' (Coleridge 1912: 297, line 16) is not only generic woman, but alludes specifically to Mary Wollstonecraft and her loveless predicament in

Scandinavia, then it appears here that Wollstonecraft is doubly subjected: once by her actual lover, Imlay, and again by the poet who inscribes her, Coleridge.

However, it is too simple, too binary almost, to assume that 'Kubla Khan' straightforwardly subjects women and accomplishes mastery and sublimity. Stanza 3 actually breaks the binary law of sexual difference which attributes power to men and makes women the passive recipients of male mastery. In this stanza the poet desires to eliminate sexual and textual difference, so he turns to the Abyssinian maid, wishing to appropriate her song; the gesture has its literal analogue in the turning by Coleridge to Wollstonecraft's text and his plagiarism of it. The project is defeated, however, by the stubborn otherness of the woman's voice, which both eludes the poet and elucidates his own incompleteness.

The stanza begins by making an initial difference between the damsel and the poet. The poet wants to deny this difference: he wishes to assimilate the woman-as-muse, and to incorporate her song within himself. However, this is no easy task: the muse possesses something the poet does not; she has a language of her own, a 'symphony and song' (an *écriture féminine* perhaps?), which is other than the poet's patriarchal language, and which he cannot speak. The stakes are high here: if only he could borrow, plagiarize, revive an other woman's language, then the poet would fully realize his creative potential. His poem would be complete, and he would be master of all words and worlds:

> Could I revive within me
> Her symphony and song,
> To such a deep delight 'twould win me,
> That with music loud and long,
> I would build that dome in air.
>
> (Coleridge 1912: 298, lines 42–6)

And yet, of course, it is precisely this that he fails to do. As a consequence, the imaginary 'dome in air', which expands to encompass irreconcilable opposites such as sun and ice, and is what Geoffrey Yarlott calls 'the ultimate in creative originality' (Yarlott 1967: 148), is never built. At the end of the poem, as Stephen Bygrave has noted, the fulfilment, the completion of the dome, and the poem, is a potential rather than a vicarious one: 'At the end of "Kubla Khan" narrative in the simple past switches to the modals of possibility: "could", "would" and "should" – a series of conditionals to represent a potential revival' (Bygrave 1986: 133).

In the context of poetic unfulfilment sensibility is as important a consideration as sublimity. Poets of sensibility commonly shared the burden of creativity after Milton, and much poetry of the 1760s, especially Collins's 'Odes' is preoccupied with the problem of writing poetry in an Age of Feeling without 'Great Men'. The muse of Collins's 'Ode to Fear' is the 'mad nymph' who belongs to a different realm from the poet and is beyond his reach. It is not insignificant that sensibility itself was taken by many of the age to be responsible for the increasing feminization of literature and culture. Pope's *Dunciad* is only one hostile response to the perceived effeminacy of his age, an effeminacy which is taken to be one of the reasons for the chaotic visions and unruly imaginations of men like Young and Collins. In the world of *The Dunciad* the disorder which chaos produces coalesces in the figure of the Goddess Dulness, and Dulness herself, of course, is a woman. What is more, she is a woman who writes improperly, collapsing the distinction between poetry and prose:

> Here to her Chosen all her works she shews;
> Prose swell'd to verse, verse loit'ring into prose:
> (Pope 1963: 732, lines 273–4)

The Dunciad presents a picture of woman as the corruptor of male poetic standards; her 'chosen' few are the denizens of Grub Street who privilege commerical concerns above literary value. In Collins's 'Odes' a woman again is made culpable for the perceived decline in poetic standards and the inability of the male poet to conceive of himself as a figure of poetic authority. In the 'Ode to Fear', for example, the poetic muse, who is female, creates an instability of representation, casting the very project of writing poetry into doubt.

Paradoxically, perhaps, the female muse deserts the poet who embraces emotion and implicitly sanctions femininity, while aiding and abetting the macho poetics of one such as Milton. And it is Milton, together with Shakespeare, who the poets of the 1760s, as well as Coleridge, turned to for reassurance that it was possible to write 'true poetry'. In the context of sensibility and the feminization of culture which was perceived to be occurring in the last four decades of the eighteenth century, it is not difficult to understand Coleridge's respect for Milton and Shakespeare, a respect which arose in part from the masculine strength he detected in their lines.[6] In 'Kubla Khan' it is a woman yet again who interrupts the scene of writing, and it is she who puts the promise of poetic fulfilment permanently in flight. What the poem cannot master is woman: starting out from the assumption that the poet once saw 'A damsel with a dulcimer / In a vision', the poem's final stanza ends with a vision of female beauty and harmony that is only a vision: for the male poet, the woman's song is ineffable and intangible. Elusive and unknown, the harmony of the Abyssinian maid is placed beyond his cognitive reach. What is more, it is exactly at the moment when the poet fails to master woman that he fails also to be the master of himself, of his own actions: the dome is never built and the poem, at least the poem the preface promises, is never finished.

And they are never likely to be, since the materials needed for their completion, music and air, have already been placed in the poem within a feminine economy, or the economy of an *écriture féminine*. I do not suggest that it is only the figure of woman, as other, who destabilizes representation in Romantic poetry. Wordsworth's 'evermore about to be', however much it appears as a compromise, a solution, to the problem faced by the poet in *The Prelude* when he yearns to reach a goal, but fails to get there, defers and therefore questions the possibility of sublimity. What I do want to point to, however, is the problem which the difference of woman poses to the poet who desires sublime oneness. Not only does woman introduce the lack which makes sublimity both desirable and impossible, she also, like the sublime, seduces and tyrannizes the poet. As always other than the subject, always outside the subject's reach, ineffable and inexpressible, the sublime object exposes the lack which is the cause and symptom of his desire; so, too, does the figure of woman.

Constructed as a subject that represents pure nature, woman intervenes between man and the chaos of his own creating; and man turns to woman, to woman-as-nature as the site of his lost innocence. As the poet in Wordsworth's 'Tintern Abbey' puts it:

> Oh! yet a little while
> May I behold in thee what I was once,
> My dear, dear, Sister!
>
> (Wordsworth 1940–9: II, 262, lines 119–21)

On the other hand, it is precisely woman's lack of learning and mastery which makes her not only a source of solace and inspiration for the male poet, but also the discomforting reminder of a remainder, of a difference, that he might potentially fail to conquer and erase, thus exposing his own lack.

The fear of not being *all* man is one that in Coleridge's writing derives from the failure to subordinate the different female other, especially when that other makes its mark on his own character. Coleridge perceived his inadequacies, his procrastinations, plagiarisms and what he called his 'diseased volition', as peculiarly feminine traits which made him a lesser man, and not so manly a poet, as, say, John Donne or Wordsworth.[7] 'Of all the men I ever knew', said Coleridge, 'Wordsworth has the least femineity [*sic*] in his mind. He is *all* man' (Coleridge 1951: 296).

Coleridge's plagiarism of Wollstonecraft's text might finally be seen, then, as a failed attempt to quell his fear of not being all man by killing off the otherness of an other woman's text. To turn women into men, to kill off the taint of femininity that men may fearfully discover within themselves, might ultimately be the self-defeating project of Romanticism: self-defeating not only because the trace of the other always inhabits the self-same text or sex, but also because the collapse of otherness leads inevitably to death. In Suskind's fiction the price paid for the crowds' consuming passion for the other-as-the-self-same is Grenouille. In Romanticism the price paid is woman. There thus results the chilling possibility that Romanticism is a literary movement that is not so much life-affirming as life-denying: the affirmation of one life, the life of the male subject, is made possible only by another's death, or the death of the other, who is woman. Could it be, then, that the difference made by who is speaking is finally the difference of life and death itself?

NOTES

1 Coleridge's notebook for September–October 1796 lists the entry: 'Epistle to Mrs. Wolstonecraft [*sic*] urging her to Religion. Read her Travels' (Coleridge 1957–73: I, f. 76, 261. G 258). I use the abbreviated title *A Short Residence*, rather than simply *Letters*, to distinguish this text (Wollstonecraft 1989: VI) from Wollstonecraft's letters which have been collected and published (Wollstonecraft 1979).

2 For work which draws on Lacanian psychoanalysis to theorize the construction of desire and subjectivity in Romanticism, see Belsey 1982 and Swann 1988.

3 For an excellent essay on 'Gender theory and the Yale School', see Johnson 1989: 32–41.

4 I have drawn here on Patricia Yaeger's suggestion that 'For Shelley and Wordsworth the sublime mode permits a normal retrieval of mythic powers that are initially alienated in order to insure their internalization' (Yaeger 1989: 210).

5 For an analysis of the more famous ruse in chapter 13 of Coleridge's *Biographia Literaria*, see Belsey 1982: 67–80. See especially p. 77, where Belsey refers to the 'totally fictitious' letter from a friend which defers publication of the theory of subjectivity which Coleridge had promised to produce. See also Gayatri Spivak, 'The letter as cutting edge' (Spivak 1987: 3–14). Spivak argues that the letter from a friend which stops publication of the original chapter 13 is '"a figment of Coleridge's imagination", another way of saying, "Coleridge himself"' (Spivak 1987: 4).

6 Coleridge 1983: II, 19–28.

7 Cleanth Brooks has argued that Donne's 'masculinity' was the reason that he found favour with Coleridge. 'Donne's masculine strength and his fire', writes Brooks, 'come in for genuine praise'; it is 'Donne's masculine power that elicits Coleridge's genuine admiration' (Brooks 1973: 141–2). See also John Barrell's comments on Coleridge's admiration of Milton's 'masculine syntax' (Barrell 1988: 44–78, esp. 64–9).

9

DE QUINCEY AND WOMEN

Angela Leighton

> Woman, sister, there are some things which you do not execute as well as your brother, man; no, nor ever will. Pardon me if I doubt whether you will ever produce a great poet from your choirs, or a Mozart, or a Phidias, or a Michael Angelo, or a great philosopher, or a great scholar. . . .
>
> Yet, sister woman . . . I acknowledge that you can do one thing as well as the best of us men – a greater thing than even Milton is known to have done, or Michael Angelo: you can die grandly.
>
> (De Quincey 1889–90: V, 406–7)

In the middle of his essay on 'Joan of Arc', De Quincey breaks off to applaud the great talent of woman. She may not be able to write, compose, draw or philosophize like her 'brother man', but in one thing she is his equal: she can die. What is more, she can die in a way which is not just a matter of her common mortality. She can die 'grandly', with an art comparable to a Milton's or a Michelangelo's. The prospect of the woman about to die elicits from De Quincey, in 1847, a curiously emphatic and innocent enthusiasm. The scene of woman's death is the scene of her artistic, emotional and even political success. She is thus generously compensated for her unquestioned intellectual inferiority.

The outrageous and punishing sentimentality of this exclamation conceals, however, other, more complex attitudes. De Quincey had good reason to associate women with death. The story of his own life is tragically landmarked by the deaths of the women he knew and loved. The first, and most crucial of these losses, occurred when he was six. His adored older sister Elizabeth died of hydrocephalus in 1792, at the age of nine, and the event seems to have established a pattern of experience which repeated itself throughout Thomas's life, and sent its dream-echoes far into his future. When, in June 1812, Wordsworth's three-year-old daughter Catherine died, De Quincey was plunged into an almost hysterical condition of grief-stricken prostration, no doubt exacerbated by his habit of spending the summer nights lying on her grave in Grasmere (De Quincey 1970: 372). Catherine was De Quincey's favourite of Wordsworth's children, and the one he had jealously claimed as his own. 'Catherine is to be taught by nobody but *me*' (Jordan 1963: 185), he reminded Dorothy in 1809. The coincidence of her death occurring in June, in the same month as his sister's, helped to fix in De Quincey's mind a prevailing irony of summer's tropical luxuriance turned hollow at the core, which was also the irony of his own life's promise turned empty at the start.

The idea of summer retains this negative relation with a dead female figure throughout De Quincey's work, and gives him the paradigmatic model for his theory of '*involutes*', those 'perplexed combinations of *concrete* objects' which represent 'compound experiences' in the memory. 'The summer we see, the grave we haunt with our thoughts; the glory is around us, the darkness is within us', he explains in the 'Suspiria' (De Quincey 1985: 103). This superimposition of summer on death, glory on darkness, provides De Quincey with a deeply pessimistic model of knowledge, in which appearances are always haunted by antagonistic forces. Furthermore, it is a model of knowledge which is inextricably tied to a consciousness of gender. The Romantic anxiety that there is hollowness at the core, that the centre cannot hold, is linked, as it is for many Victorian Romantics, to a quite specific and literal anxiety about women.

This sense of death in midsummer provides De Quincey with a ruling pattern of experience, which is then repeated throughout his life, as subsequent events seem to confirm the first trauma of his childhood. The sickly twin daughters of his tutor, for instance – deaf and disfigured as they were, and cruelly put to work as servants in the house – became the objects, as he tells us in the 'Autobiography', of his pitying affection (De Quincey 1889–90: I, 104). After their deaths, within a week of each other, he seemed to see reflected in the guilty looks of their parents 'visionary twin sisters, moving for ever up and down the stairs' (ibid.: I, 104). His own visionary inclinations were, from an early age, motivated by a combination of household tyranny, victimization and guilt. The prostitute Ann whom, according to the *Confessions*, the seventeen-year-old boy befriended during his year as a down-and-out in London, returns obsessively in his dreams as an elusive, familiar, always fading face, ominously intimating her own mortality. Much later, in 1837, De Quincey's wife Margaret, worn out probably as much by her husband's erratic lifestyle and perpetual debts as by the rearing of eight children, died of typhus. She thus fell prey to a female fate that was already deeply written in De Quincey's imagination.

Certainly, to read through his works is to travel a path strewn, either casually or traumatically, with dead women, some real, some fictional: a woman who nearly drowned as a child, a girl who foresees her death on her wedding day, a blind beggar's dead daughter, a particular niece of Lord Monboddo's who fell off a precipice, a jilted girl who wastes away. De Quincey snatches at these examples with an almost comical urgency. They seem to feed an insatiable appetite in him for female victims. His youthful notes, in the *Diary*, towards a projected novel concern, not surprisingly, a heroine dying on an island of a lake, by an open window, in midsummer (De Quincey 1927: 156). Finally, the career of 'The English Mail-Coach' leaves a trail of damage done to women: mothers bereaved, a lover run down, a boatload of girls drowned, a maid who sinks into a quicksand. De Quincey's narratives are a veritable graveyard of luckless women.

Clearly, the multiple female accidents in these writings stem not only from the facts of personal tragedy, but also from a certain imaginative preference. For it was the death of Elizabeth, not the death of his father a year later, which gave Thomas the primary emotional motif of his writing. It was the disappearance of Ann, not the death of his brother William at about the same time, which haunted his dreams. It was the death of Margaret, his wife, rather than the death of his favourite son some three years before, which inspired the few fictional stories he ever wrote. De Quincey's compulsion to repeat the same narrative of the child-woman's death draws not only on the chance facts of life but also on the fictional predilections of the imagination. The dead woman suits those predilections better than the dead man.

However, if the figure of the dead woman is a tragic idiosyncrasy of De Quincey's own experience, it is also, like so much of that experience, an intriguingly overexposed expression of certain literary worries and beliefs. Like Mary Wollstonecraft, Mary Shelley and Dorothy Wordsworth, De Quincey uses his 'inferior' art of prose at times to challenge the self-contained figurativeness of Romantic poetry. Dead children and dead women are, for *him*, connected with structures other than those of the pure imagination. His own Lucy was a real child who died: Elizabeth or Catherine. As a result, there is a continual conflict in his work between the sublime ambition of the imagination, on the one hand, and the sympathies of real life, on the other; between an aesthetics of woman as pure and perfect and therefore figuratively dead and a politics of woman as the actual victim of some external destructive force. The clash of these two perspectives is one of the distinctive marks of his writing.

On the one hand, De Quincey is a pure rhetorician, a daring dreamer, whose work often constitutes a biographer's nightmare of fantasies and fine lies. But on the other hand, he suffers from an inferiority complex of the imagination towards his contemporary Romantic poets which makes him, perhaps in spite of himself, true to certain prosaic realities of the power relations between human beings, and in particular between men and women. The connections between the aesthetic and the ideological purposes of literature have tended to be obscured by the polarization of criticism into the deconstructive on the one hand, and the historical on the other, into the formalist and the ideological. But De Quincey's writing about women resists easy accommodation to the perspectives of either school. The figure of the woman may provide him, as in 'Suspiria', with a still point for the caducean 'meanderings' of his 'narrative' (De Quincey 1985: 93) – a point of origin or of imaginative difference, from which the dream can take its bearings; but the figure of the woman is also shaped by historical and biographical events, and draws strongly on the women De Quincey knew and loved. The free play of the aesthetic imagination, in his work, is constantly called to account by the moral and ideological context. The subject of opium, for instance, which is both the inspiration and the theme of the *Confessions* (1821), can provoke either a voluptuous celebration of creativity or a guilt-ridden defensiveness in the author. From the start, he shuffles awkwardly between the two. 'Guilt, therefore, I do not acknowledge: and, if I did, it is possible that I might still resolve on the present act of confession' (De Quincey 1985: 2), he declares, half admitting the very sin he denies. Throughout the work, the pure aesthetic pleasures of opium are set against its moral pains. Two kinds of discourse are in constant conflict, making the narrative ever more unstable and devious. Guilt is, indeed, deeply embedded in De Quincey's consciousness. He is, it could be said, a Romantic aesthete who feels perennially guilty about it.

De Quincey the aesthete, the dreamer, the pure stylist, certainly lends himself, as recent critics have noticed (for instance, Jacobus, Reed, Spector), to deconstructive readings. His fondness for linguistic metaphors of the mind, and his playful celebration of style for its own sake, make him seem to pre-empt the preoccupations of recent theorists. 'In the question of style', writes Derrida, in *Spurs/Eperons: Nietzsche's Styles*, 'there is always the weight . . . of some pointed object. At times this object might be only a quill or a stylus. But it could just as easily be a stiletto or a rapier' (Derrida 1979: 37). De Quincey's essay 'On murder considered as one of the Fine Arts' (1827) might just as easily be about 'Art as one of the Fine Murders'. This essay jokingly proposes an aesthetic of absolute stylistic purity, from which human motivation, literal fact and moral responsibility have all been banished. Like Derrida, De Quincey is fascinated by the open-ended and self-contained nature of language, which can proliferate meanings in some seemingly airtight region of the subconscious.

The idea that style might be more significant than content, effect than truth, writing than suffering, is a possibility which De Quincey, like any imaginative writer, embraces with a certain rhetorical delight. In the essay 'On murder', the lecturer, who is giving his speech to the Society of Connoisseurs in Murder, dismisses with disdain the work which is motivated by vulgar ideological purpose: by hatred, revenge or, worst of all (as too often in Ireland, he suggests) by 'politics' (De Quincey 1889–90: XIII, 65). Instead, he stands by the purity of the text. In this line of art, the perfect masterpiece will be 'a murder of pure voluptuousness, entirely disinterested' (ibid.: XIII, 110). Its only purpose and significance will be in its style. In one subtle side-thrust at Wordsworth, the speaker asserts that 'from our art, as from all the other liberal arts when thoroughly mastered, the result is, to humanise the heart' – an aim best fulfilled if the subject has 'a family of young children wholly dependent on his exertions' (ibid.: XIII, 48). The whole essay depends for its comic effect, not only on a prolonged *double-entendre*, but also on a characteristic doubleness of perspective. 'Everything in this world has two handles. Murder, for instance, may be laid hold of by its moral handle (as it generally is in the pulpit and at the Old Bailey) . . . or it may also be treated *aesthetically*' (ibid.: XIII, 13), De Quincey writes. The aesthetics of murder, like those of art, are in opposition to morality, which is dismissed as the province of church and court. De Quincey, like Nietzsche after him, and then Derrida, displays the anarchic potential of art, in which meaning is set free from conventional codes of behaviour, and acts by new laws of association. In this heady atmosphere of rhetorical free play, style is indeed (literally) also a 'stiletto'.

However, unlike Derrida's abstract puns from the etymology of 'spurs', De Quincey's play on murder and the fine arts is intended to shock. The semi-documentary nature of the work, which comments on two actual, contemporary murders, ensures that the reference is always strongly at work in opposition to the academic urbanity of the style. In De Quincey, indeed, there are always 'two handles', and the pull of the one is felt against the other. Without the contrary friction of the literal, the figure of pure speech and the effects of pure style become empty. It is the contradiction of reality which makes the play of language here tense and exhilarating. The real reference constantly ironizes the words, the facts incriminate the rhetoric. Thus, the more the speaker adopts the clichés of an entirely aesthetic criticism, the more self-accusing does that language become. For instance, he claims of the returning maid in the Marrs' murder, that, 'considered as a member of a household, she had this value, viz. that she, if caught and murdered, perfected and rounded the desolation of the house. The case being reported, as reported it would be all over Christendom, led the imagination captive. The whole covey of victims was thus netted; the household ruin was thus full and orbicular' (De Quincey 1889–90: XIII, 89). This suave formalism, applied to the subject of a domestic mass murder, becomes brilliantly scandalous. The stylistic pranks of the essay 'On murder' rely for their *effect* on the literal horror of their reference.

The relationship between the aesthetic and the ideological (or what De Quincey calls the 'moral') is one of ironic connection rather than of mutual exclusion. Text and context, style and reference, are dialogically related, so that the one frets against the other. Art for art's sake is challenged by murder for murder's sake. Aesthetic pleasure is challenged by ideological guilt. Disinterested style is challenged by literal meaning. Thus, while De Quincey can seem seductively modern in his sense of writing as an originating metaphor for experience – in his description of childhood, for instance, in 'Suspiria', as a 'handwriting' which the adult must interpret (De Quincey 1985: 113, note), of the brain as a 'palimpsest' (ibid.: 144), of memory, in the *Confessions*, as an unveiling of 'the secret inscriptions on the mind' (ibid.: 69) – none the less, those descriptions remain attached to a humanist account of the individual's moral and social responsibilities. It is his descriptions of women, in particular, which carry this burden of the contextual. Unlike Nietzsche's and Derrida's freely figurative generalizations about woman as an embodiment of art or truth, De Quincey's generalizations tend to be guilty and socialized. 'It is impossible to dissociate the questions of art, style and truth from the question of the woman' (Derrida 1979: 71), claims Derrida, echoing Nietzsche. But, as De Quincey's own essay on 'Style' makes clear, 'the question of the woman' is not pure and unrelated, but is also a question of the woman's fathers, husbands and brothers.

In his essays on 'Language' (1851) and on 'Style' (1840), De Quincey struggles to formulate a very un-Wordsworthian aesthetics of style for style's sake. 'On the contrary', he writes, in the essay on 'Language', 'style has an *absolute* value, like the product of any other exquisite art, quite distinct from the value of the subject about which it is employed' (De Quincey 1973: 1). The essay on 'Style' begins by attributing the English distrust of style to a misplaced and gender-specific sense of moral superiority: to 'the manliness of the British character' (ibid.: 63). Style then, by contrast, is feminine. It is to be found in that which 'manliness' has ignored or dismissed: 'the mother tongue, [which] survives only amongst our women and children' (ibid.: 64). A quite distinct gender politics of style is being worked out here, beneath the claims for a kind of aesthetic freedom. Such a politics leads naturally to 'the question of woman'. It is not, according to De Quincey, either the innocent child-woman or the housewifely matron who keeps the secret of style, but 'the class of unmarried women above twenty-five' who 'have renounced all prospects of conjugal and parental life'. These are the ones who preserve the 'idiomatic', 'racy' and 'delicate' (ibid.: 67) register of the mother tongue. Their sense of style, then, is in direct proportion to their lack of 'conjugal and parental' control. Characteristically, the question of woman has sent De Quincey's aestheticism veering into implicit social criticism. His feminization of style cannot ignore the power complexes of the lives of actual women.

Certainly, the evidence of De Quincey's own life is that, diminutive and insecure as he was himself, he found women the objects of natural identification and affection. He was proud, for instance, of having been reared in the girls' nursery, rather than among 'horrid pugilistic brothers' (De Quincey 1985: 96). Many years later, he greeted the birth of a first grandchild with overtly biased pleasure: 'I am glad, according to my ancient doctrine, that it is a *daughter* – not a son' (Page 1877: II, 82). But one of his most interesting portraits of women is that of Dorothy Wordsworth, whom he fondly remembers in the *Recollections of the Lakes and the Lake Poets*, not simply as the poet's sister, but as an author in her own right. It is De Quincey who suggests that Dorothy's natural gifts as a writer may have been subtly inhibited, and may have thus contributed to her madness in later life (De Quincey 1970: 205). At the same time she appears to him 'the very wildest' (ibid.: 201) of human beings, and is rather vividly contrasted with the 'angelic' and 'womanly' (ibid.: 129) Mrs Wordsworth, who is silent and housewifely. Dorothy, he claims, was 'an intellectual creature from her cradle' (ibid.: 200) – a description which directly echoes a self-description in the *Confessions*: 'from my birth I was made an intellectual creature' (De Quincey 1985: 2). It is he who detects in Dorothy a kind of blocked energy, a 'self-baffled utterance' (De Quincey 1970: 188), which he regrets was never freed by a more professional pursuit of her own writing, even if it meant her becoming that hated thing: 'a blue-stocking' (ibid.: 204). The word 'self-baffled' (ibid.: 207) is then used soon afterwards to describe his own anxieties about meeting Wordsworth for the first time. Beside the figure of the great poet, with his massive back, and his habit, as he walked, of gradually edging his companions off the road (ibid.: 136), De Quincey was always doomed to feel himself insignificant (literally, only just above five feet tall), but in other ways, too, diminutive, effeminate and inarticulate. Dorothy was not only, as his sister Jane enviously noted, the sort of woman De Quincey admired (De Quincey 1891a: II, 2); she was also, in her 'self-baffled' relationship to William, something of a kindred spirit.

Dorothy clearly provides one of the models for those 'unmarried women above twenty five' who know instinctively how to write. She, who had remained free of 'conjugal and parental life', seemed to De Quincey to have kept her natural style of writing free from taint. Her very lack of conventional femininity, her impulsive energy and wildness, are associated with the unvitiated purity of her language. De Quincey's celebration of idiomatic style as the province, in particular, of women, relies on a quiet undercurrent of criticism of the social and sexual structures, whether 'conjugal' or 'parental', in which most women are caught. This is not, therefore, a simple Romantic idealization of woman 'as the site of nature, feeling, and purity', as Mary Jacobus claims (Jacobus 1989: 132). It is, rather, a complicated and conscience-stricken perception of the real inhibiting context of women's lives – even if that perception comes from De Quincey's own subjective self-identification with them.

Yet although he can feel for the Dorothy Wordsworths of his time, De Quincey's sense of gender difference also proves an insuperable barrier. He is no advocate of Romantic androgyny. Style is sexed, and 'manliness' – that mixture of common sense, chivalry and English superiority – remains an obstacle to it. Consequently, the secret of true style can only be unlocked in a movement of violent expropriation, which has ringing sexual overtones to it. De Quincey advises his fellow reader that, if he would discover a truly natural style, he must 'steal the mail-bags, and break open all the letters in female handwriting' (De Quincey 1973: 67). This male reader is a mail reader, who can only obtain the secret of style by criminally breaking open the seals of the feminine text. 'I often borrow their seals from young ladies – when closing my letters', he remarks, disarmingly, in 'Suspiria' (De Quincey 1985: 147). This writer of what Baudelaire considered a distinctly '*feminine* style' (McFarland 1987: 97) knows that he can only 'borrow' the outer seals of the feminine, or else 'steal' them. Otherwise, its authentic language is forever sealed up in those tantalizing letters by 'racy' spinsters, which men may not read. Theft, intrusion or sexual violation are implicit in this profoundly gendered aesthetics. In the end, it seems that the guilt of masculinity or 'manliness' dogs all De Quincey's writing about women. Unlike his Romantic predecessors, gender difference is not a source of self-validating androgyny, but of self-distrustful guilt and criminality. The figure of the dead woman bears witness, not only to a macabre, Victorian sentimentality in the writer, but also, more interestingly, to this profound anxiety about sexual power in him.

'Yet, sister woman . . . I acknowledge that you can do one thing as well as the best of us men . . . you can die grandly' (De Quincey 1889–90: V, 406–7). The grandeur of the woman's death, De Quincey goes on to reveal in 'Joan of Arc', is connected with its public pathos. Searching for 'the grandest sight' which might be offered to some extraterrestrial viewer, from among all the sights of earth, he chooses 'a scaffold on the morning of execution' (ibid.: V, 407). This startling pronouncement draws, not only on De Quincey's fixation with executions, about which he wrote innumerable descriptions as a journalist, and not only on the saintly martyrdom of Joan, but also on the resonances of a more recent political event: 'How', he asks, 'if it should be some Marie Antoinette . . . coming forward on the scaffold . . . ?' or, 'if it were the noble Charlotte Corday . . . ?' (ibid.: V, 407). The domestic feminization of moral values, which could be seen to characterize the climate of Victorian England, finds in the spectacle of the executed women of France, a rich source of outraged sentimentalism. The pathos provided by those beautiful martyrs had been brilliantly exploited, even before the event, in Burke's *Reflections on the Revolution in France*. 'I thought ten thousand swords must have leaped from their scabbards to avenge even a look that threatened her with insult' (Burke 1989: 126–7), Burke declaimed, in a vignette which became powerfully famous. The author who, to the annoyance of Mary Wollstonecraft and Tom Paine, called on male chivalry to avenge the wrongs of the Revolution, was much admired by De Quincey, and in 'Rhetoric' was hailed by him as 'the supreme writer of his century' (De Quincey 1973: 122). The scandal of Jacobinism and revolution abroad was thus subtly connected with a scandal concerning women. The public exhibition of innocent wives and mothers becomes a call to husbands to raise their protective swords. It is as if the scene of events in the Place de la Révolution haunts the Victorian English mind as a horror to be avenged particularly by the chivalrous re-domestication of women.

In 1838, the year after Margaret's death from typhus, De Quincey published two short stories, 'The Avenger' and 'The Household Wreck'. These appear, on the surface, to be highly sentimental tales, which fulsomely promote an ideology of hearth and home. Yet, interestingly, both are also tales in which domestic privacy is forcefully violated by public exposure and scandal.

In 'The Avenger', a son wreaks vengeance for his Jewish mother's public humiliation and execution by carrying out a series of assassinations amongst those who condoned it. The son's revenge is narrated with an emotional intensity which is, both obsessive and repetitive. 'The Household Wreck' similarly plays on the ideological opposition of the private and the political. It is a highly charged tale about a beloved wife who is incriminated for shop-lifting by a malicious suitor. She is put on public trial for the offence, and eventually dies after her distraught husband rescues her from prison. It is not so much her unjust imprisonment, however, as the scandal of her appearing in a public trial, which horrifies the narrator. He appalls his imagination by thinking of the men and boys who will see her. Hints of rape, theft and murder, committed both by the suitor and by the world at large, underlie this weird fantasy of a planted muff and some stolen lace. Simply the removal of the woman from the home is an insult levelled against her person – an insult charged with sexual intentions: 'the domestic seclusion and privacy within which it was her matronly privilege to move had already undergone a rude violation' (De Quincey 1889–90: XII, 187). The idea of the home or the 'household', for De Quincey, is heavy with all the Victorian connotations of a well-upholstered, propertied sexuality. Against the forces of revolution abroad, the woman is guarded as the angel of the hearth.

However, the curious point about both these stories is that she is not guarded faithfully enough. The pieties which De Quincey so enthusiastically reproduces are strangely at risk, not only from without, where a system of anarchic injustice prevails, but also, more insidiously, from within. There is someone, besides an angel, in the home. In 'The Avenger', for instance, the killer spreads panic in the town by planting himself, mysteriously, 'within the house' (ibid.: XII, 236) of his chosen victim. The significance of this threatening intimacy is then brought out in the fact that he indirectly kills his own wife, who is called, not by chance, Margaret. The work is charged with an atmosphere of guilt-ridden claustrophobia. The murderer, after all, is not the outsider but the familiar, and, as in the essay 'On murder', the idea of a total 'extermination' of 'separate households' (ibid.: XII, 235) is strangely alluring and satisfying.

In 'The Household Wreck', the breaking down of the protective barrier between inside and outside, private and public, has something to do with the husband's failure of will. At crucial moments, he is struck with a paralysing and vaguely complicitous sense of guilt. He cannot move when the police come to the door, and when his wife is sent for trial, he falls into a fever (which happens to be typhus), and remains unconscious for no less than seven weeks. This queer failure of attention in the man reflects the moral failure both stories enact. Chivalrous good intentions in the male are fatally undermined, so that the woman, in spite of everything, meets her destined fate. The external motives of revenge or sexual malice seem insignificant by comparison with this threat from within. In both stories, the creaking mechanism of the plot disguises another narrative: a dark, internal sense of guilt lurks, like the murderer, deep within the house of Victorian piety and propriety.

Thus, beneath the idealism of hearth and home as refuges from the historic scene of execution, or, as Josephine McDonagh puts it, from the scene of contemporary sexual and economic 'circulation' (McDonagh 1989: 128), there is a betraying sub-text. The refuge is violated and the household wrecked, not by political interference from without, but rather by suspect guardianship from within. The death of the woman is, secretly and subconsciously, perpetrated by the one man who should be her defence: in both stories it is the husband. In the fine tradition of Gothic horror, De Quincey turns the politics of revolution inwards – into the house of the subconscious, where it becomes, of course, a sexual politics of domestic relations.

In general, it could be said that, while the women of Romantic poetry are largely sexual creatures, whether fairies and enchantresses who tempt, or semi-incestuous sisters, emanations and epipsyches, who are invoked as imaginative twins, the innumerable child-women of later Victorian literature tend to be pre-sexual or post-sexual, children or matrons, if not some strange combination of the two. The wife in 'The Household Wreck', for instance, has a 'childlike innocence', a 'sweet feminine timidity' and a 'cherub loveliness' (De Quincey 1889–90: XII, 165). One of the consequences of this stunting infantilism is a certain necrophiliac fascination with the absolutely passive nature of femininity. Victorian 'morbidity' seems to be part of that ideological movement indoors which characterizes the post-Romantic English mind, and which establishes the woman as the guardian of that retreat. At the heart of De Quincey's stories, however, lurks the knowledge that the angel of the house is hardly safe. His domestic piety and his chivalry ring hollow. The woman, instead of being protected within the household, falls victim to a relentless machinery of death. It is a machinery, in the end, not only of the political system outside, but also of the domestic system inside; not of the unknown murderer, but of the familiar husband. The 'conjugal' relationship itself is subtly implicated in these outwardly sentimental and sensationalist tales.

At one point, in 'The Household Wreck', the husband feels a 'sudden horror' at realizing that there might be 'a guilty design in what before had seemed accident' (ibid.: XII, 212). The complicity of 'accident' and 'design', of disinterestedness and purpose, characterizes both the work of art and the work of the subconscious. If De Quincey's women are surprisingly 'accident prone', as Mary Jacobus puts it (Jacobus 1989: 133), they are also prone to all kinds of dark and deliberate designs. This doubleness, which lies deep in the imagined sanctuary of the home, and deep in the male consciousness metonymized by the home, requires that the woman not only 'can die', but also *must* die. The relentlessness with which women die in De Quincey's writings is not just a matter of personal obsession, but also, whether consciously or subconsciously, of ideological design. Women are victims of the very powers which should protect them, in the very context where they should be most safe: the home.

Yet, the women portrayed by De Quincey are by no means all either angelic or murdered. 'The Spanish Military Nun', a short story published in 1847, is a fantastic, picaresque tale, in which an unwanted daughter, who has been put by her father in a convent, escapes, makes herself a pair of trousers, and embarks on a life of roving adventures in South America. The girl is called, poignantly and no doubt deliberately, Kate. Thus the Lucy-like fate of the real Catherine Wordsworth is rewritten as a rollicking Byronic epic, full of morally and sexually ambiguous energy. Kate takes up with pirates, soldiers and buccaneers. She fights against men and is wooed by women. She is full of 'energy and indomitable courage' (De Quincey 1889–90: XIII, 165). Her colourful life comes to seem like a subtle form of revenge, not only on a poor brother whom she mistakenly kills, but, more emphatically, on her thoroughly pusillanimous father: 'that sublime of crocodiles, *papa*' (ibid.: XIII, 171). Obscurely, through all his life and writings, De Quincey hints that it is the very closeting protection of men, of fathers, husbands and brothers, which kills women. Those, like Joan of Arc and the Spanish military nun, who escape the home, 'can die', but on their own terms, and in their own cause. Those others, who stay indoors, are artistically and inevitably murdered.

It is interesting, therefore, that the death of Kate the nun is made a subject of mysterious, sly secretiveness. De Quincey refuses to impart the facts, and then gives this reticence a quite pointed purpose: 'it has been a secret for more than two centuries; and to man it remains a secret for ever and ever!' (ibid.: XIII, 237). The death of Kate is a way of sealing her identity 'for ever', as a 'secret' kept from men. Kate, in De Quincey's fictional re-invention of her, does not die at home, under 'the conjugal and parental' roof, but mysteriously in a foreign land. She is not the victim of any of those hidden, household fine arts, practised by accidentally designing men. Above all, it is tempting to say, she is not the victim of one particular family man, who loomed so equivocally large and great in De Quincey's admiring yet resentful eyes: 'that sublime of crocodiles, *papa*'. If this is the story in which De Quincey imagines an alternative life for his beloved Kate Wordsworth, it is also one which issues an unequivocal condemnation of patriarchal prejudices. Kate, in the end, and all women after her, are to be given their 'natural birthright of liberty' (ibid.: XIII, 167), the sign of which is a 'papal indulgence' (ibid.: XIII, 235) that they may all, like Kate, wear trousers.

'Then turning round, I sought my sister's face. But the bed had been moved; and the back was now turned. Nothing met my eyes but one large window wide open' (De Quincey 1985: 103). The death of his sister Elizabeth is the originating experience of all De Quincey's imaginative writing. The six-year-old boy in his sister's death chamber experiences the displacement which will then mark his whole attitude to life. Instead of the face, there is the window. Instead of features, there is a blank. Immediately he falls into a state of stunned trance, in which his mind traumatically wanders from one thing to another, for the space of several pages. This is the psychological origin of all De Quincey's characteristic narrative digressions and dream-wanderings, as he himself acknowledges in 'Suspiria' (ibid.: 138). That original substitution of the window for the face is the first, disinheriting impulse of all his memories. Instead of a last meeting, face to face, there is a lapse of purpose, attention and desire; and in that lapse the narrative of the bereaved, male imagination extends itself.

This powerful moment of human loss is explicitly presented also as a birth of consciousness. The sister's face is averted, and as a result, for the boy, the faces of all women will seem elusive, different, hard to read. But not only is the face turned away. It is also brutally substituted by the empty prospect of the open window. Right from the beginning, the familiar features from which the child should take his bearings give way to that view of bewildering vacancy, in a movement of substitution more delicate and memorable than any in Derrida, though Derrida, perhaps, gives an equivalent account when he writes that 'style thereby protects the presence, the content, the thing itself, meaning, truth – on the condition at least that it should not *already* be that gaping chasm' (Derrida 1979: 39). For the six-year-old De Quincey, the condition is not met, and the 'gaping chasm' of the open window is '*already*' a substitute for the familiar 'presence'. The beginning of his dream life is thus founded on the shock of this different view, which opens out, to his imagination, a dreadful receding prospect of blue sky, in which desire meets no object and thought finds no resting-place. The natural first idiom of the sister's face turns into a blank page; the primal scene into a mere differential of endless time. 'What is life?' De Quincey asks in 'The Household Wreck', and answers, in a spirit much bleaker than Shelley's, 'Darkness and formless vacancy for a beginning, or something beyond all beginning; then next a dim lotos of human consciousness afloat upon the bosom of waters' (De Quincey 1889–90: XII, 158). That first encounter with the sister's averted face plants a seed of dread in De Quincey's memory that something was lost at the beginning, and that the story of his life starts with a crucial lapse, from truth, innocence, authenticity and femininity. The dead sister gives him a lifelong figure for the discrepancy and difference of the male imagination, which punishingly forfeits the very object of its desire, and is lost and guilty ever after.

But it also gives him a figure for the woman, whose secret is thus preserved against the emotional and literary appropriation of men. It is a secret of character and of style, a mysterious, illegible text of identity, which is always somehow sealed from the man's gaze. The dream woman at the cottage door, who reappears over a period of twenty-five years in De Quincey's dreams, and who is Elizabeth, Catherine, Ann and Margaret in one, looks 'broken with a woe that no man could read' (De Quincey 1891b: I, 20). Such a text may be either violently appropriated, by breaking the 'seals', or else it must remain, like the death of Kate the nun, 'to man . . . a secret for ever and ever!' (De Quincey 1889–90: XIII, 237). It is perhaps worth noting that just such a secret was kept by another, nun-like woman, who very probably found in De Quincey, not only her own dream of the imperial crocodile, but also the idea of a female death-pose, which she too could turn from a figure of victimization to a figure of female speech. It was Christina Rossetti who wrote: 'I tell my secret? No indeed, not I' (Rossetti 1979–90: I, 47).

Thus, the traumatic primal scene in the death chamber of his sister gives to De Quincey a motif of difference, which is both the gender difference of his broken relation with his sister, and the perennial difference of the displaced imagination, which wanders, like his own narratives, in the face of 'vacancy'. The two remain obsessively connected. Perhaps because of his own real bereavements, his highly developed sense of guilt, his 'feminine' insecurities as a writer of prose among luminary poets, or perhaps, simply, because of that streak of Victorian responsibility and realism in him, which turned the abstract sublimities of Romanticism into terrible mental torments and persecutions, De Quincey remains one of the most searchingly sceptical of writers – sceptical, at some level of his nerve-strung consciousness, of the very pieties he seems to espouse. Above all, he remains an obsessively and intriguingly gender-specific dreamer, who finds in woman, not a legible muse or a kind nature spirit, but a sister, wife or daughter, who is the victim, not the justification, of man's ambitious aestheticism.

The work which most strongly and brilliantly expresses this anxiety at the heart of De Quincey's writing is 'The English Mail-Coach'. It was first published in *Blackwood's* in 1849, but its subject harks back to the revolutionary decades of the early part of the century, and therefore to the Romanticism with which De Quincey always, if uneasily, identified himself. It seems to describe a journey of patriotic and patriarchal triumph, as the news of English victory in the Napoleonic wars is carried to the provinces. But in fact, as the journey enters into its nightmare transfigurations, the coach becomes an undisguised apparatus of state power. At first, in the form of the Bath mail, presided over by that figure which comes straight from De Quincey's opium dreams – the sinisterly metamorphosing crocodile, 'grandpapa' (De Quincey 1985: 196) – and then as the London mail, it proceeds to run down all the innocent females in its path. De Quincey's tragic sense of the feminine, here, is richly invested with all the political and psychological connotations of his dreams. Thus, for instance, by comparison with the 'imperial arms' of the mail, the luckless, fragile carriage of the two lovers is painted all over with an indecipherable writing, which, together with the carriage's overintimate proximity, seems, to the travellers on the mail, to be 'sufficiently jacobinical' (ibid.: 191). The 'feminine' text, written on the lovers' carriage, and subtly associated with revolution, is thus contrasted to the clear imperial emblem of the mail. Once again, a stylistic difference expresses a gender difference, which is itself slyly suggestive of a larger political opposition. While the mail represents Englishness, reaction and moral authority, the feminine obstacles in its path develop loose associations with sensibility, Jacobinism and France.

The narrative at first seems to ride, like De Quincey himself, on the triumphant forward progress of the mail. The exhilarated speaker tells us how 'Upholding the morality of the mail, *a fortiori* I upheld its rights, I stretched to the uttermost its privilege of imperial precedency, and astonished weak minds by the feudal powers which I hinted to be lurking constructively in the charters of this proud establishment' (ibid.: 191). However, as the mail continues in its destructive career, this perspective comes to seem less and less sympathetic, and the speaker becomes more troubled and uncertain. Gradually translating into the experience of a dream, the exhilaration of speed starts to falter, for the speaker: 'The palsy of doubt and distraction hangs like some guilty weight of dark unfathomed remembrances upon my energies, when the signal is flying for *action*' (ibid.: 219). This very De Quinceyan sense of paralysis and digression derives from a characteristic load of guilt and memory, which are then realized in the dream sequences which follow. It is precisely the '*action*' of the mail which causes the traumatically repeated destruction of the various hapless women. 'Did ruin to our friends couch within our own dreadful shadow?' the speaker asks. 'Was our shadow the shadow of death?' (ibid.: 226). The visionary female figures of the 'Dream-Fugue' which follows, however emblematically funerary before the oncoming juggernaut, are also, as the language constantly implies, literal victims of a system of political power. This symbol of English victory and pride is, for them, a symbol of 'death'.

De Quincey thus emphasizes, throughout 'The English Mail-Coach', something that has been present in all his work. The reckless career of the male imagination, which rushes into strange sublime fantasies of power, is connected to other powers and other systems of domination. The mail's 'relations to the state' (ibid.: 191) are discreet, but unmistakable. As the documentary and historical realism of the first part insidiously slides into surrealistic nightmare, De Quincey seems to expose the hollowness of Victorian patriotism and patriarchy, from the point of view of the female outsider. The mail of English victory rushes past all the mourning mothers, and brutally bears down on the woman in the carriage, the girl in the quicksand and finally the infant in the graveyard. Its onward progress scatters victims in all directions, and those victims, true to De Quincey's earliest perceptions, are mainly women. The mail is as murderous as any of his males, and the murdered are those who, having no place on its privileged seats, are always liable to be run down.

'Woman, sister . . . you can die.' In the end, the death of the sister-woman is caused by the vast consolidation of power, both imaginative and institutional, emotional and social, which the mail-coach represents. The visionariness of the imagination and the ideology of masculinity come together in it, in a destructive collusion, which De Quincey, throughout his writing, in all the rich, digressing contradictions of his dream narratives, has made gradually more apparent.

10

WOMEN WRITING REVOLUTION: NARRATIVES OF HISTORY AND SEXUALITY IN WOLLSTONECRAFT AND WILLIAMS

Vivien Jones

History, in the form of a poem celebrating the fall of the Bastille, briefly disturbs the otherwise impeccably private world of Helen Maria Williams's sentimental novel *Julia*. It does so at a climactic moment of reconciliation when the 'remorseless tyranny' of illicit desire has been subdued by a woman's 'open and ingenuous heart' (Williams 1790: 240). Frederick Seymour, for whom the 'paroxysm of passion' ultimately proves fatal, is reconciled to his wife Charlotte by her 'generous affection', as she in turn reconciles herself to her friend and cousin Julia, the unwilling object of Seymour's attentions. This (feminine) moment of restored 'cordiality and friendship' is interrupted – or confirmed – by the sublime moment of revolutionary violence: a visitor reads to the two women a 'prophetic' poem on the Bastille which hails the goddesses Philosophy and Freedom:

> 'Tis thine to love all nature's weal;
> To give each gen'rous purpose birth
> And renovate the gladden'd earth.
>
> (Williams 1790: 239, 267, 271)

This brief conjunction of sentimental sexual narrative with historical event is suggestive of the way in which the French Revolution liberated Williams from an identity as acceptably decorous female poet and novelist. Its momentary destabilization of sentimental norms anticipates the pervasive transgression of gendered ideological and generic boundaries which characterizes her later writings. After *Julia*, Williams's narrative energies were almost exclusively devoted to her *Letters* and *Sketches* (1790–1819), accounts of revolutionary and postrevolutionary France which established her as one of the major recorders and mediators of the French Revolution for a British public.

Mary Wollstonecraft's writings follow an interestingly comparable trajectory. *Mary, a Fiction* and the nascent feminism of a text like *Thoughts on the Education of Daughters* were transformed by the Revolution into the powerful radicalism of the two *Vindications*, and followed in 1794 by historical narrative in the unfinished *Historical and Moral View of the Origin and Progress of the French Revolution*, and in 1796 by *A Short Residence in Sweden, Norway and Denmark*, a text which defies any easy categorization by either content or genre.

I

As radical histories, by women, Williams's *Letters from France* and Wollstonecraft's *Historical and Moral View* manifest a double pressure: ideologies of femininity and writing intensify and complicate the general threat to Enlightenment progressivism posed by the Terror. In the eyes of anti-Jacobin propagandists, the spectacle of women writing republican history was a triple violation – of sexual morality and generic decorum as well as national political loyalty. Richard Polwhele's poem *The Unsex'd Females* mobilizes the eighteenth-century discourse of 'proper' female writing to attack the 'Wollstonecraftians':

> Ah! once the female Muse, to NATURE true,
> The unvalued store from FANCY, FEELING drew;
> Won, from the grasp of woe, the roseate hours,
> Cheer'd life's dim vale, and strew'd the grave with flowers.
> But lo! where, pale amidst the wild, she draws
> Each precept cold from sceptic Reason's vase.
>
> (Polwhele 1798: 11–12)

And in one of his vicious footnotes, Polwhele professes amazement at what he sees as Williams's change of identity: 'is it not extraordinary . . . that the fair Helen, whose notes of love have charmed the moonlight vallies, should stand forward, an intemperate advocate for Gallic licentiousness' (ibid.: 19). Williams is attacked as having left the feminized, picturesque landscape of sentimentalism for the public stage, the privileged masculine arena; having thus broken generic decorum, she is herself transformed from the object of sentimental fantasy to 'intemperate' Fury. Polwhele's 'female Muse' is dependent on the dominant ideological identification of femininity with chaste sensibility, at the heart of which is a rhetoric of sexual control: sensibility is simultaneously natural – restricting women to the spheres of feeling and domesticity – and unnatural, in its association with active sexuality.[1] Radical women are thus caught in these conservative representations in a classic double bind: they have either betrayed their sex by espousing 'cold . . . sceptic Reason', or they are subject to a dangerously uncontrolled sensibility. Both aberrations, predictably, manifest themselves as sexual licence – Wollstonecraft's 'brothel feats of wickedness' (*Anti-Jacobin Review* 1801: 519) – as the propagandist's prurient gaze effects a constant slippage between ideology and biography, writing and writer.

These are extreme examples, but they differ only in degree from the normative ideology of propriety which Wollstonecraft deconstructed, but failed to escape completely, in *Vindication of the Rights of Woman*. As the *Vindication* and these hysterically defensive conservative texts amply demonstrate, competing definitions of sensibility – and thus of sexuality – were a crucial site of struggle as the Revolution released new possibilities for femininity.

The conjunction of (feminine) novel paradigms with (masculine) history in both *Letters from France* and the *Historical and Moral View* is an interesting articulation of that struggle. In Williams's text, the fluid letter form so characteristic of the 1790s effects a constant negotiation between history and fiction, sublimity and sensibility, public and private: her encounter with the French Revolution becomes an 'affair of the heart' (Williams 1975: I, 66),[2] a sentimental narrative recorded 'to the moment' (Richardson 1964: 316), in which emotional constancy is finally rewarded after the nightmare of political disillusionment and 'a heart almost broken' (Williams 1975: V, 174). Williams seeks to redeem the Terror and justify revolutionary principles to a British audience by rewriting the tales of necromancy told by British propagandists:

> To me, the land which these mighty magicians have suddenly covered with darkness, where, waving their evil wand, they have reared the dismal scaffold, have clotted the knife of the assassin with gore, have called forth the shriek of despair, and the agony of torture – to me, this land of desolation appeared dressed in additional beauty beneath the genial smile of Liberty.
>
> (ibid.: I, 217)

Wollstonecraft's strategic narrative persona is very different. In the preface to the *Historical and Moral View*, she warns against 'the erroneous inferences of sensibility', claiming instead to bring 'the cool eye of observation' to bear on 'these stupendous events' (Wollstonecraft 1989: VI, 6). But just as Williams's self-conscious reliance on 'sympathy' is challenged by her allegiance to 'impartial history' and comprehensive coverage (Williams 1975: IV, 181), so Wollstonecraft's rationalist account is dependent at moments of crisis on the kind of fictional paradigms deployed more pervasively in Williams's text.

Specifically, of course, the generic mixture is a response in kind to Burke's prescriptive chivalric 'romance' (Williams 1975: IV, 145), the feminized 'sentimental jargon' which Wollstonecraft first attacked in *Vindication of the Rights of Men* (Wollstonecraft 1989: V, 30). Gender is central to the competing accounts of historical change offered by both Burke and his antagonists. With characteristic complexity, Burke mourned the loss of that '*sensibility* of principle', which he defined as '*manly* sentiment and heroic enterprise' (Burke 1989: 127; my emphases). Enlightenment history, on the other hand, could associate cultural progress with female emancipation, in such texts as William Alexander's *History of Women* (1779). For Alexander, women become the touchstone of constitutional maturity as the position of British women, their 'privileges and immunities' secured by 'the laws of their country', is compared with that of women under European chivalry, 'complimented and chained' with only the 'influence of politeness' to rely on:

> we shall almost constantly find women among savages condemned to every species of servile, or rather, of slavish drudgery; and shall as constantly find them emerging from this state, in the same proportion as we find the men emerging from ignorance and brutality, and approaching to knowledge and refinement; the rank, therefore, and condition, in which

> we find the women in any country, mark out to us with the greatest precision, the exact point in the scale of civil society, to which the people of such country have arrived.
>
> (Alexander 1779: II, 313; I, 102, 103)[3]

A tantalizing footnote in Volney's *Les Ruines* brings out some of the contradictions implicit in Alexander's bland optimism. The note expands on the comment that 'paternal tyranny laid the foundation of political despotism':

> Numberless facts demonstrate, that with every infant people, in every savage and barbarous state, the father, the chief of the family, is a despot, and a cruel and insolent despot. The wife is his slave, the children his servants. . . . Similar to this is the state of our own uncivilized peasants. In proportion as civilization spreads, the manners become milder, and the condition of women improves, till, by a contrary excess, they arrive at dominion, and then a nation becomes effeminate and corrupt.
>
> (Volney 1853: 199)

This exposes the fundamental tension in radical accounts of historical development. The perfectibilist project demands that the Fall be dispelled, and tyranny recuperated as a necessary precursor to enlightened rationalism. But far from Alexander's confident progressivism, Volney describes an apparently inevitable movement from despotism to effeminacy, and history becomes an endless cycle of deprivation and excess. Enlightenment texts never entirely dispel this threat of inescapable tyranny – whether in the form of regression from a state of nature, or, as here, a cycle of subjection and retaliation.[4]

From the point of view of a female radical writing within the Enlightenment tradition, this complicates an already problematic project. Wollstonecraft implicitly recognizes this collusion between Burkean chivalry and a 'progressivism' which explicitly objectifies women when she refuses to give any such account in *Vindication of the Rights of Woman*:

> I shall not go back to the remote annals of antiquity to trace the history of woman; it is sufficient to allow that she has always been either a slave, or a despot, and to remark, that each of these situations equally retards the progress of reason.
>
> (Wollstonecraft 1989: V, 123)

In Alexander, no less than in Burke, women and/or femininity are simply the object against which the progress of civilization, or corruption, can be measured: in either narrative, the enlightened feminine subject is a structural impossibility. In the polemical *Vindication*, Wollstonecraft begins to write that subjectivity precisely as a means of breaking the cycle of despotic masculinity, Volney's 'paternal tyranny': 'my own sex, I hope, will excuse me, if I treat them like rational creatures' (Wollstonecraft 1989: V, 75).

What becomes of that project when women write revolutionary history? Both *Letters from France* and the *Historical and Moral View* are attempts to redeem the Revolution's degeneration into violence and to turn it towards progressivist narrative. They deploy powerful fictional paradigms to contain and demystify 'paternal tyranny', plots of sentiment and sexuality to transform the violent sublime. But those plots, actively rejected by the *Vindication*'s sublimatory rationalism, inevitably carry with them a reactionary politics of gender and writing. In refusing that, the *Vindication* is unable to endorse or envisage the possibility of an active female sexuality; it sets up, in Cora Kaplan's words, 'heartbreaking conditions for women's liberation' (Kaplan 1986: 39). To what extent can Wollstonecraft's and Williams's rewritings of history succeed in also rewriting gender, producing new narratives of sexuality for the 'rational creatures' of the *Vindication*? Or does the tyranny of reiterated plots condemn femininity to a depressing essentialism, in which 'history evaporates, leaving us in an immutable present of male oppression' (Merck 1988: 101)?[5]

II

The mob's entry into the royal apartments at Versailles in October 1789 is one of those points of crisis in Wollstonecraft's *Historical and Moral View* when the linear rationalist narrative, the 'cool eye of observation', is disrupted by more novelistic paradigms. Wollstonecraft's anxieties in the face of revolutionary excess are manifest in her depiction of the Parisian women ('the lowest refuse of the streets', 'with the appearance of furies', 'monsters, . . . hunting after blood or plunder' – Wollstonecraft 1989: VI, 196, 197, 205), and in her uneasy elevation of Marie Antoinette to the status of innocent victim, the heroine of a 'silly novel' (Wollstonecraft 1989: V, 257):

> The sanctuary of repose, the asylum of care and fatigue, the chaste temple of a woman, I consider the queen only as one, the apartment where she consigns her senses to the bosom of sleep, folded in it's arms forgetful of the world, was violated with murderous fury.
>
> (Wollstonecraft 1989: VI, 209)

Wollstonecraft writes history here as Richardsonian Gothic fiction. In an almost Burkean defence of social order and (feminized) bourgeois privacy, domestic space, moral/religious value and female body are interchangeable, the 'chaste temple' penetrated by class violence. And Wollstonecraft's attempt to strip Marie Antoinette of her royal status, in defiance of Burke – 'I consider the queen only as [a woman]' – at best only succeeds in putting her back on the throne of idealized (and therefore, according to the *Vindication of the Rights of Woman*, degraded) womanhood.

But Wollstonecraft's account differs from Burke's in various important ways. Burke had taken the events out of context, giving them an originary and extraordinary status as the beginning of 'the most important of all revolutions . . . I mean a revolution in sentiments, manners, and moral opinions' (Burke 1989: 131). In defence of that 'new constitution of mind', Wollstonecraft's 'historical view' locates them within a standard Enlightenment narrative, according to which the revolution is 'the natural consequence of intellectual improvement, gradually proceeding to perfection in the advancement of communities, from a state of barbarism to that of polished society' (Wollstonecraft 1989: VI, 52, 6–7). And that in turn depends on a still larger context:

> We must get entirely clear of all the notions drawn from the wild traditions of original sin: the eating of the apple, the theft of Prometheus, the opening of Pandora's box, and other fables, too tedious to enumerate, on which priests have erected their tremendous structures of imposition, to persuade us, that we are naturally inclined to evil: we shall then leave room for the expansion of the human heart.
>
> (ibid.: VI, 21–2)

Throughout the *Historical and Moral View*, Wollstonecraft draws on Rousseau's *Discourse on Inequality* with its depiction of society as a state of corrupting competitive dependency. As in *Vindication of the Rights of Men*, or Paine's *Rights of Man*, revolutionary excesses then become the regrettable but demonstrably transient effect of earlier despotism and corruption:

> The deprivation of natural, equal, civil and political rights, reduced the most cunning of the lower orders to practise fraud, and the rest to habits of stealing, audacious robberies, and murders. And why? because the rich and poor were separated into bands of tyrants and slaves, and the retaliation of slaves is always terrible.
>
> (ibid.: VI, 234)

But that 'terrible' retaliation inevitably carries with it the sub-text of inescapable despotism, the possibility made horribly manifest in the Terror, and registered in the narrative intensity and ideologically charged fictional paradigms of Wollstonecraft's proleptic account of Versailles.

In the *Historical and Moral View*, the *ancien régime* is depicted in standard bourgeois radical terms as a complementary degeneracy of aristocracy and lower class: 'the depravity of the higher class, and the ignorance of the lower respecting practical political science, rendered them equally incapable of thinking for themselves'. The account of the march to Versailles mobilizes an interestingly sexualized version of this fatal collusion between two 'unnatural' classes. Finding it 'scarcely probable' from her middle-class vantage-point that 'a body of women should put themselves in motion to demand relief of the king', Wollstonecraft adopts what was in fact a conservative reading of events, seeing the women as puppets of the Duke of Orléans's ambition:

> Whilst nature shudders at imputing to any one a plan so inhuman, the general character and life of the duke of Orleans warrant the belief, that he was the author of this tumult. And when we compare the singularly ferocious appearance of the mob, with the brutal violation of the apartment of the queen, there remains little doubt, but that a design was on foot against the lives of both her and the king.
>
> (ibid.: VI, 142, 207, 206)

At the risk of attributing revolutionary events to individual will rather than historical necessity, Wollstonecraft provides a novelistic description of the duke's 'general character and life', a character study which links political ambition with private vice, and produces the duke as archetypal sexual villain:

> To a disposition for low intrigue was added also a decided preference of the grossest libertinism, seasoned with vulgarity, highly congenial with the manners of the heroines, who composed the singular army of the females.
>
> Having taken up his abode in the centre of the palais royal, a very superb square, yet the last in which a person of delicacy, not to mention decorum, or morality, would choose to reside; because, excepting the people in trade, who found it convenient, it was entirely occupied by the most shameless girls of the town, their hectoring protectors, gamesters, and sharpers of every denomination. In short, by the vilest of women; by wretches, who lived in houses from which the stript bodies, often found in the Seine, were supposed to be thrown – and he was considered as the grand sultan of this den of iniquity.
>
> (ibid.: VI, 207)

This standard evocation of the seraglio recalls and reworks Richardson's specific version of that motif: Lovelace among the prostitutes at Mrs Sinclair's. In *Clarissa*, as in so many novels, middle-class morality flirts with an aristocratic aesthetic through the sexual plot. Arguably, Lovelace is partly the instrument of the prostitutes' vicarious revenge on innocence: monstrous lower-class female sexuality goads the libertine into rape, and the ambivalence of Richardson's text allows for the plausible rake to be partly absolved.[6] In Wollstonecraft, interestingly, the ambivalent aristocratic figure is female, and the violation of Marie Antoinette's apartment, the 'chaste temple', is actually carried out by the women, but firmly revealed to be motivated by the physically absent – and unequivocally abhorrent – male.

This writing in of the duke's role is a further crucial difference between Wollstonecraft's account and Burke's – not just because it shifts Burke's attribution of blame from a working-class mob on to their aristocratic motivator, but because it continues the critique of Burke's 'chivalric' aesthetic, with its associated feudal and sexual politics, which Wollstonecraft had begun in *Vindication of the Rights of Men*. The 'libertine imagination' which Wollstonecraft exposes there as the motivating presence in Burke's text, is here realized in the figure of the duke, graphically demonstrating the sexual and political violence masked by Burke's 'Gothic affability', his 'sentimental jargon' (Wollstonecraft 1989: V, 46, 17, 30).

That last phrase is part of Wollstonecraft's commentary on

Burke's depiction of the Versailles crowd as 'furies of hell, in the abused shape of the vilest of women' (Burke 1989: 122):

> Probably you mean women who gained a livelihood by selling vegetables or fish, who never had any advantages of education; or their vices might have lost part of their abominable deformity, by losing part of their grossness. The queen of France – the great and small vulgar claim our pity; they have almost insuperable obstacles to surmount in their progress towards true dignity of character; still I have such a plain downright understanding that I do not like to make a distinction without a difference.
>
> (Wollstonecraft 1989: V, 30)

In refusing to make a 'distinction without a difference' Wollstonecraft's earlier text enacts that true rational 'dignity of character' which, unlike Burke, can see through the 'decent draperies' of class difference to pity 'the great and small vulgar' as equally the victims of inadequate education.

That gender-directed pity is still demonstrably in operation in the less confidently radical *Historical and Moral View*. Before her transformation into female victim at Versailles, Marie Antoinette had appeared, more predictably, as the personification of aristocratic luxury, queen of an 'emasculated . . . circean court'. But this depiction of Marie Antoinette as sexual temptress is actually preceded by a more complex psychological portrait of 'the unfortunate queen of France', dedicated to demonstrating that 'education, and the atmosphere of manners in which a character is formed, change the natural laws of humanity'. The explanatory mode contrasts significantly with the Duke of Orléans's unmotivated, and thus implicitly inexplicable, villainy. They come, however, from the same Gothic plot, with the young Marie Antoinette as anti-heroine, innocence successfully corrupted by the combined patriarchy of church, family ambition and domestic sexual tyranny. As such, she invites comparison with the women of Paris who are seen as having 'thrown off the virtues of one sex *without having power* to assume more than the vices of the other' (Wollstonecraft 1989: VI, 73, 72, 197; my emphasis):

> But her opening faculties were poisoned in the bud; for before she came to Paris, she had already been prepared, by a corrupt, supple abbe, for the part she was to play; and, young as she was, became so firmly attached to the aggrandizement of her house, that, though plunged deep in pleasure, she never

> omitted sending immense sums to her brother, on every occasion. The person of the king, in itself very disgusting, was rendered more so by gluttony, and a total disregard of delicacy, and even decency in his apartments: and, when jealous of the queen, for whom he had a kind of devouring passion, he treated her with great brutality, till she acquired sufficient finesse to subjugate him.
>
> (ibid: VI, 73)

The monstrosity of Circe or of female furies is engendered by the distorting power of feudal patriarchy – whether in the form of supple Gothic abbés or of libertine dukes.

III

Or, in Williams's *Letters from France*, of tyrannic enchanters whose plots threaten to rewrite her love affair with the Revolution: 'though I have survived such scenes, they have left upon my heart that settled melancholy which never can be dissipated'. The 'scenes' responsible include visiting the prison chamber where the executioner's scissors 'cut off the lavish tresses of the youthful beauty, and where he tied her tender hands behind her waist with cords' (Williams 1975: VI, 100). In a metaphorical rape, the punitive hand of tyranny destroys female sensuality ('lavish tresses') before executing its victim. This generalized violation is a variant of the main romance narrative which gradually emerges from the *Letters*: they tell the tale of Liberty, the beautiful and adored heroine who is persecuted, abducted and temporarily disfigured by the 'monster' Robespierre, 'to whom nature, by some strange deviation, has given a human form' (ibid.: IV, 185). Williams's despair coincides with the most disturbing moment in the story – when Liberty seems irredeemably corrupted:

> In the first days of the revolution, when liberty and philosophy went hand in hand together, what a moral revolution was instantly effected throughout Europe. . . . But what eternal regrets must the lovers of Liberty feel, that her cause should have fallen into the hands of monsters ignorant of her charms, by whom she has been transformed into a Fury, who, brandishing her snaky whips and torches, has enlarged the limits of wickedness, and driven us back into regions of guilt hitherto unknown!
>
> (ibid.: VI, 211–12)

This is disturbing not least because the moment of crisis seems to reproduce the reactionary gender politics used by the anti-Jacobins against Williams herself: a female sexuality carefully circumscribed by 'charm' is activated into a terrifying and guilt-inducing excess which is apparently ('eternal regrets') irreversible. Though Liberty is the victim of monsters, tyrannic monstrosity is nevertheless displaced onto the woman.

In the end, of course, Liberty is freed and nature restored to her former beauty by the death of the enchanter:

> Upon the fall of Robespierre, the terrible spell which bound the land of France was broken; the shrieking whirlwinds, the black precipices, the bottomless gulphs, suddenly vanished; and reviving nature covered the wastes with flowers, and the rocks with verdure.
>
> (ibid.: VII, 190)

And in the final volume of the *Letters*, in spite of former despair, Liberty is presented as having emerged from her ordeal, like Richardson's Clarissa, essentially inviolate – though, like Clarissa, her charms are now 'divine' rather than physical:

> Upon the whole, the cause of liberty is not the less sacred, nor her charms less divine, because sanguinary monsters and sordid savages have defiled her temple, and insulted her votaries.
>
> (ibid.: VIII, 178)

That '[u]pon the whole' betrays a narrative and ideological anxiety at the heart of Williams's ultimately optimistic account. Can the spell of violent tyranny really be broken for ever? And can defiled femininity survive violation in a world where conduct literature ideology decreed that 'the least slip in a woman's honour, is never to be recovered' (Wilkes 1766: 114)? To present Robespierre as wicked enchanter is to make his spells reversible, to create the transformative possibility of undoing rape. But it is also to abandon the Enlightenment progressivism which Williams's text generally endorses, for faith that 'Heaven' will miraculously 'bring good out of evil' to produce the happy ending (Williams 1975: IV, 223).

Alongside the romance paradigm, however, Williams's *Letters* follow another narrative of sensibility which offers different affirmative possibilities. In this account, the experience of the Revolution is written as an educative sentimental journey, with Sterne as authority for the inseparability of 'particular sympathy' and 'general philanthropy'. Williams's own exemplary ability to 'blend the feelings of private friendship with my sympathy in public blessings' effects a continuity not simply between private and public feeling, but between passivity and activity. The *Letters* thus potentially intervene in, as well as simply recording, the course of the Revolution by posing the optimistic agency of 'generous minds' against the Burkeans – 'narrow-minded, splenetic, or selfish men' – whose 'predictions . . . were in a great measure the causes of the evils they foretold'. The short exemplary narratives and sentimental vignettes through which history is played out in the *Letters* are the means of effecting in England the political education in feeling Williams describes as happening in France: the text's constructed readers are, precisely, the 'generous minds'. The 'enthusiasm of the virtuous affections' which these narratives record and evoke becomes an alternative sublime, capable of transforming tyranny, 'the throb of indignant horror', to 'the glow of sympathetic admiration' during the Terror (Williams 1975: I, 25, 71–2; IV, 216–17; VI, 103). When the Terror is over, it breaks the cycle of extremity, the desire for retribution, by offering an alternative mode:

> While that desire of retribution, which is natural to the human mind, was satisfied in contemplating the great criminals dragged to punishment by the strong arm of national justice, sensations of softer pleasure were excited by observing the delightful transition which these momentous scenes produced in the situation of private individuals: – as after some terrible tempest, some mighty convulsion of nature, . . . the minuter objects of the landscape partake also the reviving influence of a benign sky, and all nature rejoices.
>
> (ibid.: VIII, 52)

And this attention to 'the minuter objects of the landscape' is the means of producing the progressivist reading which makes the Terror unrepeatable:

> the whole nation, roused into a sense of its danger by the terrible lesson it has been taught, can be oppressed no more. There scarcely exists a family, or an individual in France, that has not been bereaved by tyranny of some dear relation, some chosen friend, who seems from the grave to call upon them with a warning voice to watch over the liberties of their country.
>
> (ibid.: V, 258)

In both narratives, the new dispensation is a feminine world of beauty and feeling, replacing the Gothic landscape of 'black precipices' and 'bottomless gulphs'. In one way, then, her treatment of the Revolution could be seen simply to reinscribe Williams in the acceptably picturesque landscape of 'moonlight vallies' (Polwhele 1798: 19). But in the second narrative, the transformation of sublimity into beauty is effected by, in Wollstonecraft's phrase, '*active* sensibility' (Wollstonecraft 1989: I, 144; original emphasis), an interestingly androgynous quality given contemporary ideologies of gender.[7] Williams's text plays off a traditional narrative of (redeemed) female victimization against a more subversive destabilization of gender boundaries – and not least in the way the generic fluidity of the letter form allows these feminine narratives of sensibility to be mapped onto a comprehensive 'impartial history'. In spite of ritual apologies for a woman's inadequacy when faced with political arguments – 'how many fine-spun threads of reasoning would my wandering thoughts have broken' – the *Letters* offer an authoritative analysis of revolutionary debates, complete with appendices and interpolated evidence from a variety of sources (Williams 1975: IV, 181; I, 195).

IV

An important part of that analysis consists in careful discrimination between revolutionary factions, an attempt to convince an English readership blinded by the homogenizing rhetoric of anti-French propaganda that a clear understanding of events in France depends on an appreciation of difference. This difference is very clearly class-based, as Williams defends a bourgeois commercial ethic against, first, 'that shocking *inequality* which disfigured human society' under the *ancien régime*, and then against the 'destruction of commerce' by Robespierre's 'horrible levellers'. Between the two is an English ideal:

> a long series of classes of well-informed and worthy men, in the middling ranks of society, who connect the rich with the poor, and the men of large property with those who have none.
>
> (Williams 1975: IV, 252; VI, 166; IV, 253)

Like the *Historical and Moral View, Letters from France* asserts not only a distinct class consciousness, but also a national identity.

A constitutionally (in all senses) sound English middle class is in both texts the missing term which would save France from destruction.

As defenders of the bourgeois revolution, and women, Wollstonecraft and Williams provide a particularly revealing example of the process described by Foucault:

> one of [the bourgeoisie's] primary concerns was to provide itself with a body and a sexuality – to ensure the strength, endurance, and secular proliferation of that body through the organization of a deployment of sexuality. This process, moreover, was linked to the movement by which it asserted its distinctiveness and its hegemony. There is little question that one of the primordial forms of class consciousness is the affirmation of the body; at least, this was the case for the bourgeoisie during the eighteenth century. It converted the blue blood of the nobles into a sound organism and a healthy sexuality.
>
> (Foucault 1979: 125–6)

For Wollstonecraft, this 'conversion' of the nobles into a 'sound' body politic has been a commercial rapprochement with progressive moral consequences:

> just sentiments gain footing only in proportion as the understanding is enlarged by cultivation, and freedom of thought, instead of being cramped by the dread of bastilles and inquisitions. In Italy and France, for example, where the mind dared to exercise itself only to form the taste, the nobility were in the strictest sense of the word, a cast, keeping aloof from the people; whilst in England they intermingled with the commercial men, whose equal and superior fortunes made the nobles overlook their inequality of birth.
>
> (Wollstonecraft 1989: VI, 70)

But this 'intermingling' is not always effected by men – or, indeed, by an English propriety. In the Versailles passage it happens before our eyes as Marie Antoinette is transformed through (feminine) pity into the violated bourgeois heroine – the 'chaste temple of a woman, I consider the queen only as one' (ibid.: VI, 209). And in another climactic passage, Wollstonecraft ends a brief history of the domestication of human happiness with an uncharacteristic expression of admiration for French women:

> in France, the women have not those factitious, supercilious manners, common to the english; and acting more freely, they have more decision of character, and even more generosity . . . their coquetry is not only more agreeable, but more natural: and not left a prey to their unsatisfied sensations, they were less romantic indeed than the english; yet many of them possessed delicacy of sentiment.
>
> It is, perhaps, in a state of comparative idleness – pursuing employments not absolutely necessary to support life, that the finest polish is given to the mind, and those personal graces, which are instantly felt, but cannot be described: and it is natural to hope, that the labour of acquiring the substantial virtues, necessary to maintain freedom, will not render the french less pleasing, when they become more respectable.
>
> (ibid.: VI, 148)

In its perfectibilist hope that upper-class grace and polish can be recuperated for a dissenting middle-class 'respectability' this is a rationalist expression of the fictive transformation of Marie Antoinette, another example of that bourgeois fascination with an aristocratic aesthetic which is central to the novel of seduction. Material and sexual freedom are to be converted into moral freedom in a feminized version of Godwin's upward progress in *Political Justice* from the 'man of taste and liberal accomplishments' to the ideal 'man of benevolence' (Godwin 1976: 394–5).

Cora Kaplan has argued that, in *Vindication of the Rights of Woman* at least, Wollstonecraft's role model is an 'idealized bourgeois male' (Kaplan 1986: 46). But the rational masculine persona in Wollstonecraft's polemical texts is always importantly modified by a feminine rhetoric of pity, right feeling and true refinement, a concern to demonstrate the possibility of that '*active* sensibility' (Wollstonecraft 1989: I, 144) already identified as operative in Williams's writing. For Wollstonecraft, this instrumental femininity is continuous with rather than disruptive of rationality: in *Vindication of the Rights of Men*, for example, she attempts to redefine, and forge a link between, Burke's aesthetic categories:

> should experience prove that there is a beauty in virtue, a charm in order, which necessarily implies exertion, a depraved sensual taste may give way to a more manly one – and *melting* feelings to rational satisfactions.
>
> (Wollstonecraft 1989: V, 46)

This can be read as an earlier, more rigidly moralistic, attempt to prove perfectibility by redeeming, transforming even, a 'depraved sensual taste'. In the passage from the *Historical and Moral View*, Wollstonecraft flirts much more dangerously with 'depravity' as French aristocratic women become a kind of model, a representative stage in the progressive incorporation of beauty into (sublime) 'substantial virtues'. The implicit narrative invites comparison with the often ignored second half of Rousseau's *Nouvelle Héloïse* where Julie, rehabilitated and domesticated, can be seen as the ideal middle way between St Preux's excessive sensibility and Wolmar's rationalism.[8]

But as the analogy also makes clear, the hope of improvement through a rationalized femininity carries with it the possibility of loss: 'it is natural to hope, that the labour of acquiring substantial virtues . . . will not render the french less pleasing, when they become more respectable'. That moment of transgressive longing for a 'respectable' aesthetic/sexual pleasure captures exactly the threat of regulation, as active femininity released by the revolutionary moment is reappropriated for the 'sound organism and healthy sexuality' of male bourgeois hegemony.

In Williams, as I have already suggested, the 'sound organism' is personified in the 'classes of well-informed and worthy men'. The partner of these solid, but distinctly uninteresting, Englishmen is liberty, but liberty 'seen in her matron state', 'beheld with sober veneration' rather than desire. French liberty in contrast is 'adorned with the freshness of youth' and 'loved with the ardour of passion' (Williams 1975: IV, 253; I, 71), but as Williams's narrative so clearly demonstrates, she is therefore vulnerable to abduction and corruption. On one level, then, the Revolution's degeneration into the Terror becomes a familiar cautionary tale, yet another demonstration of the necessary containment of female sexuality into the respectable 'matron state' in the interests of social and commercial stability.

But this is a moral Williams's text, at least, seems ultimately unwilling to draw. In the *Letters*, the return of natural order at Robespierre's fall is reinforced in a series of sentimental vignettes which certainly emphasize a maternal femininity: the young woman 'straining her infants to her breast, and, while she bathes them with her tears, telling them that they shall see again their father!'; and the bourgeois family restored to itself at the gates of the prison:

> There they wait in panting expectation: – The girl no sooner perceives her mother than she springs upon her neck, the father strains his boy in his arms, and the crowd assembled at the door gaze upon this family interview with all the luxury of sympathetic delight.
>
> (ibid.: VIII, 54–5)

But discourses of respectability and pleasure maintain an uneasy coexistence here as the language of feeling libidinizes even these normative representations: Williams's text refuses to choose between sexuality and maternity.

As Robespierre's spell begins to break, sexual difference is celebrated in less disturbingly voyeuristic terms. The death of Hébert, for example:

> was the signal for throwing off the hideous masquerade of sansculottism, in which all the world had been arrayed during the winter, in submissive deference to his interpretation of equality. Immediately after his execution, the scene suddenly changed: black wigs, red caps, sailors' jackets, and pantaloons were cast aside; and the eye was refreshed with the sight of combed locks, clean linen, and decent apparel; – while the women, who for some months had reluctantly bound up their hair beneath the round cap of the peasant, now unfolded their tresses, perfumed and powdered, to the vernal gales, and decorated in whatever manner they thought proper, provided the national cockade formed part of their ornaments.
>
> (ibid.: VI, 21–2)

Anarchic masquerade has replaced Gothic landscape as a means of evoking a 'hideous' denial of order, but Williams's bourgeois aesthetic ('clean linen, and decent apparel') is at odds with her equal delight in the sensuous individuality of the women and their freedom to reconstruct themselves as objects of desire. And later, after the fall of Robespierre:

> The women indulge in their dress the full extent of female caprice, as well as extravagance. This day the peruque blonde converts the dark-complexioned nymph into a fair beauty; tomorrow she reassumes her jetty locks, and thus varies her attractions.
>
> 'How many pictures of one nymph we view,

'All how unlike each other, all how true!'
(ibid.: VII, 9)

The tone again is celebratory and transgressive, quoting Pope's couplet in order to subvert rather than endorse the dismissive criticism, echoing throughout the century, which it normally carries. Such passages must, of course, be read against the more normative – even conservative – representations of femininity already cited. The carnival atmosphere of Robespierre's fall legitimates extravagances which would be dismissed in other circumstances. But it is striking that, for Williams, one response to the end of the Terror is a celebration of restored sexual difference in which women take delight in their sexuality.

V

In *Letters from France* and the *Historical and Moral View*, then, novelistic paradigms write historical necessity in terms of confrontations of sensibility and sublimity, class and sexuality. The female body is the victim and focus of violence, but femininity (however circumscribed) is also presented as instrumental in the process of rational, or sensible, moral improvement, an active role which threatens to subvert the objectifying versions of feminization in the standard histories.

In the *Historical and Moral View*, however, the dominant rationalism and tragic sexual narrative produce a defensively desexualized femininity. Kaplan, again, argues that in *Vindication of the Rights of Woman*: 'What the argument moves towards, but never quite arrives at, is the conclusion that it is male desire that must be controlled and contained if women are to be free and rational' (Kaplan 1986: 46). The *Historical and Moral View* repeats the asymmetry of the *Vindication* in its failure to extend the careful exposition of women's social construction to men. In the *Vindication* Wollstonecraft had claimed that 'men are certainly more under the influence of their appetites than women', going on to cite 'want of chastity in men' as the 'one grand cause' behind 'all the causes of female weakness, as well as depravity, which I have already enlarged on'. As it stands, of course, this does not necessarily rule out an analysis of that 'want of chastity' as itself a social construct and subject to rational improvement. But the conduct-book discourse in the *Vindication*, with its focus on making women worthy of their 'peculiar duties' tends to reify male sexuality (Wollstonecraft 1989: V, 207, 208, 132) – a tendency even more evident in the fictional paradigm (also present in conduct literature) which takes libertinism beyond class, to give it demonic status – in the *Historical and Moral View*, as I suggested earlier, the Duke of Orléans's 'depravity' remains an unmotivated given.

Williams's transformative romance version of the seduction/abduction plot more easily accommodates varieties of femininity which include moments of guilt-free female pleasure. Her fluid text is thus in some ways better able to imagine new narratives of sexuality and subjectivity than is Wollstonecraft's more rigorous historical polemic. But again there is the problem of imagining a new masculinity: Robespierre's tyrannic corruption is replaced in Williams's *Sketches from France* (1801) by the authoritative heroism of Bonaparte, and the effect of the abduction plot in the *Historical and Moral View*, Marie Antoinette and the Duke of Orléans as archetypal victim and villain, is to produce masculinity as the 'natural'/fallen category responsible for turning progressivist possibilities back into the cycle of tyranny. In spite of Wollstonecraft's opening imperative, then, the discourse of sexuality in the *Historical and Moral View* ultimately reasserts 'wild traditions of original sin' (Wollstonecraft 1989: VI, 21). Though the blame for the Fall is transferred to the male, the cycle remains unbroken.

The struggle to break the tyrannic binarism of Richardsonian Gothic and sentimental romance continues throughout the period in the 'feminine' novel. New plots of sexuality are painfully tested in the fictions of Hays, Inchbald, Opie, Smith, and Wollstonecraft herself (and later Charlotte Brontë), as radical women seek ways of rewriting history by rewriting gender and sexuality. But that brief moment of revolutionary potential in Williams's *Julia* with which I began is in many ways paradigmatic: there, the retributive death of the hero destroys the balanced 'cordiality and friendship' which might have transformed a conventional triangle of relationships, and in the final paragraph of the novel, the memory of passion, 'that one unconquered weakness', disrupts the female community of Julia and Charlotte (Williams 1790: 267, 282). In various ways, that ambivalent articulation of failed possibilities reverberates through the novels of the postrevolutionary period.

NOTES

I want to thank John Whale and Angela Keane for discussion and comments which have been invaluable in writing this essay.

1 On the relationship between sexuality and sensibility in contemporary definitions of femininity, and on ideas of propriety as they affect women's writing, see Jones 1990, Poovey 1984, Spencer 1986, Todd 1986. For influential contemporary expressions of the necessary exclusion of women from politics and from writing (though not reading) history, see Hester Chapone, *Letters on the Improvement of the Mind*, 1773, and Laetitia Matilda Hawkins, *Letters on the Female Mind, its Powers and Pursuits*, 1793 (in Jones 1990: 104–6, 117–20).

2 The bibliography of *Letters from France* is extremely complicated. For convenience, references are to Janet Todd's facsimile reprint, but for the sake of clarity, I have added volume numbers as follows:

I: *Letters from France, in the summer of 1790, to a friend in England containing various anecdotes relative to the French Revolution and memoirs of M. and Mme. du F* –, 5th edn, London, 1796.

II: *Letters from France: containing many new anecdotes relative to the French Revolution, and the present state of French manners*, 2nd edn, London, 1792, vol. 2.

III and IV: *Letters from France: containing a great variety of interesting and original information concerning the most important events that have lately occurred in that country, and particularly respecting the campaign of 1792*, 2nd edn, London, 1796, vols 3, 4.

V and VI: *Letters containing a sketch of the politics of France from the thirty-first of May 1793, till the twenty-eighth of July 1794, and of the scenes which have passed in the prisons of Paris*, London, 1795, vols 1, 2.

VII: *Letters containing a sketch of the scenes which passed in various departments of France during the tyranny of Robespierre, and of the events which took place in Paris on the 28th of July 1794*, London, 1795, vol. 3.

VIII: *Letters containing a sketch of the politics of France, from the twenty-eighth of July 1794, to the establishment of the Constitution in 1795, and of the scenes which have passed in the prisons of Paris*, London, 1796, vol. 4.

3 On the Enlightenment association of progress with feminization, see Tomaselli 1985. I have also had the benefit of reading an unpublished paper by Jane Rendall, 'Virtue and propriety: the Scottish Enlightenment and the construction of femininity' (1989).

4 In Rousseau's *Discourse on Inequality*, for example, the progress of civilization is also a regression to 'the complete law of the strongest, and so to a new state of nature . . . the consequence of excessive corruption' (Rousseau 1973: 114); in *Political Justice*, Godwin's defence of 'sound philosophy' hardly matches up to his terrifying version of

the opposing view in which 'the whole of the history of the human species . . . appears a vast abortion' (Godwin 1976: 400); and, perhaps most symptomatic, in *Les Ruines* itself the rationalist intervention to break the cycle of despair is ambivalently represented in the form of dream-vision.

5 Merck's comment is from her critique of Andrea Dworkin's reiteration of certain kinds of sexual narrative in *Intercourse*.

6 For a full exposition of this reading of *Clarissa*, see Wilt 1977.

7 See, for example, Burke's famous comparison of the feminine 'softer virtues' with those 'of the sublimer kind' (Burke 1958: 110–11).

8 Cf. Deane 1988: chapter 4.

11

WORDSWORTH AND THE USE OF CHARITY

Robin Jarvis

> the manna must be scattered in the wilderness for the poor to claim as a right and not left in the power of anothers charity for them to solicit as a blessing for then thousands will be sent empty away.
>
> (Clare 1984: 447)

'The Old Cumberland Beggar' has never been among Wordsworth's most popular poems. One possible cause of the distaste it arouses was pinpointed by Charles Lamb, who considered it a fault 'that the instructions conveyed in it are too direct and like a lecture: they don't slide into the mind of the reader, while he is imagining no such matter' (Lamb 1935: I, 239). Such unease has obviously been intensified for some considerable time by the many versions of formalist and expressive literary theory opposed to anything in poetry that smacks of didacticism, propaganda or incitement to action; and ironically, at a time when the material contexts and purposes of poetry are at last finding serious critical attention, the sentiments expressed in 'The Old Cumberland Beggar' seem destined to keep it still longer in the critical closet. In this chapter, I propose to resuscitate and re-explore the radical discomfort occasioned in Lamb and others by the poem's hortatory discourse. Our own time is one of rapidly expanding domestic and international charitable activity, and 'The Old Cumberland Beggar' speaks loudly yet obliquely to a present that can use its historical distance from the text for purposes of both criticism and self-criticism.

My working assumption is that the poem is concerned principally with private charity and its implications for both donor and recipient, rather than, as the rudimentary historical element in much criticism would seem to suggest, with the administration of poor relief or the debate on Poor Law reform.[1] These are relevant issues, but they are not the end-focus of the poem, as the prefatory note of 1800, with its description of informal, voluntary almsgiving, would seem to confirm:

> The class of Beggars to which the old man here described belongs, will probably soon be extinct. It consisted of poor, and, mostly, old and infirm persons, who confined themselves to a stated round in their neighbourhood, and had certain fixed days, on which, at different houses, they regularly received charity; sometimes in money, but mostly in provisions.[2]

However, the so-called Fenwick note, written in 1843 against the more immediate background of the 1834 Poor Law Amendment Act, has been partly responsible for a misunderstanding concerning the poem's relation to contemporary attitudes and policies towards the poor. The note records that a real-life equivalent to the Beggar was observed in childhood 'with great benefit to my own heart', and that the poem was written at Racedown and Alfoxden[3] at a time when 'The political economists were . . . beginning their war upon mendicity in all its forms, and by implication, if not directly, on Almsgiving also'; Wordsworth adds that this 'heartless process' has been carried still further by the Poor Law Amendment Act, which aims to force the poor 'into a condition between relief in the Union poor-house, and Alms robbed of their Christian grace and spirit, as being *forced* rather from the benevolent than given by them' (Wordsworth 1963: 306).

The old Poor Law is a notorious historical minefield, with scholars disagreeing widely over the interpretation of sources which are themselves unusually variegated and contradictory; but scholarship at this level is irrelevant to my purposes, even were I competent to evaluate it. What is practicable and worthwhile is to highlight certain features of the public debate on poverty in the late eighteenth century that can be set against Wordsworth's poem, and which can later be placed in mutual interrogation with aspects of current debate on the same issue.[4] The immediate material context of 'The Old Cumberland Beggar' was the increasing strain imposed on the Poor Law system in the final quarter of the eighteenth century by demographic change and economic upheaval, and which came to crisis point in the mid-1790s with a succession of bad harvests and a proliferation of vagrancy caused by soldiers returning from the war. This led to the more widespread use of outdoor relief and to the introduction of a varied system of wage supplementation. It was the alleged social consequences of this system, which was accused of encouraging large families for which no independent provision could be made, as well as the inflated cost of the system thus inaugurated, which created the climate from which the 1834 Act eventually emerged.

While even this relatively 'factual' summary is open to disagreement, it is certain arguments marshalled in support of, or in opposition to, the Poor Law that concern us here. One of the remarkable features of the Poor Law debate is the way very different, and sometimes conflicting, theses intersect and overlap in places. Thus arguments in favour of the utility of poverty occur throughout the eighteenth century, but may be primarily economic (stressing the need for low wages to maximize profits) or moral (stressing the need to discourage idleness and improvidence) in character. Workhouse schemes were attacked in some quarters for humanitarian reasons, but elsewhere were championed on the same grounds. Most interesting for the present discussion is the overlap between Poor Law abolitionists and apologists, in respect of a shared belief in the reciprocal duties of rich and poor and a preference for private charity. Both groups, that is, could object to forced charity on the grounds that it dissolved the natural moral bonds between the different social orders, although the latter group would acknowledge that individual benevolence would not be sufficient to fill the gap. More extreme positions were, of course, on offer: Joseph Townsend, in his *Dissertation on the Poor Laws* (1786), adopted the position that *all* charity, public *or* private, had deleterious effects on the poor, since 'it is only hunger which can spur and goad them on to labour' (Townsend 1786: 23); and Thomas Malthus gave influential expression to the economic case that poor laws worsened the condition of the poor, since their tendency was to 'increase population without increasing the food for its support', and thereby to 'create the poor which they maintain' (Malthus 1970: 97). But these more unequivocally hawkish contributions to the debate are part of an evolving discourse in which moral attitudes, social prejudices and economic principles are often confusingly interwoven.

One of the fascinating indices of this confusion is the convergence of minds between William Wordsworth and his erstwhile antagonist, Richard Watson, the Bishop of Llandaff. Watson's Westminster sermon of 1785, the 1793 appendix to which prompted

Wordsworth's unpublished republican *Letter*, is a wholly representative document in the charity debate. Watson praises private charity as a Christian duty, tied to the divinely sanctioned institution of private property. God, he states,

> never meaned that the idle should live upon the labour of the industrious, or that the flagitious should eat the bread of the righteous: he hath therefore permitted a state of property to be every where introduced; that the industrious might enjoy the rewards of their diligence, and that those who would not work, might feel the punishment of their laziness.
>
> (Watson 1793: 2)

He admits the difficulty of persuading the poor of the justice of this dispensation, but makes the point that the chief ingredients of happiness are equally dispersed by God: 'air, and light, and sleep, the warmth of the sun, and the dew of Heaven' (ibid.: 9). Wordsworth finds similar grounds for optimism in 'The Old Cumberland Beggar'. The rich, according to Watson, have a duty to ensure that the poor do not lack the means necessary for the preservation of life, and to treat them with 'fellow feeling kindness'; conversely, the poor have a duty to be grateful to the rich 'for all the good they receive from them', to make provision for their old age, and not to surrender to envy or despair. Were all men on a level, Watson concludes, the better-off would find themselves in a spiritual quandary: 'the rich not being called upon to part with his property, would not know whether he was the servant of Mammon or of God' (Watson 1793: 14–15). In 1793 Wordsworth had expressed the hope that 'the class of wretches called mendicants will not much longer shock the feelings of humanity' (Wordsworth 1974: I, 43), but by 1797, when 'The Old Cumberland Beggar' is written, just how far is he from Watson's smug prescriptions?

Charity, as Raymond Williams has observed, was originally synonymous with 'Christian love, between men and God, and between men and their neighbours' (Williams 1983: 54–5), and only later acquired the narrowed sense of help to the needy. It is under the umbrella of this traditional Christian conception of charity that Wordsworth shelters with the Bishop, and formulates the message of 'The Old Cumberland Beggar'. It is mistaken to argue that Wordsworth's invective in this poem is aimed primarily at the engineers of a system of poor relief which held to the workhouse as the best way of discouraging the irresponsible and the work-shy. For despite a counter-impulse represented by Pitt's abandoned bill of 1796, which proposed a massive programme of workhouse construction, the whole movement in the 1790s was towards the expansion and diversification of outdoor relief.[5] Wordsworth was acquainted with this state of affairs, and it seems implausible that he would write a poem targeted mainly at the workhouse system at a time when public policy, despite dissonant voices, was repudiating or downgrading that system under the pressure of circumstances. In so far as 'The Old Cumberland Beggar' is implicated in contemporary debate over poor relief, therefore, it is by virtue of its covert awareness of the abolitionist case that had been gathering momentum in the last quarter of the century; more specifically, Wordsworth's preoccupation was with the rationale advanced by political economists for the counter-productive and depraving effects of institutional toleration of dependent poverty, since this had sinister implications for the practice of *private* charity. The Cumberland Beggar does not appear to be in receipt of any parish assistance, and if he and his ilk are to become extinct, as the prefatory note suggests, it will not be so much because they have all been shunted into workhouses, but more because, Wordsworth fears, attitudes to charity (on the part of either donor or recipient) will become too negatively charged. Just such an ideological victory – that is, the creation of an overt social stigma for charity – is commonly observed to have been won by mid-Victorian times. The tone of Wordsworth's resistance to this process, in 'The Old Cumberland Beggar', is unpalatable to many readers today, as it was then, but the *substance* of his arguments was conventional to a large degree.

One might digress at this point to say something about the Wordsworths' actual experience of beggars at about this period, of which a substantial and detailed account survives in Dorothy's journals. Evidence of this kind might seem of limited relevance to an analysis of 'The Old Cumberland Beggar', but it does help to concentrate attention on certain attitudes that are far less bluntly registered in the poem. The Grasmere journal of 1800–3 is strewn with references to beggars encountered in the street or presenting themselves at the door of Dove Cottage. One remarkable feature of these incidents is the regularity with which the Wordsworths get their money's worth of *story* out of the beggars they patronize. A poor potter who calls on 20 June 1800, for example, is required to give details of his illness, his family situation and his dealings with the parish before eventually receiving his sixpence (Dorothy Wordsworth 1952: I, 49–50). A subtler example of this form of barter occurs on 10 June: a woman is given a piece of bread only, it seems, after she has provided details of her birthplace, her normal place of residence, her husband's occupation and their reasons for being on the move. The parish overseer could scarcely ask for more. Her husband and children, she says, have gone on ahead; Dorothy continues:

> Afterwards on my road to Ambleside, beside the bridge at Rydale, I saw her husband sitting by the roadside, his two asses feeding beside him, and the two young children at play upon the grass. The man did not beg. I passed on and about 1/4 of a mile further I saw two boys before me, one about 10, the other about 8 years old, at play chasing a butterfly. They were wild figures, not very ragged, but without shoes and stockings; the hat of the elder was wreathed round with yellow flowers, the younger whose hat was only a rimless crown, had stuck it round with laurel leaves. They continued at play till I drew very near, and then they addressed me with the begging cant and the whining voice of sorrow. I said 'I served your mother this morning'. (The Boys were so like the woman who had called at the door that I could not be mistaken.) 'O!' says the elder, 'you could not serve my mother for she's dead, and my father's on at the next town – he's a potter.' I persisted in my assertion, and that I would give them nothing. Says the elder, 'Come, let's away', and away they flew like lightning. They had however sauntered so long in their road that they did not reach Ambleside before me, and I saw them go up to Matthew Harrison's house with their wallet upon the elder's shoulder, and creeping with a beggar's complaining foot.
>
> (ibid.: I, 47)

There is a conspicuous tension in Dorothy's narrative. On the one hand, there is a romanticizing tendency to picture the boys as impulsive children of nature: they are garlanded with flowers, they chase butterflies in the manner of the young Wordsworth and Dorothy themselves (see 'To a Butterfly'), they fly away 'like lightning'. On the other, there is her manifest class-conscious distaste for the boys' 'begging cant', 'whining voice[s]' and 'complaining feet'. Dorothy shows no sympathizing awareness that the 'cant' and the 'whine' are, practically speaking, the only economic leverage a beggar possesses. This point had been made by Adam Smith in *The Wealth of Nations*: he had argued, in fact, that the near-total dependence of beggars on the benevolence of their fellow citizens effectively divorced them from the rest of humanity, the arts of supplication necessarily employed inducing a closer approximation to mere animality:

> When an animal wants to obtain something either of a man or of another animal, it has no other means of persuasion but to gain the favour of those whose service it requires. A puppy fawns upon its dam, and a spaniel endeavours by a thousand attractions to engage the attention of its master who is at dinner, when it wants to be fed by him. Man sometimes uses the same arts with his brethren, and when he has no other means of engaging them to act according to his inclinations, endeavours by every servile and fawning attention to obtain their good will.
>
> (Smith 1976: I, 26)

What the beggar cannot and does not do, according to Smith, is to engage, as all other people do in the business of living, in acts of treaty, barter and purchase.[6] As I have suggested, however, the relationship between the Wordsworths and the beggars who try their luck with them may reasonably be interpreted as one of exchange, in which the beggars barter their stories – of considerable interest and utility to the poetic observer – for a few pence or a slice of bread. What Dorothy seems not to like, however, on the evidence of this passage, is *lies* from mendicant children, since this smacks of dishonest 'trading'.

The sharp practice in this instance, though, is on the Wordsworths' side, since Wordsworth was to process the incident two years later into the poem 'Beggars', and even compounded his interest on the transaction by pressing straight on over breakfast to write 'To a Butterfly'.[7] In 'Beggars', Wordsworth begins by describing the mother, now idealized into a 'fit person for a Queen / To lead those ancient Amazonian files'.[8] Then, still closely following Dorothy's report of the incident, he relates the meeting with the two boys, in whose faces he claims to have read 'Unquestionable lines of that wild Suppliant's face'. A further decorative comparison ('Wings let them have, and they might flit / Precursors to Aurora's car, / Scattering fresh flowers') pushes to the extreme the recuperation of two penniless children into the peace and plenitude of nature. Returning to the incident, Wordsworth records the boys' placid resistance to the accusations he makes towards them:

'She has been dead, Sir, many a day.' –
'Hush, boys! you're telling me a lie.'

Unlike his conversation with another celebrated liar, the child of 'Anecdote for Fathers', Wordsworth does not seem to find this encounter a positive educational experience.

The canonical reading of 'The Old Cumberland Beggar' is, I believe, one which humanizes the speaker (and implied reader) of the poem at the cost of *de*-humanizing the beggar himself. This is a tactic that bears more than a chance relation to the Wordsworth of the journal extracts or the unyielding inquisitor of 'Beggars'. If, in the latter poem, there is an asymmetry between the romantic leanings of the reflective poet who converts a woman he has never seen into an Amazonian queen, and the social attitude which requires that the poor submit themselves to DHSS-style scrutiny from every potential benefactor, in 'The Old Cumberland Beggar' there is a similar, but more brutal, disjunction between the empathizing narrative that *accompanies* the beggar as he 'plies his weary journey' and the strident rhetoric which co-opts him to the philosophical agenda of the poet.

Sight is the dominant medium and metaphor of the poem, as many critics have noted. The first line, 'I saw an aged Beggar in my walk', introduces a blandly literal description of the old man,

seated by the highway side
On a low structure of rude masonry
Built at the foot of a huge hill, that they
Who lead their horses down the steep rough road
May thence remount at ease.

(Wordsworth 1963: lines 2–6)

The beggar's immobility, negatively reinforced by allusion to those who use the stone for its intended purpose, then becomes a psychological characteristic as he draws his scraps and fragments from his bag and scans them 'with a fixed and serious look / Of idle computation' (lines 11–12). The apparent contradiction here ('fixed' and 'serious'/'idle') serves to annul any emerging impression of mental activity: the beggar's glance is fixed only in its vacancy and purposelessness, concentratedly lacking in concentration. As he eats, and crumbs fall from his 'palsied hand', it is this hand, acting in seeming independence of any directive from the brain, that attempts to 'prevent the waste'; the birds, though 'Not venturing yet to peck their destined meal', are moving in as though on a dying man. This physical and mental neutralization of the beggar is an essential preliminary to establishing him as a proper object for contemplation. Recumbent on the 'second step of that small pile', alone among the 'wild unpeopled hills', the beggar offers no resistance to the invasive gaze of the poet famous for finding sermons in stones.

This slow, circling description continues in the next section, which completes the poetic disablement of the already decrepit beggar:

> Him from my childhood have I known, and then
> He was so old, he seems not older now.
>
> (lines 22–3)

The aged beggar is curiously ageless, like a natural object – or one that gives the *impression* of permanence, like the stone pile on which he is seated. As Wordsworth now generalizes his narrative of the beggar's life, the dominant figure of oxymoron takes the form of motionless movement: the 'sauntering horseman-traveller' *stops* in order to 'safely lodge the coin / Within the old Man's hat' (lines 26–9), rather like a motorist pulling in to feed coins into an auto-toll machine. In fact, it is the woman who tends the toll-gate who is mentioned next, and one wonders how long she had to wait between seeing the beggar coming and lifting the latch in order to let him pass. The post-boy in his cart circumvents the beggar as though he were a bollard in the middle of the road, and even the 'cottage curs' get bored of barking at him; he is progressively de-animated to the point where he cannot even 'Disturb the summer dust' as he passes.

These lines effect a metonymizing reduction of a human being to one element among others of the natural scene through which he travels. In the poet's eyes, he represents no centre of conscious life:

he is capable of no sensory activity, let alone mental or emotional agitation:

> On the ground
> His eyes are turn'd, and, as he moves along,
> *They* move along the ground; and evermore,
> Instead of common and habitual sight
> Of fields with rural works, of hill and dale,
> And the blue sky, one little span of earth
> Is all his prospect. Thus, from day to day,
> Bowbent, his eyes for ever on the ground,
> He plies his weary journey, seeing still,
> And never knowing that he sees, some straw,
> Some scatter'd leaf, or marks which, in one track,
> The nails of cart or chariot wheel have left
> Impress'd on the white road, in the same line,
> At distance still the same.
>
> (lines 45–58)

The beggar's eyes function, to use another motoring metaphor, like the camera mounted on a car door that gives us unselectively the driver's unfolding 'view' – except that in this case the car is virtually stationary. A curious kind of transference seems to operate in the last three or four lines, which, even while they register a detail of the physical surroundings, seem to apply more to the beggar himself – to the monotony of his existence and the regularity of his itinerary. The reiterated synecdoche, 'His age has no companion', invokes the notion of fellowship only to withdraw it in the same gesture, not only because the beggar happens not to have a companion, but because, abstracted to a tally of years or resolved into the material signs of his longevity, he is not *fit* for companionship, has no nearer claims on any of those who, compassionately or otherwise, 'pass him by'.

The long discursive section of the poem opens with the blanket admonition of 'Statesmen' who wish to sweep the beggar and his like out of public sight, or eradicate their calling completely. There had been little in the way of open compassion in the more intimate descriptive/narrative section – nothing more personalized than the withdrawn sympathy of 'Poor Traveller', true kindliness being the prerogative of the community which maintains the beggar, and with which the speaker of the poem does little to identify. The discursive section, though, achieves a more secure and effortless distance, rather shockingly foreshadowed in the association of the beggar with 'the meanest of created things' (line 74). Wordsworth sets out, no doubt with good intentions but also with a chilling philosophical hauteur, to settle the question of the beggar's utility. Indeed, his specific target has been argued by David Simpson to be Jeremy Bentham's utilitarian case *against* mendicity, which deemed the pains of sympathy and disgust excited in tender-hearted or squeamish passers-by to outweigh the temporary pleasures of comfort occasioned in the beggar himself. Simpson is concerned particularly with Bentham's proposals for 'schools of industry', and Wordsworth's possible anxieties as one of the 'lower middle-class property owners' who would foot the bill for them; but his claim that 'Wordsworthian self-interest is not something that excludes concern for others, but rather includes it' (Simpson 1987: 169), chimes with my own interpretation of Wordsworth's argument concerning private charity. Surely the most remarkable feature of the poem is the absence of any reference to, or any attempt to divine, the feelings of the beggar himself as the recipient of charitable acts; rather, he is considered to have outrun or transcended such capacity for response. That, at any rate, is the manifest statement of the poem. But it is also transparently obvious to the modern reader that any response would be ruled out of court as an irrelevance, since Wordsworth's objective is to justify private charity from the point of view of the moral and spiritual welfare of the donor, at the expense of the self-respecting humanity of the recipient.

He conducts his argument on four fronts. First, he claims that the perennial call which the beggar makes on the goodwill of the community operates as an unconscious moral pressure on the villagers, sanctifying their involuntary kindnesses:

> The mild necessity of use compels
> To acts of love; and habit does the work
> Of reason, yet prepares that after joy
> Which reason cherishes.
>
> (lines 91–4)

– which is rather like the formation of the mind and morals of the child by the subliminal influence of natural objects which Wordsworth theorizes in Book I of *The Prelude* ('Nature by extrinsic passion first / Peopled my mind with beauteous forms or grand' (Wordsworth 1959: 1805, I, lines 572–3)). However, Wordsworth evidently does not regard himself as falling into this particular category of virtuous villager. His affiliations are more with the 'lofty minds / And meditative, authors of delight / And happiness' (lines 98–100) whom he describes in his second proposition as having received from characters like the Cumberland Beggar in childhood 'That first mild touch of sympathy and thought, / In which they found their kindred with a world / Where want and sorrow were' (lines 106–8). Presumably what Wordsworth means here by 'kindred' is an affinity, the kind of adaptation of the preternaturally other-worldly child to the reality principle also recounted in *The Prelude*; but the implication is that a real world characterized by 'want and sorrow' makes for a still more difficult adjustment. It is, one supposes, the beggar's solitariness with which the self-isolating youthful genius can identify. The irony is that the relatedness to suffering humanity thus celebrated does not seem to issue, in the poem, in a tangibly closer kinship with the old man described, who remains for the most part an object of philosophico-moral contemplation.

Wordsworth's third argument is that the beggar functions as a 'silent monitor', reminding the poor and the more comfortably-off of their relative prosperity and making them more conscious of the benefits they enjoy. The striking image of the man 'Who sits at his own door, and like the pear / Which overhangs his head from the green wall, / Feeds in the sunshine' (lines 109–11), is effective because the unreflective, purely organic existence it evokes widens, rather than closes, the gap between the villagers and the beggar, since the sense of overactive fructification is so inapposite with regard to the old man. Wordsworth's rider that the beggar makes felt the paltry blessings of others, even though he cannot 'give the fortitude / And circumspection needful to preserve' them, appears to reproduce the typical middle-class complaint about the improvidence and fecklessness of the poor, and helps to define more accurately the speaker's social identity. The final argument is the most intriguing and the most question-begging. In contrast to the 'inevitable charities' shown by ordinary, upright people to their close family, Wordsworth postulates that

the poorest poor
Long for some moments in a weary life
When they can know and feel that they have been
Themselves the fathers and the dealers out
Of some small blessings.

(lines 140–4)

Unfortunately, this humane affirmation carries with it the implication that there must always be some who cannot enjoy such voluntary charities; the spiritual uplift of those who can afford to give of their own modest means is parasitic on the need and importunity of those who have nothing to give. We may all have 'one human heart' in theory, but if the 'exhilarated heart' of the donor is the reward of moral maturity, then in practice some must have a more human heart than others. The cruellest unacknowledged irony of this poem, with its overt disdain for 'schools of industry', is that the beggar should be 'put to work' discursively for the spiritual rehabilitation of those more fortunate than himself.

This, at any rate, is the counter-current I feel disturbing the peroration in which Wordsworth, having re-established the beggar's social utility without deigning to solicit his own feelings on being an object of charity, cheerfully consigns him to the frosty air and winter snows. The rhetoric which now dedicates him to the Wordsworthian 'mountain solitudes' he is allegedly incapable of enjoying seeks to consecrate in the poet's own idiom of freedom a mode of endurance that has been appropriated; the '*natural* silence of old age' (line 175; my emphasis) is in fact a silence that has been discreetly *enforced* throughout the poem. The final triumphal prosopopoeia may be thought to conceal, by way of supplementary persuasion, a hyperbole in which the care and supervision of the institutional guardians of the poor – rejected at the level of the poem's manifest statement – has been apotheosized into the benign invigilation of nature:

> As in the eye of Nature he has lived,
> So in the eye of Nature let him die.
>
> (lines 188–9)

Benign it may just about seem to be, but this is *oversight* in both senses: a recognition of what is there and an omission to notice anything challenging the complacency of the beholder. Seeing, here as elsewhere in the poem, reconfirms the separation of observers and observed, the former receiving reassurance of their own privileges and security through the opportunities afforded to underline their superiority by giving of their superfluity. The system will always need some people who are *less* than human to keep itself intact. This is the burden of the most poignant detail in the poem, that of the beggar feeding the mountain birds unintentionally and unwillingly:

> And ever, scatter'd from his palsied hand,
> That still attempting to prevent the waste,
> Was baffled still, the crumbs in little showers
> Fell on the ground, and the small mountain birds,
> Not venturing yet to peck their destin'd meal,
> Approached within the length of half his staff.
>
> (lines 16–21)

Only the beggar, it seems, is refused the pleasure of being the 'dealer out' of small blessings, even to the birds, and therefore of constituting himself as fully human. The poem makes trouble for itself by conceiving 'kindness' (line 145) solely in terms of the provision of subsistence; but as it stands it must surely beg the question of whether we need the poor to be human.

For we are still caught in the contradictions manifested by 'The Old Cumberland Beggar'. We live in an age of massive and proliferating charitable activity. Two major features of the past ten years have been the progressive internationalization of this activity, and the emergence of spectacular one-off appeals linked to mass entertainments of one kind or another. In the latter development, we see an even more naked exchange relationship than that embodied in the charitable acts already considered. The extreme instance is one in which, for instance, a record is played on the radio only once sufficient punters have phoned in their pledges: just as, that is, the mendicants calling at the Wordsworths' back door discover that there is no such thing as a free lunch, today's tele-donors get something for their money. However, an important difference between the two cultural landscapes is the more complete alienation of the modern benefactor, especially in the context of international aid, from the object of his/her charity. The global village is a radically different entity to the village patrolled by the Old Cumberland Beggar, and the credit card pledge is an irredeemably more impersonal transaction than that conducted on the doorstep with the disadvantaged persons themselves. The 'popularity' of international aid can be partly explained by this very remoteness and impersonality: the poor and homeless within our own country are too uncomfortably close not to elicit a measure of guilt, since a consciousness that their sufferings are removable (given the necessary political action) is far more widely diffused than in Wordsworth's time, when the existence of a poor class was justified on both economic and religious grounds. In contrast, a sense of the complicity of industrialized capitalist nations in the deprivations of the Third World, and hence of actual responsibility for those afflicted, is far less widespread or acute.

Charity is increasingly popular(ized) because it is more in tune with the ideology of the New Right as a remedy for poverty than the state welfarism it has continued to supplement in modern times. For evidence of this one need look no further than the celebrated speech given by Margaret Thatcher to the General Assembly of the Church of Scotland on 21 May 1988, a speech regarded as a key statement of the ethics of Thatcherism. Although she rejects the notion that spiritual redemption and social reform are completely separate, Mrs Thatcher starts by defining the 'distinctive marks' of Christianity in spiritual terms. These amount to an assertion of individual responsibility and rational free will, for which the Crucifixion is her central icon:

> We must not profess the Christian faith and go to Church simply because we want social reforms and benefits or a better standard of behaviour, but because we accept the sanctity of life, the responsibility that comes with freedom and the supreme sacrifice of Christ.[9]

Moving on to relate these convictions to questions of public policy, Mrs Thatcher invokes St Paul to justify an emphasis on wealth creation, adding that 'the spiritual dimension comes in deciding what one does with the wealth'. In a notorious passage, she then confesses that she 'always had difficulty with interpreting the Biblical precept to love our neighbours as ourselves' until she came across the works of C.S. Lewis. 'He pointed out that we don't exactly love *ourselves* when we fall below the standards and beliefs we have accepted': in other words, compassion towards one's neighbours is ultimately, as with Wordsworth's Cumberland villagers, in the service of one's own self-image or self-regarding humanity.

The key section of the speech opens with the declared certainty 'that any set of social and economic arrangements which is not founded on the acceptance of individual responsibility will do nothing but harm. We are all responsible for our own actions.' Mrs Thatcher seems to have law-breaking chiefly in mind here, but the notion of responsibility is one that is silently extended to cover any situation in which individuals find themselves. In adding that 'We simply cannot delegate the exercise of mercy and generosity to others', the subject-position occupied and offered in the 'we' is revealingly one that defines itself in opposition to those appealing for mercy or generosity. It is also a collective designation for Christian individuals who refuse to allow their inviolable God-given freedom of thought and action to be eroded by a state that is obfuscatorily accorded little more than a counselling role. Laws, according to Mrs Thatcher, should seek to *encourage* people's best instincts and suppress the bad. In terms of neighbourliness and charity, this means that people should be encouraged to practise generosity towards their disadvantaged fellow citizens, but that if they choose not to then there is little the state can – or should – do about it.

This is qualified only somewhat in the conclusion to this section of her speech:

> In our generation, the only way we can ensure that no one is left without sustenance, help or opportunity, is to have laws to provide for health and education, pensions for the elderly, succour for the sick and disabled. But intervention by the State must never become so great that it effectively removes personal responsibility. The same applies to taxation for while you and I would work extremely hard whatever the circumstances, there are undoubtedly some who would not unless the incentive was there. And we need *their* efforts too.

It is amusing to speculate on the reaction of Mrs Thatcher's audience of presbyters and elders to this grandiloquent appeal. But it is more important to note that she has here retrenched into something like the Malthusian position that poor relief should be abolished or severely curtailed because it fosters idleness and dependency. Responsibility for one's actions easily distends into responsibility for one's poverty. The speech makes no reference to the economic system which produces broadening disparities of wealth and poverty, and structural unemployment immune to the incentives of lower taxation; on the contrary, the 'you and I', beyond the immediate context of the speech, is an invitation to identify in principle or practice with a privileged social grouping and collaborate in the maintenance of gross material inequality under the flimsy guise of a *moral* egalitarianism. It is a rhetoric that cruelly echoes that of the anti-Poor Law ideologists of the late eighteenth century.

Wordsworth's poem, then, is discomfitingly alien in its invocation of a poor yet mutually supportive rural community, as well as in the specific cast of its political polemic; yet it is astonishingly close to home in the spirit, if not the exact content, of the arguments in defence of private charity which the disconcertingly rootless narrator brings into play. This tension between a sense of cultural dislocation and a queasy over-familiarity with at least some among the range of social and political positions adopted, generates a fresh readerly discomfort with 'The Old Cumberland Beggar' that is sensitive to the ways in which it can engage and outrage the present at the same time as it makes full acknowledgement of its historical difference. Reproducing and confronting this discomfort might help, if nothing else, to render more available the kind of elementary insight offered by John Clare in the epigraph to this essay.

NOTES

1 Simpson (1987: 162–74) offers a strong alternative reading. I also listened with great interest to a paper by Nicola Trott, 'Wordsworth's "Old Cumberland Beggar": The Poor Laws and the Law of Nature', presented at the conference, 'Reviewing Romanticism', at King Alfred's College, Winchester, in April 1989, and to the ensuing discussion.

2 My text of 'The Old Cumberland Beggar' is the first published text of 1800, as printed in the Brett and Jones edition of *Lyrical Ballads* (Wordsworth 1963).

3 For an account of the composition of the poem, which makes clear that it was originally conceived purely as a descriptive piece, see Reed (1967), 342–3.

4 The necessary limitations of my research make me heavily dependent here on the work of other scholars, in particular the books by Fraser (1973), Marshall (1985), Oxley (1974) and Poynter (1969) cited in the Bibliography.

5 Thompson points out that Hawkshead (where Wordsworth went to school) had never conformed to the 1722 Act's prescription of the workhouse test, but continued to practise outdoor relief, and lists several examples of what he terms 'avoidable expenditure' (Thompson 1970: 377). However, as de Selincourt says (Wordsworth 1940–9: IV, 446), the fact that the beggar is from Cumberland would indicate that the recollection, if genuine, is of his earlier Cockermouth childhood, since Hawkshead was in neighbouring Westmorland. Administration of the Poor Law was notoriously varied from parish to parish.

6 Smith does, however, qualify this in adding that beggars may use the proceeds of their mendicancy for purposes of exchange.
7 See Dorothy Wordsworth, *Journals* (1952: I, 123).
8 The text of this poem is from the *Poetical Works* (Wordsworth 1940–9: II, 222–4). I have not deemed it necessary to give line references for a short poem.
9 I have used the official text of Mrs Thatcher's speech provided by the Press Office at 10 Downing Street.

12

SACRED OBJECTS AND THE SUBLIME RUINS OF ART

John Whale

> I make my way into a room of sculpture where a cold confusion reigns. A dazzling bust appears between the legs of a bronze athlete. Between repose and vehemence, between silliness, smiles, constrictions, and the most precarious states of equilibrium, the total impression is something quite intolerable. I am lost in a turmoil of frozen beings, each of which demands, all in vain, the abolition of all the others – not to speak of the chaos of sizes without any common scale of measurement, the inexplicable mixture of dwarfs and giants, nor even of the foreshortening of evolution presented to us by such an assemblage of the complete and the unfinished, the mutilated and the restored, the djins and the gentlemen.
> (Valéry 1960: XII, 202)

Valéry's powerful description of the bizarre juxtapositions and disorientating alignments of the museum is underwritten by a dream of order. His uncluttered understanding of the aesthetic object is threatened by establishment coercion and bourgeois philistinism. But what he takes to be an alarming and ridiculous burlesque might easily be reclaimed by others as a positive postmodern experience, a carnivalesque site of cultural difference and variety. If Valéry exits from the museum with a vague sense of the arts under threat and a splitting head, it might be because his Romantic conception of art demands a clear space for the appreciation of each unique production. The museum can be a particularly disturbing site for an aesthetics based on the extreme individuation of the artistic object.

The suggestion of inadequacy in Valéry's registering of 'confusion' is comparable with Keats's 'dizzy pain' on viewing the Elgin marbles. Such claims of inadequacy must, of course, be read alongside the other, peculiarly powerful, side of the Romantic ideology which can replace a Grecian urn with a poetic text in an imaginary museum of its own making. Indeed, Keats's 'Ode on a Grecian Urn' is perhaps one of the best instances we have of that institutional power.

If the agonized artist in the bourgeois museum gives us an insight into the appropriating power of the Romantic it also invites us to project back from Valéry's early twentieth-century view to the early nineteenth century when the museum as we know it was still being formed.

In this chapter I shall outline two stories which take us behind certain sacred objects to their problematic excavation, collection, ownership and exhibition. The first concerns the so-called 'Elgin marbles' or the Parthenon frieze; the second the Memnon's head. They stand only yards from each other in the British Museum, their respective rooms representing two different kinds of ancient culture, the one Greek, the other Egyptian. And their magnificent setting itself provides impressive evidence of this famous institution's own historical origins. Their stories are of 'djins and gentlemen', giants and dwarfs, athletes and artists. Both tales negotiate the fraught boundaries of polite and popular culture in early nineteenth-century British society; both challenge the claim that aesthetic objects can be appreciated and enjoyed in a situation of cultural purity, whether those objects be lapidary or verbal. Well-wrought urns are here already verbal icons.

The strategy involved in this analysis owes something to recent attempts to write a new kind of history into literary criticism. Despite their disabling attention to a centralized and absolute 'power' (most typically by concentrating on kingship in Renaissance studies) the variety of critical practices now known as New Historicism has performed a valuable function by disproving the existence of an autonomous aesthetic realm. Such a stable aesthetic ground is no longer available, it is claimed, once the boundaries of literary discourse and symbolic representation have been 'mapped'. But the full possibilities of such disruptive analyses can only emerge if due attention is paid to the precariousness and instability of power as well as its pervasiveness.

To uncover the archaeological expeditions, institutional wrangles and artistic appropriations which surround sublime Romantic objects is not, of course, to offer a progressive narrative or to chart the route back to their original discovery. The analysis of objects which follows moves through a series of cultural sites which construct various kinds of oppositionality and exert their own peculiar forms of power. Even at the moment when such fragments 'fail' to speak they are made to articulate the rich and strange silences of a particularly powerful aesthetic discourse. The sublime provides its own energy to speak where speech fails and to articulate what itself it claims can only be felt.

I

The story of Lord Elgin's involvement with the marble sculptures to which he attached his name is one of enlightened intervention and cultural vandalism. If few people at the time were willing to justify the behaviour of the Turks, many remained unconvinced of the role played by the English diplomat. Add to this the tale's background of practical fiasco and financial embarrassment, and it forms the potent combination which became a disconcerting artistic focus for the national consciousness.

Thomas Bruce, seventh Earl of Elgin, was appointed ambassador to the Porte in Constantinople in 1799. He soon became interested in the condition of the ancient monuments in Turkish hands and eventually received a *firman* allowing him to make drawings and to take casts from the Parthenon. It was while working with a team of artists led by Lusieri, and after witnessing further damage by the Turks, that Elgin formed the plan to remove large sections of the Parthenon and other buildings to Britain. The whole enterprise would last until 1812 and prove extremely costly. The embarrassment was aesthetic as well as economic. To save what remained of the Parthenon frieze some pieces had to be detached forcibly from the monument. And Elgin himself, not untypically for an age not yet attuned to the idea of a scientific archaeology, actually added his own name to the ruins. Misfortune was quick to follow. One of the ships – the *Mentor* – sank off Cerigo and it took three years of hard labour by a team of divers to salvage the marbles.

Back home in Britain, the supposedly enlightened motives which produced such a botched salvage act were seriously questioned. To make matters worse, even the merits of the marbles themselves were brought into question by some notable Academicians. Meanwhile the sacred classical sculptures languished in a kind of shabby gentility at the back of Elgin's house in Park Lane. In this chaotic, acrimonious context Lord Elgin's marbles inevitably became an issue of national concern. Shouldn't they be bought for the nation? Parliament considered the matter on more than one occasion before an Act was passed in July 1816 buying the marbles for the British Museum at a public cost of £35,000. Even at this stage debate in the House showed that doubts still remained as to whether the collection really was, as claimed, an enlightened rescue from a barbarous people. Honourable members, whether from jingoism or from national guilt, were determined to distinguish this civilized British intervention from what they saw as the naked military aggression of Napoleonic France which had snatched important cultural objects by force from their rightful owners. The Act itself describes Elgin as behaving with 'great Knowledge, Judgement, and Care' and does much to write his name upon the ruins. It stipulates that the collection should be 'distinguished by the Name or Appellation of "The Elgin Collection"' and should be called 'by the name of "The Elgin Marbles"'.[1]

Benjamin Robert Haydon first saw these 'Elgin marbles' in 1808 in the 'damp, dirty pent-house' or shed in Park Lane (Haydon 1950: 77). His *Autobiography* glories in such humble and inglorious origins. His narrative revels in the confidence of retrospect to such an extent that the moment of revelation is itself obscured, or, more accurately, repeated, as entry into the lowly pent-house, first with Wilkie and then with Fuseli, promotes his own immediate recognition of greatness, and the other painters' failure of perception or subsequent recantation. For Haydon the marbles are both retrospective vindication and immediate guarantee of his own aesthetic principles, his passionate belief in the importance of history painting for a national culture, in defiance of the Academy, and his unerring conviction in the power of his own creative imagination. Struck between an outmoded civic humanism and an extreme attachment to genius, Haydon simultaneously sees an inscription of his own identity and a new dawn of national cultural consciousness in the Parthenon frieze.

> That combination of nature and idea which I had felt was so much wanting for high art was here displayed to midday conviction. My heart beat! If I had seen nothing else I had beheld sufficient to keep me to nature for the rest of my life . . . when I saw, in fact, the most heroic style of art combined with all the essential detail of actual life, the thing was done at once and for ever.

> Here were principles which the common sense of the English people would understand; here were principles which I had struggled for in my first picture with timidity and apprehension; here were the principles which the great Greeks in their finest time established, and here was I, the most prominent historical student, perfectly qualified to appreciate all this by my own determined mode of study. . . .
>
> Oh!, how I inwardly thanked God that I was prepared to understand all this! . . . Now was I mad for buying Albinus without a penny to pay for it? Now was I mad for lying on the floor hours together, copying its figures? I felt the future, I foretold that they would prove themselves the finest things on earth, that they would overturn the false beau-ideal, where nature alone was nothing, and would establish the true beau-ideal, of which nature alone is the basis.
>
> I shall never forget the horses' heads – the feet in the metopes! I felt as if a divine truth had blazed inwardly upon my mind and I knew that they would at last rouse the art of Europe from its slumber in the darkness.
>
> I do not say this *now*, when all the world acknowledges it, but I said it then, *when no one would believe me*. I went home in perfect excitement.
>
> (Haydon 1950: 77–8)

By 1822 Hazlitt could use the Elgin marbles to wage a fierce onslaught on the whole idea of Reynolds's *Discourses*, which he disparagingly refers to as 'the fashionable and fastidious theory of the ideal' (Hazlitt 1930–4: XVIII, 147). According to Hazlitt's principles 'art is (first and last) the imitation of nature' (ibid.: XVIII, 147) and, significantly, as a result 'The historical is nature in action. With regard to the face, it is expression' (ibid.: XVIII, 150). With his mimeticism and empiricism Hazlitt articulates a new individualism: subjective response now feels confident enough to speak publicly.[2] It is an aesthetic 'privatization' which makes the agonized split between egotistical assertion and civic humanism in Haydon's *Autobiography* and *Journal* look all the more anachronistic and desperate. Despite these differences, Hazlitt's viewing of the marbles also produces the effect of a self-evident revelation of truth comparable with Haydon's: 'The communication of art with nature is here everywhere immediate, entire, palpable' (ibid.: XVIII, 145).

Whereas Haydon's self-justifying revelation – appropriately sanctioned by God and history – sees the light of a new dawn of European civilization issuing from British common sense, Byron's *The Curse of Minerva* provides us with a very different crepuscular vision of the Elgin marbles. The light figured forth in his poem produces some disconcerting refractions for Romantic creativity's encounter with cultural difference. Byron's satirical intelligence provides a pretty severe contextualization for this most famous set of Romantic objects.[3]

The poem opens in the brief but brilliant light of an Athenian sunset, a phenomenon which measures the difference between the north and south of Europe. The delicious reverie of the amorous poet is then turned sour by a woman's rage. Faced with Minerva's curse the poet is seen squirming with a lover's guilt. His embarrassed defence peculiarly combines the critical exile and the ferocious patriot. National identity is suddenly more particular and brittle than one might have thought. In typical Byronic fashion masculinity takes pride of place:

> A true-born Briton may the deed disclaim.
> Frown not on England; England owns him not:
> Athena! no; thy plunderer was a Scot.
>
> (Byron 1986: I, 324, lines 126–8)

In keeping with the pervasive north/south divide Elgin is compared to Alaric the Goth, but the prevailing sexual paradigm means that he must be mocked. With characteristic social hauteur Byron presents Elgin's housing of the marbles as a vulgar 'shop of stone' in which the connoisseur's masculinity is read pejoratively against the figures on the frieze. Through them he becomes the laughing-stock of the women of England.

> While many a languid maid, with longing sigh,
> On giant statues casts the curious eye:
> The room with transient glance appears to skim,
> Yet marks the mighty back and length of limb;
> Mourns o'er the difference of *now* and *then*,
> Exclaims, 'These Greeks indeed were proper men!'
>
> (ibid.: I, 326, lines 185–90)

Once Elgin's diminished manhood is seen as a prophecy already fulfilled, Minerva's curse opens out to accommodate the entire British Empire. At home there will be economic collapse; abroad bloody revolt in India. Typically, Byron invests the objects with his kind of sexual politics; Elgin is seen as a 'dull spoiler' whose interaction with the aesthetic object is equivalent to an act of cold sex. According to Byron's line of thinking the connoisseur/lover should have projected an intense warmth into the dry dust of the past, reanimating it with passion.

Because Haydon and Hazlitt see 'nature' manifest in the marbles they can make claims for a totally enabling revelation of truth. Byron too, though viewing events in a negative way, simply assumes the artistic status of the stones. They are unproblematically at one with his aesthetic values. His poetic text moves explicitly from romantic description to bitter reality as reverie gives way to execration, and the dull, diminished, Dunciad world of the north takes over from the warm south. But such obvious oppositions are premised on a collapsing of a larger sense of historical difference.

Elgin's more concrete inscription on the marbles is perhaps only the most explicit manifestation of a proprietorial relationship, and perhaps the least developed artistically of the responses we have seen. He can lay claim to the status of neither artistic theorist nor practitioner like Haydon, Hazlitt and Byron, but as collector his graffito'd signature might be read as much as poet/artist manqué as proprietor. The ambivalence of his act of artistic stewardship sounds the paradigmatic problem of certain kinds of Romantic creativity and their relationship to egotistical assertion and incipient colonialism in the construction of art. Dilettante engagement is matched by artistic inability, and might stand as a figure for the agonized Romantic poet, especially one self-conscious of a particularly problematic binary opposition of success and failure at the heart of Romanticism.

The four sonnets Keats addressed to Haydon significantly combine heroic aspiration and abject failure. Keats considers the Elgin marbles through the intense medium of Haydon's high ambition – one sign among many of the poet's exploration of the idea of fame. Yet what makes the poems so interesting is the prominence given in them to failure. This is something more than the young poet in awe of genius; failure for Keats is clearly a source of creativity – a productive mode of expression. Given Haydon's own monumental investment in the marbles, writing a definitive poem about them (and that a sonnet) would never be easy. As an admission of failure, some would say, Keats had to write two poems, the second – 'To Haydon, with a Sonnet Written on Seeing the Elgin Marbles' – by way of apology. But in imploring 'Forgive me, Haydon, that I cannot speak / Definitively on these mighty things' (Keats 1978: 93, lines 1–2) it could be argued that Keats affords them the greatest power. The very indirection and the evasion performed in these two sonnets is their characteristic representation of 'power'.

In one sense, 'On Seeing the Elgin Marbles' collapses into a succession of dashes: a desperate and failed attempt to find some suitable objective correlative for the objects in question.

My spirit is too weak – mortality
  Weighs heavily on me like unwilling sleep,
  And each imagined pinnacle and steep
Of godlike hardship tells me I must die
Like a sick eagle looking at the sky.
  Yet 'tis a gentle luxury to weep
  That I have not the cloudy winds to keep
Fresh for the opening of the morning's eye.
Such dim-conceived glories of the brain
  Bring round the heart an undescribable feud;
So do these wonders a most dizzy pain,
  That mingles Grecian grandeur with the rude
Wasting of old time – with a billowy main –
  A sun – a shadow of a magnitude.

(Keats 1978: 93)

A straight biographical reading could confirm this as a poetic expression of weakness. But if one considers such failure against its counter-image of heroic enterprise other possibilities emerge. 'On First Looking into Chapman's Homer' (Keats 1978: 64) provides a convenient example of a poem which explores this same subject of the prospect of fame and makes explicit in the other direction the correlation between Romantic poetic creativity and heroic imperialism. The outfacing conquistador – 'stout Cortez' with 'eagle eyes' – is differentiated from the common herd. Similarly, in the two other, earlier poems addressed to Haydon, 'Great spirits' and 'stout unbending champion[s]' awe the 'unnumbered souls' and strike dumb the listening nations. Cortez is another 'great spirit' imbued with all the stature of the Romantic hero – all the 'singleness of aim' and 'steadfastness' which Keats associates with Haydon's isolated and monomaniacal genius. This is the flight of the condor rather than the sick eagle. But what still puzzles commentators, after this human differentiation, is the object of attention. The Pacific, like the marbles, defies definition: it literally gets lost somewhere between the Romantic hero and the attendant crowd. Cortez's gaze remains peculiarly impenetrable to critical knowledge.

> Or like stout Cortez when with eagle eyes
> He star'd at the Pacific – and all his men
> Look'd at each other with wild surmise –
> Silent, upon a peak in Darien.
>
> (Keats 1978: 64, lines 11–14)

Though these poems suggest a peculiarly powerful originary moment based on the first sighting of an object, in both cases we are left with a powerful blindness. The Romantic sublime can always stand in for a failure of vision. Indeed, its very basis in optical theory and empirical philosophy makes it a means of writing power as failure and vice versa.

It should be noted of course that in these poems Keats does not pose power against the complete absence of power: the poet's 'failure' is as a 'sick *eagle*'. Characteristically, the poems explore reciprocal power relations. The tyranny of sight gives rise to an awed silence and the silence being contemplated is anything but tranquil – it is a forced denial of speech rather than a relaxation. In many of Keats's poems silence signals a moment of terrifying arrest – as in the transfixed metamorphoses of *Lamia*, which are the after-effects of a most tyrannical gaze, whether it be that of the poet, the lover or the philosopher. Keats's construction in the poem to Haydon – 'I cannot speak / Definitively on these mighty things' (Keats 1978: 93) – also makes available the possibility of the intractable and invasive nature of things as things, as against the provisional nature of speech and discourse.

In this attention to failure and silence Keats's poems register a kind of difference unavailable in Haydon, Hazlitt and Byron. But it is a difference still subject to the reversibility of its underlying Romantic paradigm: power/failure. Only in the construction of the idea of Keats's bourgeois belatedness might one find a more enabling difference. By invoking the figure of the vulgar interloper at the high table of art it is possible to see Keats's poetic elaborateness as transgressive. According to this scenario failed imitation can become subversive parody, overblown sensuousness enabling masturbation. Bloom's idea of 'belatedness' opens up a creative distance between past and present. Keats can then become an 'entrepreneur' of literary objects rather than an agonized poet caught in the flow of intertextuality. Keats's relationship to the displayed poems of the past can look as proprietorial and irreverent as Elgin's.[4]

'Ode on a Grecian Urn' extends the idea of the intractability of objects and the provisionality of discourse, complicating the issue by merging text and object, sound and silence. The past can speak, but only tangentially. The urn as art is never simply the past, but a finished product of it. For all its teasing exploration of the paradoxes of death and passion, art and life, the ode itself becomes a finished product, and approaches as far as such a text can (especially when aided by all the force of a New Criticism) the isolated status and inscrutability of an object. As with the evasions and indirections of Keats's failure to respond adequately to the Elgin marbles in the face of Haydon's genius, the poem dislocates itself from the realism of human response. While we are keenly aware that objects as objects cannot speak in the usual sense, we are forced to admit that the language of passion can, quite disconcertingly, be made into an object. As Marjorie Levinson puts it,

> The framing devices of Keats's poetry do not, like Wordsworth's preemptive techniques, usher us into the poem, they frame us out. Think of the 'Ode on a Grecian Urn'. The final bracketed epigram – formally, a parody of Wordsworth's closing, intersubjective immediacies – puts the entire poem and all its apparently human and authorial anguish in aesthetic space: museum space, to be precise.
>
> (Levinson 1988: 20)

II

A granite statue of Rameses II dominates the Egyptian exhibits in the British Museum. Only the head and shoulders now remain of the colossal figure which once adorned the temple at Abu Simbel, and there is a conspicuous hole drilled through its right breast. On its plinth a modest plaque records in the curt graffito of modern scientific labelling the names of Salt and Burckhardt. Such presentation conceals a troubled history, a Romantic narrative and a crisis of identity. More poetically the head might have been named 'Ozymandias' or the 'Young Memnon'. And the name omitted from those who discovered it suggests a concern to be scientifically factual rather than poetically fabulous as well as the continuing power of academic, scientific and cultural respectability. For the man whose name was most associated with this object in the early nineteenth century and whose engineering skill did much to remove it from the banks of the Nile in 1816 was Giovanni Battista Belzoni – the 'Great Belzoni'.

Belzoni's story may be said to begin twice; and each time it is generated by Napoleonic forces. His entrepreneurial wanderlust began with the unsettling French 'liberation' of his native Padua, and his discovery of the possibility of fame as an Egyptologist could only have taken place after Bonaparte's invasion in 1797. Belzoni's story switches dramatically from popular to polite culture, from freak show to gentleman traveller, from Sadlers Wells to the British Museum, from geek to artist manqué. But unlike John Keats, that vulgar Cockney, Belzoni failed to make it into the polite halls of fame. Such fame as he had was popular and therefore, almost inevitably, temporary. His name lived on not in the history books or in the academies, but in the Victorian music hall.[5]

For all his pretensions to respectable knowledge in the field of engineering and hydraulics it was Belzoni's physique – his statuesque figure – which provided him with employment as a young man in Britain in 1802. At six foot seven, with a powerful frame, he entertained audiences at Sadlers Wells in *Jack the Giant Killer* and thrilled them with his strong-man act as 'The Human Pyramid'. And he performed conjuring feats and fantastical hydraulic events across a range of audiences, all the way from the stalls of Bartholomew Fair to the thrones of the Spanish Court.

His journey to Egypt in 1814 was based on a mixture of these skills – ostensibly to introduce a more effective water-pump into the Nile valley, possibly to entertain at the Seraglio. The more utilitarian aim failed, but the acrobat, conjurer and muscle-man stayed on in Egypt, and, at the instigation of Henry Salt, diplomat and gentleman collector of antiquities, set out up the Nile to collect amongst the spectacular ruins.

The difficult feat of removing the Memnon's head and floating it down the Nile to Alexandria was only one of Belzoni's accomplishments in this field. He also made extensive exploration of the ruins at Abu Simbel and Karnac, entered the tomb of Seti I, and was the first explorer to penetrate the second pyramid at Giza. But his achievements are only grudgingly acknowledged by archaeological history. He is put down as a blundering giant stumbling and bulldozing his way through the fragile relics of antiquity. He is generally considered to be something of a vandal: trampling on the mummies of Gournou and Qurna to rob them of their papyri; and desecrating the statue of Amenhetep III with his autograph.

On his return to England Belzoni maintained his spirit of enterprise and combined it with his sense of theatre. He set off his collected antiquities to best advantage by fabricating what he called 'The Egyptian Tomb'. Middle-class Londoners of Regency England were thus treated to a museum 'experience' reminiscent of the 1980s. Belzoni's exhibition was housed in the Egyptian Hall in Piccadilly – a bizarre site at the boundaries of middle-class culture: the crossroads of the shabby-genteel. Once Belzoni's theatrical display had run its course he sold off the contents to gentlemen amateurs. His next adventure was his last: he died in 1823 of dysentery on the west coast of Africa attempting to get through to Timbuktu.

Belzoni's *Narrative of the Operations and Recent Discoveries within the Pyramids, Temples, Tombs, and Excavations in Egypt and Nubia*, published in 1820 by John Murray, was dismissed and patronized by contemporaries as a naive text written in a crude and broken English. Masquerading as a record of unspectacular factual detail it performs a fraught self-justification which splits the text into three distinct zones of cultural difference: the peoples of the Nile valley; European collectors; and the ancient Egyptians. The last are represented almost entirely by their objects. The Europeans are untrustworthy and perfidious – the serpents in an ancient paradise. The contemporary Egyptians evoke the most contradictory response, ranging from fine ethnic delineation to the crudest undifferentiation. But it is when the three planes intersect that the narrative exposes most successfully the relationship between cultural object and cultural difference. In the flux of Belzoni's text the ancient Egyptians can also be primitives; the Europeans barbarous; and the peoples of the desert at once untrustworthy and innocent. Yet however much the text is riven and driven by conflict with these different cultural groups – its contradictory construction and collapsing of difference – the ultimate power of Belzoni's book derives from contact with objects otherwise cleared of human contact. At times his isolation with them approaches a museum aesthetic in its assumption of the object's 'purification' from its culture.

On just a few occasions Belzoni's *Narrative* breaks with its expediency and beleaguered self-justification to reveal this peculiar concentration on the object. In his description of the 'discovery' of the tomb of Seti I the multitude of beautiful objects produces a familiar Romantic combination of isolation and self-assertion:

> The sun was rising, and the long shades from the various groups of columns extended over these ruins, intermixed with the rays of light striking on these masses in various directions, formed such delightful views all round as baffle description. . . . I was lost in contemplation of so many objects; and being alone in such a place, my mind was impressed with ideas of such solemnity, that for some time I was unconscious whether I were on terrestrial ground, or on some other planet. . . .
>
> How can I describe my sensations at that moment! I seemed alone in the midst of all that is most sacred in the world; a forest of enormous columns, adorned all round with beautiful figures, and various ornaments, from the top to the bottom, the graceful shape of the lotus, which forms their capitals, and is so well proportioned to the columns, that it gives to the view the most pleasing effect; the gates, the walls, the pedestals and the architraves also adorned in every part with symbolical figures in basso relievo and intaglio, representing battles, processions, triumphs, feasts, offerings, and sacrifices, all relating no doubt to the ancient history of the country; the sanctuary, wholly formed of fine red granite, with the various obelisks standing before it, proclaiming to the distant passenger, 'Here is the seat of holiness'; the high portals, seen at a distance from the openings of this vast labyrinth of edifices; the various groups of ruins of the other temples within sight; these altogether had such an effect upon my soul, as to separate me in imagination from the rest of mortals, exalt me on high over all, and cause me to forget entirely the trifles and follies of life. I was happy for a whole day, which escaped like a flash of lightning; but the obscurity of the night caused me to stumble over one large block of stone, and to break my nose against another, which, dissolving the enchantment, brought me back to my senses again.
>
> (Belzoni 1820: 152–3)

As the technical architectural details give way to an act of reciprocation between explorer and object, it becomes apparent that the aesthetic pleasure produced rests on an assumption of sacredness.

For all the claim of reciprocation the speaking objects possess a voice which is based on silence, erasure and ignorance. This moment of 'holiness' is the product of cultural ignorance. Finally, with less ceremony than a Romantic poet, Belzoni returns to the world of sense perception with a bump, restored to the practical belief that even aesthetic objects are objects. Fortunately, Belzoni's 'spot of time' only approaches epiphany.

If his entrance into the tomb of Seti I provides a painful illustration of the egotistical sublime and represents a particularly intense contact with the aesthetic object, then his desecration of the tombs at Qurna provides us with something closer to Gothic sensationalism. By comparison with the reverie on sculpture, sleeping with mummies provides a strikingly different appreciation of the relationship between aesthetic objects and human contact.

> But what a place of rest! surrounded by bodies, by heaps of mummies in all directions; which, previous to my being accustomed to the sight, impressed me with horror. The blackness of the wall, the faint light given by the candles or torches for want of air, the different objects that surrounded me, seeming to converse with each other, and the Arabs with the candles or torches in their hands, naked and covered with dust, themselves resembling living mummies, absolutely formed a scene that cannot be described. In such a situation I found myself several times, and often returned exhausted and fainting, till at last I became inured to it, and indifferent to what I suffered, except from the dust, which never failed to choke my throat and nose; and though fortunately, I am destitute of the sense of smelling, I could taste that the mummies were rather unpleasant to swallow. . . . I could not pass without putting my face in contact with that of some decayed Egyptian; but as the passage inclined downwards, my own weight helped me on; however, I could not avoid being covered with bones, legs, arms, and heads rolling from above. Thus I proceeded from one cave to another, all full of mummies piled up in various ways, some standing, some lying, and some on their heads. The purpose of my researches was to rob the Egyptians of their papyri.
>
> (ibid.: 156–7)

Belzoni's two 'poetic' moments of epiphany and Gothic horror provide counter-images of aesthetic exploration. Where human contact is made it results in disgust rather than reverie, decay of the body rather than the radiant eternity of art. The combination is not uncommon: consecrated urns are often filled with the remains of their makers. For all its populist appeal it is tempting to read Belzoni among the mummies as a precise account of artistic appropriation. Convenient for the intensification of horror, the collapsing of historical difference turns contemporary Arabs into ancient Egyptians, and through custom the explorer becomes inured to the very contact which, it is presumed, the western audience will find disgusting. There is no dream of difference here, only the nightmare of an invasion of the body. There is no dream of order either. The scene has all the chaotic ridiculousness of Valéry's scathing description of the museum experience. Both Valéry's and Belzoni's accounts have no difficulty in joining cultural superiority with a rather literal form of disorientation.

This oscillation between the religious idealization of art and a Gothic disgust at the otherness of the human body – between a natural supernaturalism and a Romantic racism – can also be found in the work of De Quincey where the oscillation ranges spectacularly from the infinity of the heavens to Nilotic mud. Brooding upon the infinity of time and space in 'System of the Heavens, As Revealed By Lord Rosse's Telescope', De Quincey travels back in time with all the authority of scholarly digression to consider 'that object which some four-and-thirty years ago in the British Museum struck me as simply the sublimest sight which in this sight-seeing world I have seen. It was the Memnon's head, then recently brought from Egypt' (De Quincey 1889–90: VIII, 17). This object goes – as is already evident from De Quincey's awestruck verbosity – beyond the limits of language. Its silence is accredited with the highest form of articulacy: spiritual truth.

> I looked at it, as the reader must suppose in order to understand the depth which I have here ascribed to the impression, not as a human, but as a symbolic head; and what it symbolised to me were: – 1. The peace which passeth all understanding. 2. The eternity which baffles and confounds all faculty of computation; the eternity which *had* been, the eternity which *was* to be. 3. The diffusive love, not such as rises and falls upon waves of life and mortality, not such as sinks and swells by undulations of time, but a procession – an emanation from some mystery of endless dawn. You durst not

> call it a smile that radiated from the lips; the radiation was too awful to clothe itself in adumbrations or memorials of flesh.
> (ibid.: VIII, 17)

Typically, the idea of symbol overrides the human. De Quincey's text conjures death in life and life in death to hail the superhuman. Such a heavenly moment of arrest, of timelessness, is countered by the famous image in the nebula of Orion, a hieroglyph from which 'the mind of man shudders and recoils' (ibid.: VIII, 18), which derives from 'another silence, from the frost and from the eternities of death'. Recalling 'Milton's "incestuous mother"' the image which formed in Herschel's mirror mixes 'the angelic and the brutal' (ibid.: VIII, 18), incest and miscegenation. Unspeakable horror has replaced the divine tranquillity of silence. Such an image speaks not of heaven, but of the abyss.

The Memnon's status here as supreme sublime object finds another counter-image in the Orientalist nightmare in *Confessions of an English Opium-Eater* where, once again, origins turn to incest and the attempt to negotiate cultural difference is absorbed into a terrifying guilt narrative:

> I was stared at, hooted at, grinned at, chattered at, by monkeys, by paroquets, by cockatoos. I ran into pagodas: and was fixed, for centuries, at the summit, or in secret rooms; I was the idol; I was the priest; I was worshipped; I was sacrificed. I fled from the wrath of Brama through all the forests of Asia: Vishnu hated me: Seeva laid wait for me. I came suddenly upon Isis and Osiris: I had done a deed, they said, which the ibis and the crocodile trembled at. I was buried, for a thousand years, in stone coffins, with mummies and sphynxes, in narrow chambers at the heart of eternal pyramids. I was kissed, with cancerous kisses, by crocodiles; and laid, confounded with all unutterable slimy things, amongst reeds and Nilotic mud.
> (De Quincey 1985: 73)

Fascinated by the Orient as a sign of tyranny, De Quincey's emotive supernaturalism can see the Memnon's head as sacred object, and at the same time fantasize his own subjection: trapped, sacrificed and tainted on the wrong side of cultural difference.

In contrast, Shelley's 'Ozymandias' seems to present us with the possibility of a rationalist Enlightenment superiority to the dangers of such an enthralling and enthralled Romanticism. But only the possibility. From its second-hand encounter with a traveller the persona, along with the reader, is assumed to be able to measure the political distance between sublime object and the ruins of empire. Fragmentation is made to illuminate a moral lesson. But the end of Shelley's poem suggests an enigmatic recuperation of the sublime by placing an inexplicable scene after the political truth – 'The lone and level sands stretch far away' (Shelley 1970: 550, line 1). Indeed Shelley's poem highlights the difficulty in an Enlightenment rational sublime maintaining a safe distance from the terrible objects of power. The Enlightenment use of an Orientalist 'other' against European tyranny is already implicated in, and can actually provide the opiate for, some of the most material dreams of power.

Napoleon's Egyptian expedition set sail in 1797 with *l'Orient* as its aptly named flagship. As military commander and director of the Institut d'Egypt, Napoleon found no difficulty in combining aggressive colonialism with Enlightenment cultural 'improvement'.[6] Volney's *Travels through Syria and Egypt* and *Considerations on the Present War with the Turks* may have been preparations for the seditious *The Ruins . . . of Empires*. As far as Napoleon was concerned, they could provide the necessary strategic information for his crushing victory over the Mamelukes and set the intellectual scene for the large-scale contemplation of Egypt as a gateway to India.

After dwelling on the stronger cultural attractions of the Orient over those of the Americas as they determined his choice of journey, Volney's preface to *Travels through Syria and Egypt* suddenly switches to more practical concerns:

> On the other hand, considering the political circumstances of the Turkish empire, for the last twenty years, and reflecting on their possible consequences, it appeared to me equally curious and useful to acquire correct notions of its internal government, in order to form a just estimate of its real power and resources.
>
> (Volney 1787: I, iii)

Similarly, *Considerations on the Present War with the Turks*, for all its profession of the dangers of French involvement, contains the following hostage to libertarian fortune: 'The inhabitants of Turkey are on many accounts, fitter subjects for legislation than those of Europe' (Volney 1788: 83). In such ways Volney's texts become complicit with the enterprise which famously combined the intellectual and the militaristic: producing short-term military aggression and the long-term, monumental *Description de l'Egypte* (1809–28) – altogether, perhaps, the most important founding event in the history of Orientalism.

III

'It is in the Orient that we must search for the highest Romanticism.' Edward Said's *Orientalism* could be seen as ironically reversing the words of Friedrich Schlegel which it cites (Said 1978: 98). His study characteristically focuses on the exteriority of its chosen cultural construction: 'It is clear, I hope, that my concern with authority does not entail analysis of what lies hidden in the Orientalist text, but analysis rather of the text's surface, its exteriority to what it describes' (ibid.: 20). Among its wealth of concerns the book charts a collusion of Romantic supernaturalism and the scientific descendants of an Enlightenment rationalism. With a dream of taxonomy Orientalism found a powerful base in the new science of philology and an influential individual in the figure of Ernest Renan, with his belief in the '*exact science* of mental objects' (ibid.: 132). Said's diagnosis of the power problem in conjuring meaning from the relationship between words and objects might stand as a particularly impressive warning of the dangers of a Romantic investment in sacred objects. But at the same time it fails to resolve a distinction between cultural constructivism and political empiricism:

> The special value of linguistics (as the new philology was then often called) is not that natural science resembles it, but rather that it treats words as natural, otherwise silent objects, which are made to give up their secrets. Remember that the major breakthrough in the study of inscriptions and hieroglyphs was the discovery by Champollion that the symbols on the Rosetta stone had a *phonetic* as well as a semantic component. To make objects speak was like making words speak, giving them circumstantial value, and a precise place in a rule-governed order of regularity.
>
> (ibid.: 140)

Said's polemic provides a strategic counter to Enlightenment, Orientalist and structuralist dreams of an absolute order, but its capacity to deal with the subject/object dialectic of Romanticism would seem more questionable. Despite its initial claim to place the emphasis, in its analysis of the Orientalist text, on 'the evidence . . . for such representations *as representations*' (ibid.: 21), Said's book is fraught with a concealed empiricism and a problematic relegation of 'representation' to secondary status. The political necessity of dealing only with exteriority – 'the text's surface' – has the effect of undercutting the dynamic nature of representation. The critique of Renan is a reversal: it turns discourse back into an object. The various representations we have witnessed are subject not to a monolithic and synchronic authority, but to a binary play which is just as coercive and dangerous, especially when it enacts the fiction of its own collapse. The appropriating power of the Romantic ideology takes place side by side with claims of its own incapacity: sublime abstraction continuous with bodily disgust; critiques of power alongside worship of power. The relationship between these strategies of Romanticism and their objects has also to be measured against their contexts – what Said refers to above as their 'circumstantial value'. Failures in their own right, Haydon and Belzoni can appear tragic and ridiculous, at once challenging and confirming, at their different levels of cultural practice, the surety of the Romantic pantheon. Of course, their failures can easily be absorbed by a sublime aesthetic, but exhibiting them within the imaginary museum of Romanticism might at least make revisiting that institution – following Keats and Valéry – a more constructively vertiginous experience.

NOTES

1 See Acts of Parliament 1816: 56 Geo. III, c.99, 470–1.
2 See Barrell 1986: 308–43.
3 See Larrabee 1943: 151–8.
4 See Aske 1985 and Levinson 1986.
5 See Mayes 1959.
6 See Thompson 1952: 107–33.

BIBLIOGRAPHY

Abrams, M.H. (1986) 'Construing and deconstructing', in M. Eaves and M. Fischer (eds) *Romanticism and Contemporary Criticism*, Ithaca and London: Cornell University Press, 127–83.

Aeschylus (1952) *Suppliant Maidens. Persians. Prometheus. Seven Against Thebes*, trans. H. Weir Smyth, Loeb Classical Library, Cambridge, Mass.: Harvard University Press.

Alexander, William (1779) *The History of Women, from the earliest antiquity, to the present time; giving some account of almost every interesting particular concerning that sex, among all nations, ancient and modern*, 2 vols, London: Strahan & Cadell.

Anderson, Perry (1976) *Considerations on Western Marxism*, London: New Left Books.

Anti-Jacobin Review (1801) 'The vision of liberty', 9: 515–20.

Arac, J. (1987) *Critical Genealogies: Historical Situations for Postmodern Literary Studies*, New York: Columbia University Press.

Aske, M. (1985) *Keats and Hellenism: An Essay*, Cambridge: Cambridge University Press.

Austen, Jane (1971) *Northanger Abbey*, ed. with intro. John Davie, notes and biblio. James Kinsley, London: Oxford University Press.

Austin, Rev. Gilbert (1806) *Chironomia: or a Treatise on Rhetorical Delivery*, London.

Bakhtin, M.M. (1981) *The Dialogic Imagination: Four Essays*, ed. Michael Holquist, trans. Caryl Emerson and Michael Holquist, Austin, Texas: University of Texas Press.

Barker, Francis *et al.* (eds) (1982) *1789: Reading Writing Revolution: Proceedings of the Essex Conference on the Sociology of Literature: July 1981*, Colchester: University of Essex.

Barrell, John (1986) *The Political Theory of Painting from Reynolds to Hazlitt: 'The Body of the Public'*, New Haven and London: Yale University Press.

——(1988) *Poetry, Language and Politics*, Manchester: Manchester University Press.

Barthes, R. (1968) 'The death of the author', in David Lodge (ed.) (1988) *Modern Criticism and Theory: A Reader*, London and New York: Longman, 166–72.

Beattie, James (1783) 'On fable and romance', in *Dissertations Moral and Critical*, London: Strahan.

Belsey, C. (1982) 'The Romantic construction of the unconscious', in Francis Barker *et al.* (eds) *1789: Reading Writing Revolution: Proceedings of the Essex Conference on the Sociology of Literature: July 1981*, Colchester: University of Essex, 67–80.

Belsey, C. and Moore, J. (eds) (1989) *The Feminist Reader: Essays in Gender and the Politics of Literary Criticism*, London: Macmillan Education.

Belzoni, G. (1820) *Narrative of the Operations and Recent Discoveries within the Pyramids, Temples, Tombs, and Excavations in Egypt and Nubia, and of a Journey to the Coast of the Red Sea, in Search of the Ancient Berenice and another to the Oasis of Jupiter Ammon*, London: John Murray.

Bennett, Tony (1979) *Formalism and Marxism*, London: Methuen.

Bewell, Alan J. (1986) 'The political implications of Keats's classicist aesthetics', *Studies in Romanticism* 25: 220–31.

Blackstone, William (1767–9) *Commentaries on the Laws of England*, 3 vols, Oxford: Clarendon Press.

Blake, William (1971) *The Complete Poems*, ed. W.H. Stevenson, London: Longman.

——(1980) *The Letters of William Blake, with Related Documents*, ed. Geoffrey Keynes, Oxford: Clarendon.

——(1982) *The Complete Poetry and Prose of William Blake*, ed. David V. Erdman, New York: Anchor.

Bloom, H. (1959) *Shelley's Mythmaking*, New Haven: Yale University Press.

——(1971) *The Ringers in the Tower: Studies in Romantic Tradition*, Chicago: University of Chicago Press.

Boswell, James (1934–50) *Life of Johnson*, ed. George Birkbeck Hill, rev. and enl. L.F. Powell, 6 vols, Oxford: Clarendon Press.

Bové, P. (1986) *Intellectuals in Power: A Genealogy of Critical Humanism*, New York: Columbia University Press.

Bowie, M. (1988) *Freud, Proust and Lacan: Theory as Fiction*, Cambridge: Cambridge University Press.

Brewster, Sir David (1832) *Letters on Natural Magic, Addressed to Sir Walter Scott*, London.

Brooks, C. (1973) 'Coleridge as metaphysical poet', in D. Thoburn and G. Hartman (eds) *Romanticism: Vistas, Instances, Continuities*, Ithaca and London: Cornell University Press, 134–54.

Brown, John (1757) *An Estimate of the Manners and Principles of the Times*, London: Davis.

Bucco, M. (1981) *Rene Wellek*, Boston: Twayne Publishers.

Bürger, P. (1984) *Theory of the Avant-Garde*, trans. M. Shaw, foreword by J. Schulte-Sasse, Manchester: Manchester University Press.

Burke, Edmund (1958) *A Philosophical Enquiry into the Origin of our Ideas of the Sublime and the Beautiful*, ed. J.T. Boulton, London: Routledge & Kegan Paul.

——(1989) *Reflections on the Revolution in France*, in *The Writings and Speeches of Edmund Burke*, VIII, *The French Revolution 1790–1794*, ed. L.G. Mitchell, Oxford: Clarendon Press.

Butler, Marilyn (1979) *Peacock Displayed: A Satirist in His Context*, London: Routledge & Kegan Paul.
——(1981) *Romantics, Rebels and Reactionaries: English Literature and its Background, 1760–1830*, Oxford: Oxford University Press.
——(1982) 'Myth and myth-making in the Shelley circle', *English Literary History* 49: 50–72.
——(1985a) 'Nymphs and nympholepsy: the visionary woman and the Romantic poet', in R. Breuer, W. Huber and R. Schöwerling (eds) *English Romanticism: the Paderborn Symposium*, Essen: Verlag die Blaue Eule, 11–31.
——(1985b) 'Druids, bards and twice-born Bacchus: Peacock's engagement with primitive mythology', *Keats–Shelley Memorial Bulletin* 36, 57–76.
——(1988) 'Romanticism in England', *Romanticism in National Context*, ed. Roy Porter and Mikuláš Teich, Cambridge: Cambridge University Press, 37–67.
——(1989) 'Romantic Manichaeism: Shelley's "On the devil and devils" and Byron's mythological dramas', in J.B. Bullen (ed.) *The Sun is God: Painting, Literature and Mythology in the Nineteenth Century*, Oxford: Clarendon Press, 13–37.
Buxton, J. (1978) *The Grecian Taste: Literature in the Age of Neo-Classicism, 1740–1820*, London: Macmillan.
Bygrave, S. (1986) *Coleridge and the Self: Romantic Egoism*, Basingstoke: Macmillan.
Byron, Lord (1986) *The Complete Poetical Works*, ed. Jerome J. McGann, 5 vols, Oxford: Clarendon Press.
Cameron, K.N. and Reiman, D.H. (eds) (1961–86) *Shelley and his Circle, 1773–1822*, 8 vols to date, I–IV ed. Cameron, V–VIII ed. Reiman, Cambridge, Mass.: Harvard University Press.
Chandler, James K. (1984) *Wordsworth's Second Nature: A Study of the Poetry and Politics*, Chicago and London: University of Chicago Press.
Clairmont, Claire (1968) *The Journals of Claire Clairmont*, ed. Marion Kingston Stocking, Cambridge, Mass.: Harvard University Press.
Clare, John (1984) 'If the necessitys of the poor' (fragment), in *John Clare*, ed. Eric Robinson and David Powell, The Oxford Authors, Oxford and New York: Oxford University Press, 447.
Coleridge, H. (1822) 'On the poetical use of the heathen mythology', *The London Magazine* 5 (February 1822): 113–20.
Coleridge, S.T. (1912) *Complete Poetical Works of S.T. Coleridge*, ed. E.H. Coleridge, 2 vols, Oxford: Clarendon Press.
——(1936) *Coleridge's Miscellaneous Criticism*, ed. T.M. Raysor, Cambridge, Mass.: Harvard University Press.
——(1951) *Inquiring Spirit: A New Presentation of Coleridge from his Published and Unpublished Prose Writings*, ed. Kathleen Coburn, New York: Pantheon Books.
——(1956–71) *Collected Letters of Samuel Taylor Coleridge*, ed. E.L. Griggs, 6 vols, Oxford: Clarendon Press.
——(1957–73) *Notebooks*, ed. Kathleen Coburn, 3 vols, London: Routledge & Kegan Paul.
——(1960) *Coleridge's Shakespeare Criticism*, ed. T.M. Raysor, London: Dent.

——(1969) *The Friend*, ed. Barbara Rooke, 2 vols, *The Collected Works of S.T. Coleridge*, IV, London: Routledge & Kegan Paul; Princeton, N.J.: Princeton University Press.

——(1972) *Lay Sermons*, ed. R.J. White, *The Collected Works of S.T. Coleridge*, IV, London: Routledge & Kegan Paul; Princeton, N.J.: Princeton University Press.

——(1976) *On the Constitution of the Church and State*, ed. John Colmer, *The Collected Works of S.T. Coleridge*, X, London: Routledge & Kegan Paul; Princeton, N.J.: Princeton University Press.

——(1978) *Essays on His Times*, ed. David V. Erdman, 3 vols, *The Collected Works of S.T. Coleridge*, III, London: Routledge & Kegan Paul; Princeton, N.J.: Princeton University Press.

——(1983) *Biographia Literaria*, ed. James Engell and Walter Jackson Bate, 2 vols, *The Collected Works of S.T. Coleridge*, VII, London: Routledge & Kegan Paul; Princeton, N.J.: Princeton University Press.

——(1984) *Marginalia*, ed. George Whalley, 2 vols, *The Collected Works of S.T. Coleridge*, IV, London: Routledge & Kegan Paul; Princeton, N.J.: Princeton University Press.

Colley, Linda (1986) 'Whose nation? Class and national consciousness in Britain 1750–1830', *Past and Present* 113: 97–117.

Coloquhoun, J.C. (1833) *Report of the Experiments on Animal Magnetism made by a Committee . . . of the French Royal Academy of Sciences*, Edinburgh.

Colwell, F.S. (1979) 'Shelley on sculpture: the Uffizi notes', *Keats–Shelley Journal* 28: 59–77.

Constable, J. (1968) *John Constable's Correspondence*, ed. R.B. Beckett, 6 vols, Ipswich: Suffolk Records Society.

Crook, Nora and Guiton, Derek (1986) *Shelley's Venomed Melody*, Cambridge: Cambridge University Press.

Culler, Jonathan (1988) *Framing the Sign: Criticism and its Institutions*, Oxford: Basil Blackwell.

Curran, Stuart and Wittreich Jr, Joseph (1972) 'The dating of Shelley's "On the devil and devils"', *Keats–Shelley Journal* 21: 83–94.

Darnton, Robert (1968) *Mesmerism and the End of Enlightenment in France*, Cambridge, Mass.: Harvard University Press.

Dawson, P.M.S. (1981) 'Shelley and the *improvvisatore* Sgricci; an unpublished review', *Keats–Shelley Memorial Bulletin* 32: 19–29.

——(1986) '"A sort of natural magic": Shelley and animal magnetism', *The Keats–Shelley Review* 1: 15–34.

Deane, Seamus (1988) *The French Revolution and Enlightenment in England 1789–1832*, Cambridge, Mass., and London: Harvard University Press.

de Bolla, Peter (1989) *The Discourse of the Sublime: Readings in History, Aesthetics and the Subject*, Oxford: Basil Blackwell.

de Man, P. (1982) 'Sign and symbol in Hegel's *Aesthetics*', *Critical Inquiry* 8(4): 761–75.

——(1983) 'Hegel on the Sublime', in M. Krupnick (ed.) *Displacement: Derrida and After*, Bloomington: Indiana University Press, 139–54.

——(1984a) 'The intentional structure of the Romantic image', in *The Rhetoric of Romanticism*, New York: Columbia University Press, 1–17;

first published in translation in H. Bloom (ed.) (1970) *Romanticism and Consciousness*, New York: Norton.

——(1984b) 'Phenomenality and materiality in Kant', in G. Shapiro and A. Sica (eds) *Hermeneutics: Questions and Prospects*, Amherst: University of Massachusetts Press.

De Quincey, Thomas (1833–4) 'Animal magnetism' (anonymous article), *Tait's Edinburgh Magazine* 4 (October 1833–January 1834): 456–74.

——(1889–90) *The Collected Writings of Thomas De Quincey*, ed. David Masson, 14 vols, Edinburgh: Adam & Charles Black.

——(1891a) *De Quincey Memorials*, ed. Alexander H. Japp, 2 vols, London: Heinemann.

——(1891b) *The Posthumous Works of Thomas De Quincey*, ed. Alexander H. Japp, 2 vols, London: Heinemann.

——(1927) *A Diary of Thomas De Quincey (1803)*, ed. Horace A. Eaton, London: Noel Douglas.

——(1970) *Recollections of the Lakes and the Lake Poets*, ed. David Wright, Harmondsworth: Penguin.

——(1973) *De Quincey as Critic*, ed. John E. Jordan, London: Routledge.

——(1985) *Confessions of an English Opium-Eater and Other Writings*, ed. Grevel Lindop, Oxford: Oxford University Press.

Derrida, J. (1979) *Spurs/Eperons: Nietzsche's Styles*, trans. B. Harlow, Chicago and London: University of Chicago Press.

de Staël Holstein, Mme (1807) *Corinne, or Italy*, trans. D. Lawler, 5 vols, London.

de Villers, Charles (1986) *Il magnetizzatore innamorato*, ed. Lucio Sarno, Palermo.

Dodds, E.R. (1951) *The Greeks and the Irrational*, Berkeley: University of California Press.

Eagleton, Terry (1982) *The Rape of Clarissa: Writing, Sexuality and Class Struggle in Samuel Richardson*, Oxford: Basil Blackwell.

——(1983) *Literary Theory: An Introduction*, Oxford: Basil Blackwell.

——(1986) *Against the Grain: Essays 1975–1985*, London: Verso.

——(1990) *The Ideology of the Aesthetic*, Oxford: Basil Blackwell.

Ellis, Kate Ferguson (1989) *The Contested Castle: Gothic Novels and the Subversion of Domestic Ideology*, Urbana: University of Illinois Press.

Engell, James (1981) *The Creative Imagination: Enlightenment to Romanticism*, Cambridge, Mass., and London: Harvard University Press.

Euripides (1960) *Bacchae*, ed. E.R. Dodds, Oxford: Clarendon Press.

Everest, Kelvin (ed.) (1983) *Shelley Revalued: Essays from the Gregynog Conference*, Leicester: Leicester University Press.

Falk, Doris V. (1969) 'Poe and the power of animal magnetism', *Publications of the Modern Language Association of America* 84: 536–46.

Fisher, Michael (1982) 'Morality and history in Coleridge's political theory', *Studies in Romanticism* 21: 457–60.

Flaxman, John (1799) *A Letter to the Committee for Raising the Naval Pillar*, London.

Fleming, D.H., and Bailyn, B. (eds) (1969) *The Intellectual Migration: Europe and America, 1930–1960*, Cambridge, Mass.: Harvard University Press.

Foucault, Michel (1969) 'What is an author?', trans. Joseph V. Harari, in D. Lodge (ed.) (1988): *Modern Criticism and Theory: A Reader*, London and New York: Longman, 196–210.

——(1973) *The Birth of the Clinic: An Archeology of Medical Perception*, trans. A.M. Sheridan Smith, London: Tavistock.

——(1979) *The History of Sexuality*, I, *An Introduction*, trans. Robert Hurley, London: Allen Lane.

——(1980) *Power/Knowledge: Selected Interviews and Other Writings 1972–1977*, ed. Colin Gordon, Brighton: Harvester Press.

Fraser, D. (1973) *The Evolution of the British Welfare State: A History of Social Policy since the Industrial Revolution*, London: Macmillan.

Freud, Sigmund (1955) 'Medusa's head', in *Standard Works*, trans. and ed. J. Strachey, XVIII: 273–4, London: Hogarth Press.

Gallini, Clara (1983) *La Somnambula meravigliosa: magnetismo e ipnotismo nell' Ottocento italiano*, Milan: Feltrinelli.

Gallop, Jane (1982) *The Daughter's Seduction: Feminism and Psychoanalysis*, London: Macmillan.

——(1985) *Reading Lacan*, Ithaca and London: Cornell University Press.

Godwin, William (1976) *Enquiry Concerning Political Justice and its Influence on Modern Morals and Happiness*, ed. with intro. I. Kramnick, Harmondsworth: Penguin.

——(1987) *Memoirs of the Author of 'The Rights of Woman'*, in R. Holmes (ed.) *A Short Residence in Sweden and Memoirs of the Author of 'The Rights of Woman'*, Harmondsworth: Penguin.

Graff, G. (1987) *Professing Literature: An Institutional History*, Chicago: University of Chicago Press.

Green, G. (1982) *Literary Criticism and the Structures of History: Erich Auerbach and Leo Spitzer*, Lincoln and London: University of Nebraska Press.

Hamilton, Paul (1983) *Coleridge's Poetics*, Oxford: Basil Blackwell.

——(1989) 'Keats and critique', in M. Levinson (ed.) *Rethinking Historicism: Critical Readings in Romantic History*, Oxford: Basil Blackwell, 108–42.

Handwerk, G.J. (1985) *Irony and Ethics in Narrative: From Schlegel to Lacan*, New Haven: Yale University Press.

Hartman, G. (1980) *Criticism in the Wilderness: The Study of Literature Today*, New Haven and London: Yale University Press.

Haskell, Francis and Penny, Nicholas (1981) *Taste and the Antique: The Lure of Classical Sculpture, 1500–1900*, New Haven and London: Yale University Press.

Haydon, Benjamin Robert (1926) *The Autobiography of Benjamin Robert Haydon (1786–1846)*, ed. from his Journals by T. Taylor, intro. A. Huxley, London: Peter Davies.

——(1950) *Autobiography and Journals (1786–1846)*, ed. M. Elwin, London: Macdonald.

——(1960) *The Diary of Benjamin Robert Haydon*, ed. W. Bissell Pope, Cambridge, Mass.: Harvard University Press.

Hayley, William (1968) *An Essay on Epic Poetry*, intro. Sister M. Celeste Williamson, Gainesville: Scholars' Facsimiles and Reprints.

Hayter, Alethea (1968) *Opium and the Romantic Imagination*, London: Faber.

Hazlitt, William (1930–4) *Complete Works*, ed. P.P. Howe, centenary edn, 21 vols, London and Toronto: Dent.

Hegel, G.W.F. (1975) *Aesthetics: Lectures on Fine Art*, trans. T.M. Knox, Oxford: Clarendon Press.

——(1977) *Phenomenology of Spirit*, trans. A.V. Miller, intro. J.N. Findlay, Oxford: Clarendon Press.

Hillis Miller, J. (1963) *The Disappearance of God: Five Nineteenth-Century Writers*, Cambridge, Mass.: Harvard University Press; London: Oxford University Press.

Hobbes, Thomas (1968) *Leviathan*, ed. C.B. Macpherson, Harmondsworth: Penguin.

Hobsbawm, E.J. (1990) *Nations and Nationalism since 1780: Myth, Programme, Reality*, Cambridge and New York: Cambridge University Press.

Hodges, William (1787) *A Dissertation on the Prototypes of Architecture, Hindoo, Moorish, and Gothic*, London.

Hohendahl, P.U. (1982) *The Institution of Criticism*, Ithaca and London: Cornell University Press.

Holmes, R. (1974) *Shelley: The Pursuit*, London: Weidenfeld & Nicolson.

——(ed.) (1987) *A Short Residence in Sweden and Memoirs of the Author of 'The Rights of Woman'*, Harmondsworth: Penguin.

Hunt, L. (1818) *Foliage; or Poems Original and Translated*, London: C. & J. Ollier.

——(1820a) 'Spirit of the ancient mythology', *The Indicator* 15 (19 January 1820): 113–16.

——(ed.) (1820b) *The Indicator*, 2 vols, London: Joseph Appleyard.

Hurd, Richard (1762) *Letters on Chivalry and Romance*, London.

——(1811) *Moral and Political Dialogues, with Letters on Chivalry and Romance*, in *Works*, 8 vols, London: Cadell.

Indicator, The (1820) 'Rousseau's scène lyrique "Pygmalion and Galathea"', XXXI (Wednesday 10 May).

Isaak, Jo-Anna (1987) 'Seduction without desire', *Vanguard* 16: 3.

Jacobus, M. (1979) 'The difference of view', in C. Belsey and J. Moore (eds) (1989) *The Feminist Reader: Essays in Gender and the Politics of Literary Criticism*, London: Macmillan Education, 49–62.

——(1984) 'The art of managing books: Romantic prose and the writing of the past', in Arden Reed (ed.) *Romanticism and Language*, London: Methuen, 215–46.

——(1989) *Romanticism, Writing and Sexual Difference: Essays on 'The Prelude'*, Oxford: Clarendon Press.

Jardine, Alice A. (1985) *Gynesis: Configurations of Women and Modernity*, Ithaca, N.Y.: Cornell University Press.

Jardine, Alice A. and Smith, Paul (eds) (1987) *Men in Feminism*, New York and London: Methuen.

Jeffrey, F. (1820) Review of *Endymion: A Poetic Romance* (1818) and *Lamia, The Eve of St Agnes and other Poems* (1820) by John Keats, *Edinburgh Review* 34 (August 1820): 203–13.

Johnson, Barbara (1988) *A World of Difference*, Baltimore, Maryland: Johns Hopkins University Press.

Jones, Vivien (ed.) (1990) *Women in the Eighteenth Century: Constructions of Femininity*, London and New York: Routledge.
Jordan, John E. (1963) *De Quincey to Wordsworth: A Biography of a Relationship*, Berkeley: University of California Press.
Jordanova, Ludmilla (ed.) (1986) *Languages of Nature: Critical Essays on Science as Literature*, London: Free Association Books.
Kames, Henry Home, Lord (1785) *Elements of Criticism*, 6th edn, 2 vols, Edinburgh.
Kant, I. (1928) *The Critique of Judgement*, trans. J.C. Meredith, Oxford: Clarendon Press.
——(1933) *Critique of Pure Reason*, trans. Norman Kemp Smith, 2nd imprint (corrected), London: Macmillan.
——(1953) *Prolegomena to Any Future Metaphysics that will be able to present itself as a Science*, trans. Peter G. Lucas, Manchester: Manchester University Press.
Kaplan, Cora (1986) *Sea Changes: Essays on Culture and Feminism*, London: Verso.
Kaplan, F. (1975) *Dickens and Mesmerism: The Hidden Springs of Fiction*, Princeton, N.J.: Princeton University Press.
Kauffman, L. (ed.) (1989) *Gender and Theory: Dialogues on Feminist Criticism*, Oxford: Basil Blackwell.
Keats, John (1978) *John Keats: Complete Poems*, ed. Jack Stillinger, London: Heinemann.
Klancher, Jon P. (1987) *The Making of English Reading Audiences 1790–1832*, Madison: University of Wisconsin Press.
——(1989) 'English Romanticism and cultural production', in H. Aram Veseer (ed.) *The New Historicism*, New York and London: Routledge, 77–88.
Kristeva, J. (1983) 'Within the microcosm of "the talking cure"', cited in J. Smith and W. Kerrigan (eds) *Interpreting Lacan*, New Haven and London: Yale University Press, 33.
Lacan, J. (1977) *Ecrits: A Selection*, trans. Alan Sheridan, London: Tavistock.
——(1979) *The Four Fundamental Concepts of Psycho-Analysis*, ed. Jacques-Alain Miller, trans. Alan Sheridan, Harmondsworth: Penguin.
Lacoue-Labarthe, P. and Nancy, J.-L. (1988) *The Literary Absolute: The Theory of Literature in German Romanticism*, trans. P. Barnard and C. Lester, Albany: State University of New York Press.
Lamb, C. (1935) *The Letters of Charles and Mary Lamb*, ed. E.V. Lucas, 3 vols, London: Dent.
Larrabee, Stephen (1943) *English Bards and Grecian Marbles*, New York: Columbia University Press.
Leask, Nigel (1988) *The Politics of Imagination in Coleridge's Critical Thought*, Basingstoke: Macmillan.
Lempriere, J. (1818) *A Classical Dictionary*, 10th edn, London: T. Cadell & W. Davies.
Lentricchia, F. (1980) *After the New Criticism*, Chicago: University of Chicago Press.
Levere, Trevor (1980) 'S.T. Coleridge and the human sciences: anthropology, phrenology and mesmerism', in M.P. Hanen, M.J. Osler and

R.G. Weyant (eds) *Science, Pseudo-Science and Society*, Waterloo, Ontario: Wilfred Laurier, Humanities, 171–92.

Levinson, Marjorie (1986) *The Romantic Fragment Poem: A Critique of a Form*, Chapel Hill: University of North Carolina Press.

——(1988) *Keats's Life of Allegory: The Origins of a Style*, Oxford: Basil Blackwell.

——(ed.) (1989) *Rethinking Historicism: Critical Readings in Romantic History*, Oxford: Basil Blackwell.

Literary Gazette, The (1820) Anonymous review of *Prometheus Unbound*, 9 September: 580–2.

Lockhart, J.G. (1817a) 'Remarks on Greek tragedy', *Blackwood's Edinburgh Magazine* 1: 39–42.

——(1817b) 'Remarks on Greek tragedy', *Blackwood's Edinburgh Magazine* 2: 147–52.

——(1817c) 'Remarks on Greek tragedy', *Blackwood's Edinburgh Magazine* 3: 352–7.

——(1817d) 'Remarks on Greek tragedy', *Blackwood's Edinburgh Magazine* 4: 593–6.

——(1819) Review of *The Revolt of Islam*, *Blackwood's Edinburgh Magazine* 4: 475–82.

——(1820) Review of *Prometheus Unbound*, *Blackwood's Edinburgh Magazine* 7: 679–87.

Lodge, David (ed.) (1988) *Modern Criticism and Theory: A Reader*, London and New York: Longman.

[Gold's] *London Magazine* (1820) Anonymous review of *Prometheus Unbound*, II (October): 382–91.

Lonsdale Magazine, The (1820) Anonymous review of *Prometheus Unbound*, I (November): 498–500.

Lonsdale, R. (ed.) (1969) *The Poems of Thomas Gray, William Collins and Oliver Goldsmith*, London and Harlow: Longmans, Green.

Lovejoy, A.O. (1936) *The Great Chain of Being: A Study of the History of an Idea*, Cambridge, Mass.: Harvard University Press.

——(1941) 'The meaning of Romanticism for the historian of ideas', *Journal of the History of Ideas* 2: 257–78.

——(1944) 'Reply to Professor Spitzer', *Journal of the History of Ideas* 5: 204–19.

——(1948) *Essays on the History of Ideas*, Baltimore: Johns Hopkins University Press.

Lowes, J.L. (1978) *The Road to Xanadu: A Study in the Ways of the Imagination*, London: Constable.

McDonagh, Josephine (1989) 'Do or die: problems of agency and gender in the aesthetics of murder', *Genders* 5: 120–34.

McFarland, Thomas (1987) *Romantic Cruxes: The English Essayists and the Spirit of the Age*, Oxford: Clarendon Press.

McGann, Jerome J. (1983) *The Romantic Ideology: A Critical Investigation*, Chicago and London: University of Chicago Press.

——(1989) 'The *Biographia Literaria* and the contentions of English Romanticism', in Frederick Burwick (ed.) *Coleridge's 'Biographia Literaria': Text and Meaning*, Columbus: Ohio State University Press, 233–54.

Madoff, Mark (1979) 'The useful myth of Gothic ancestry', in Roseann Runte (ed.) *Studies in Eighteenth-Century Culture*, 8, Madison: Wisconsin University Press.

Malthus, T.R. (1970) *An Essay on the Principle of Population and A Summary View of the Principle of Population*, ed. with intro. A. Flew, Harmondsworth: Penguin.

Maniquis, Robert (1969) 'The puzzling mimosa: sensibility and plant symbols in Romanticism', *Studies in Romanticism* 8: 129–55.

Marshall, J.D. (1985) *The Old Poor Law 1795–1834*, 2nd edn, London: Macmillan.

Marx, K. (1974) From *Introduction to the Critique of Political Economy*, in L. Baxandall and S. Morawski (eds) *Karl Marx, Friedrich Engels on Literature and Art*, New York: International General, 136–8; first published in German in 1857.

Marx, K. and Engels F. (1970) *The German Ideology*, London: Lawrence & Wishart.

Matthews, G.M. (1957) 'A volcano's voice in Shelley', *English Literary History* 24: 191–228.

Mayes, Stanley (1959) *The Great Belzoni*, London: Putnam.

Medwin, Thomas (1824) *Conversations of Lord Byron*, 2nd edn, London.

——(1834) *The Angler in Wales*, 2 vols, London.

——(1847) *The Life of Percy Bysshe Shelley*, 2 vols, London.

Mellor, Anne K. (ed.) (1988) *Romanticism and Feminism*, Bloomington and Indianapolis: Indiana University Press.

Merck, Mandy (1988) 'Bedroom horror: the fatal attraction of *Intercourse*', *Feminist Review* 30: 89–103.

Montagu, Elizabeth (1777) *An Essay on the Writings and Genius of Shakespear . . . To which are now first added, Three Dialogues of the Dead*, London: Dilly.

——(1813) *The Letters of Elizabeth Montagu*, ed. Matthew Montagu, 4 vols, London: Cadell.

Mukarovsky, J. (1964) 'The esthetics of language', in P.L. Garvin (trans. and ed.) *A Prague School Reader on Esthetics, Literary Structure, and Style*, Washington: Georgetown University Press, 31–70.

Mullan, John (1988) *Sentiment and Sociability: The Language of Feeling in the Eighteenth Century*, Oxford: Clarendon Press.

Murray, E.B. (1983) 'Shelley's *Notes on sculptures*: the provenance and authority of the text', *Keats–Shelley Journal* 32: 150–71.

Nairn, Tom (1981) *The Break-Up of Britain*, 2nd edn, London: Verso.

Napier, Elizabeth (1987) *The Failure of Gothic: Problems of Disjunction in an Eighteenth-Century Literary Form*, Oxford: Clarendon Press.

Neubauer, John (1967) 'Dr. John Brown (1735–88) and early German Romanticism', *Journal of the History of Ideas* 28: 367–82.

Newman, Gerald (1987) *The Rise of English Nationalism*, London: Weidenfeld & Nicolson.

Nietzsche, F. (1966) *Beyond Good and Evil*, trans. Walter Kaufmann, New York: Vintage.

——(1968) *The Birth of Tragedy out of the Spirit of Music*, in *Basic Writings of Nietzsche*, trans. Walter Kaufmann, New York: The Modern Library, 15–144.

——(1974) *The Gay Science*, trans. Walter Kaufmann, New York: Random House.

Nisbet, H.B. (ed.) (1985) *German Aesthetic and Literary Criticism: Winckelmann, Lessing, Hamann, Herder, Schiller, Goethe*, Cambridge: Cambridge University Press.

Nussbaum, Felicity and Brown, Laura (eds) (1988) *The New Eighteenth Century: Theory, Politics, English Literature*, New York and London: Methuen.

Ogilvie, John (1801) *Britannia: A National Epic Poem*, Aberdeen.

Oxley, G.W. (1974) *Poor Relief in England and Wales, 1601–1834*, Newton Abbot and London: David & Charles.

Page, H.A. (1877) *Thomas De Quincey: His Life and Writings*, 2 vols, London.

Paley, Morton D. (1983) *The Continuing City: William Blake's Jerusalem*, Oxford: Clarendon Press.

Peacock, T.L. (1924–34) *The Halliford Edition of the Works of Thomas Love Peacock*, ed. H.F.B. Brett-Smith and C.E. Jones, 10 vols, London: Constable.

Plotz, Judith (1988) 'On guilt considered as one of the Fine Arts: De Quincey's criminal imagination', *The Wordsworth Circle* 19: 83–8.

Pocock, J.G.A. (1975) *The Machiavellian Moment: Florentine Political Thought and the Atlantic Republican Tradition*, Princeton: Princeton University Press.

——(1985) *Virtue, Commerce, and History: Essays on Political Thought and History, Chiefly in the Eighteenth Century*, Cambridge: Cambridge University Press.

Poe, Edgar Allen (1978) *Collected Works of Edgar Allan Poe*, 3 vols, Cambridge, Mass.: Harvard University Press.

Polidori, John (1911) *The Diary of John William Polidori*, ed. W.M. Rossetti, London: Elkin Mathews.

——(1966) 'The vampyre', in E.F. Bleiler (ed.) *Three Gothic Novels and a Fragment of a Novel by Lord Byron*, New York: Dover.

Polwhele, R. (1798) *The Unsex'd Females: A Poem, addressed to the author of The Pursuits of Literature*, London: Cadell & Davies.

Poovey, Mary (1984) *The Proper Lady and the Woman Writer: Ideology as Style in the Works of Mary Wollstonecraft, Mary Shelley, and Jane Austen*, Chicago and London: University of Chicago Press.

Pope, Alexander (1963) *The Poems of Alexander Pope: A One Volume Edition of The Twickenham Pope*, ed. John Butt, London: Methuen.

Porter, Roy (1985) 'Under the influence: mesmerism in England', *History Today* 35, ix (September): 22–9.

Porter, Roy and Teich, Mikuláš (1988) *Romanticism in National Context*, Cambridge: Cambridge University Press.

Pott, J.H. (1782) *An Essay on Landscape Painting*, London.

Poynter, J.R. (1969) *Society and Pauperism: English Ideas on Poor Relief, 1795–1834*, London: Routledge & Kegan Paul.

Pressly, William L. (1981) *The Life and Art of James Barry*, New Haven and London: Yale University Press.

Punter, David (1980) *The Literature of Terror: A History of Gothic Fictions from 1765 to the Present Day*, London: Longman.

Raben, J. (1983) 'Shelley the Dionysian', in K. Everest (ed.) *Shelley Revalued: Essays from the Gregynog Conference*, Leicester: Leicester University Press, 21–36.

Rajan, Tilottama (1985) 'Displacing post-structuralism: Romantic studies after Paul de Man', *Studies in Romanticism* 24: 449–74.

Reed, Arden (1978) 'Abysmal influence: Baudelaire, Coleridge, De Quincey, Piranesi, Wordsworth', *Glyph* 4: 189–206.

——(ed.) (1984) *Romanticism and Language*, London: Methuen.

Reed, Mark (1967) *Wordsworth: The Chronology of the Early Years 1770–1799*, Cambridge, Mass.: Harvard University Press.

Reeve, Clara (1785) *The Progress of Romance*, Colchester: Keymer.

Reiman, D.H. (ed.) (1972) *The Romantics Reviewed: Contemporary Reviews of British Romantic Writers*, 3 parts, 9 vols, New York: Garland.

Reynolds, Joshua (1975) *Discourses on Art*, ed. Robert R. Wark, New Haven: Yale University Press.

Richardson, Alan (1988) 'Romanticism and the colonisation of the feminine', in Anne K. Mellor (ed.) *Romanticism and Feminism*, Bloomington and Indianapolis: Indiana University Press, 13–25.

Richardson, Samuel (1964) *Selected Letters of Samuel Richardson*, ed. John Carroll, Oxford: Clarendon Press.

——(1985) *Clarissa: or, The History of a Young Lady*, ed. Angus Ross, Harmondsworth: Penguin.

Risse, Gunter (1970) 'The Brownian system of medicine: its theoretical and practical implications', *Clio Medica* 5: 45–51.

Ross, Marlon B. (1988) 'Romantic quest and conquest: troping masculine power in the crisis of poetic identity', in Ann K. Mellor (ed.) *Romanticism and Feminism*, Bloomington and Indianapolis: Indiana University Press, 26–51.

Rossetti, Christina (1979–90) *The Complete Poems of Christina Rossetti*, ed. R.W. Crump, 3 vols, Baton Rouge: Louisiana State University Press.

Rousseau, Jean-Jacques (1973) *The Social Contract and Discourses*, trans. G.D.H. Cole, rev. and aug. J.H. Brumfitt and John C. Hall, London: Dent.

Said, Edward W. (1978) *Orientalism*, London and New York: Routledge.

St Clair, William (1967) *Lord Elgin and the Marbles*, London: Oxford University Press.

Schlegel, A.W. (1815) *A Course of Lectures on Dramatic Art and Literature*, trans. John Black, 2 vols, London: Baldwin, Cradock & Joy.

Schlegel, F. (1984) 'Ideen', in K. Wheeler (ed.) *German Aesthetic and Literary Criticism: The Romantic Ironists and Goethe*, Cambridge: Cambridge University Press.

Seward, Anna (1811) *Letters*, 6 vols, Edinburgh: Ramsay.

Shelley, Mary (1922) *Proserpine and Midas: Two Unpublished Mythological Dramas by Mary Shelley*, ed. A. Koszul, London: Oxford University Press.

——(1987) *The Journals of Mary Shelley 1814–1844*, ed. Paula R. Feldman and Diana Scott-Kilvert, 2 vols, Oxford: Clarendon Press.

Shelley, P.B. (1970) *Complete Poetical Works*, ed. T. Hutchinson, corrected by G. Matthews, London: Oxford University Press.

——(1949) 'A discourse on the manners of the ancient Greeks relative to the subject of love', in James A. Notopoulos (ed.) *The Platonism of Shelley: A Study of Platonism and the Poetic Mind*, Durham, N.C.: Duke University Press.

——(1964) *The Letters of Percy Bysshe Shelley*, ed. F.L. Jones, 2 vols, Oxford: Clarendon Press.

——(1988) *Shelley's Prose: The Trumpet of a Prophecy*, ed. David Lee Clark, London: Fourth Estate.

Simpson, D. (1987) *Wordsworth's Historical Imagination: The Poetry of Displacement*, New York and London: Methuen.

Siskin, C. (1988) *The Historicity of Romantic Discourse*, New York and Oxford: Oxford University Press.

Smith, A. (1976) *An Inquiry into the Nature and Causes of the Wealth of Nations*, ed. R.H. Campbell, A.S. Skinner, and W.B. Todd, Oxford: Clarendon Press.

Smith, Horace (1821) *Amarynthus, the Nympholept: A Pastoral Drama, in Three Acts. With Other Poems*, London: Longman, Hurst, Rees, Orne & Brown.

——(1845) *Love and Mesmerism*, 3 vols, London: Longman, Hurst, Rees, Orne & Brown.

Smith, J. and Kerrigan, W. (eds) (1983) *Interpreting Lacan*, New Haven and London: Yale University Press.

Snyder, Robert Lance (1986) 'De Quincey's literature of power: a mythic paradigm', *Studies in English Literature 1500–1900* 26: 691–711.

Solkin, David (1982) *Richard Wilson: The Landscape of Reaction*, London: Tate Gallery.

Southey, Robert (1951) *Letters from England: by Don Manuel Alvarez Espriella. Translated from the Spanish* (1807), ed. J. Simmons, London: Cresset Press.

Spacks, P.M. (1967) *The Poetry of Vision: Five Eighteenth-Century Poets*, Cambridge, Mass.: Harvard University Press.

Spector, Stephen J. (1979) 'Thomas De Quincey: self-effacing autobiographer', *Studies in Romanticism* 18: 501–20.

Spencer, J. (1986) *The Rise of the Woman Novelist: From Aphra Behn to Jane Austen*, Oxford: Basil Blackwell.

Spitzer, L. (1941) 'History of Ideas versus Reading of Poetry', *Southern Review* 6: 584–609.

——(1944) '*Geistesgeschichte* vs. History of Ideas as applied to Hitlerism', *Journal of the History of Ideas* 5: 191–203.

Spivak, Gayatri Chakravorty (1987) *In Other Worlds: Essays in Cultural Politics*, New York and London: Methuen.

——(1989) 'The New Historicism: political commitment and the post-modern critic', in H. Aram Veseer (ed.) *The New Historicism*, New York and London: Routledge, 277–92.

Staum, Martin (1980) *Cabanis: Enlightenment and Medical Philosophy in the French Revolution*, Princeton, N.J.: Princeton University Press.

Strelka, J. (ed.) (1984) *Literary Theory and Criticism – Festschrift in Honor of Rene Wellek*, Bern, Frankfurt, New York: Peter Lang.

Suskind, P. (1987) *Perfume: The Story of a Murderer*, trans. John E. Woods, Harmondsworth: Penguin.

Swann, K. (1988) 'Harassing the muse', in Anne K. Mellor (ed.) *Romanticism and Feminism*, Bloomington and Indianapolis: Indiana University Press, 81–92.

Tatar, Maria (1978) *Spellbound: Studies in Mesmerism and Literature*, Princeton, N.J.: Princeton University Press.

Thelwall, John (1801) *Poems Chiefly Written in Retirement*, Hereford.

Thoburn, D. and Hartman G. (eds) (1973) *Romanticism: Vistas, Instances, Continuities*, Ithaca and London: Cornell University Press.

Thompson, J.M. (1952) *Napoleon Bonaparte: His Rise and Fall*, Oxford: Basil Blackwell.

Thompson, T.W. (1970) *Wordsworth's Hawkshead*, ed. R. Woof, London: Oxford University Press.

Tickner, Lisa (1988) 'Feminism, art history, and sexual difference', *Genders* 3 (Fall): 92–128.

Todd, Janet (1986) *Sensibility: An Introduction*, London and New York: Methuen.

Tomalin, C. (1974) *The Life and Death of Mary Wollstonecraft*, London: Weidenfeld & Nicolson.

Tomaselli, Sylvana (1985) 'The Enlightenment debate on women', *History Workshop Journal* 20: 101–24.

Townsend, J. (1786) *A Dissertation on the Poor Laws. By a Well-wisher to Mankind*, London.

Valéry, Paul (1960) *The Collected Works of Paul Valéry*, trans. David Paul, 14 vols, New York: Pantheon Books.

Veseer, H. Aram (ed.) (1989) *The New Historicism*, New York and London: Routledge.

Volney, Count Constantin François de (1787) *Travels through Syria and Egypt in 1783, 1784, 1785: Translated from the French*, 2 vols, London.

——(1788) *Considerations on the Present War with the Turks: Translated from the French*, London.

——(1853) *The Ruins: or, a Survey of the Revolutions of Empires, translated from the French*, London: T. Allman.

Walker, W.S. (1821) Review of *Prometheus Unbound*, *Quarterly Review* 26 (October 1821): 168–80.

Walpole, Horace (1937) *Correspondence with the Rev. William Cole*, ed. W.S. Lewis and A. Dayle Wallace, 3 vols, New Haven: Yale University Press.

——(1941) *Correspondence with George Montagu*, ed. W.S. Lewis and Ralph S. Brown Jr, 2 vols, New Haven: Yale University Press.

——(1961) *Correspondence with Hannah More*, ed. W.S. Lewis, Robert A. Smith and Charles H. Bennett, New Haven: Yale University Press.

Warton, Thomas (1774) 'Dissertation of the origin of Romantic fiction in Europe', in *The History of English Poetry*, 3 vols, London.

——(1802) 'Verses on Sir Joshua Reynolds's painted window at New College, Oxford', in *The Poetical Works,* ed. Richard Mant, Oxford: Hanwell.

Watson, R. (1793) *A Sermon Preached Before the Stewards of the Westminster Dispensary at their Anniversary Meeting in Charlotte-Street Chapel, April 1785. With An Appendix*, London: T. Cadell & T. Evans.
Webb, T. (ed.) (1982) *English Romantic Hellenism 1700–1824,* Manchester: Manchester University Press.
Wellek, R. (1936) 'Theory of literary history', *Traveux du Circle Linguistique de Prague* 6.
——(1937) 'Literary criticism and philosophy', *Scrutiny* 5: 375–83.
——(1941) 'Literary history', in N. Foerster (ed.) *Literary Scholarship: Its Aims and Methods,* Chapel Hill: University of North Carolina Press.
——(1949) 'The concept of Romanticism, in literary history', *Comparative Literature* I: 1–23, 147–72.
——(1963) *Concepts of Criticism*, New Haven and London: Yale University Press.
——(1982) *The Attack on Literature,* Brighton: Harvester Press.
Weyant, Robert (1980) 'Proto-science, pseudo-science, metaphors and animal magnetism', in M.P. Hanen, M.J. Osler and R.G. Weyant (eds) *Science, Pseudo-Science and Society*, Waterloo, Ontario: Wilfred Laurier, Humanities, 77–114.
Wilkes, Rev. Mr Wetenhall (1766) *A Letter of Genteel and Modest Advice to a Young Lady*, 8th edn, London: Hawes, Clarke & Collins.
Williams, Helen Maria (1790) *Julia, a Novel,* Dublin: Chamberlaine & Rice.
——(1975) *Letters from France 1790–96,* ed. Janet Todd, 2 vols, New York: Scholars' Facsimiles and Reprints.
Williams, R. (1983) *Keywords: A Vocabulary of Culture and Society*, rev. edn, London: Fontana.
Wilt, Judith (1977) 'He could go no farther: a modest proposal about Lovelace and Clarissa', in *Publications of the Modern Language Association of America* 92: 19–32.
Wollstonecraft, Mary (1979) *Collected Letters of Mary Wollstonecraft*, ed. R. Wardle, Ithaca and London: Cornell University Press.
——(1989) *The Works of Mary Wollstonecraft*, ed. Janet Todd and Marilyn Butler, 7 vols, London: William Pickering.
Wordsworth, D. (1952) *Journals of Dorothy Wordsworth*, ed. E. de Selincourt, 2 vols, London: Macmillan.
Wordsworth, W. (1940–9) *The Poetical Works of William Wordsworth*, ed. E. de Selincourt and H. Darbishire, 5 vols, Oxford: Clarendon Press.
——(1959) *The Prelude or Growth of a Poet's Mind*, ed. E. de Selincourt, second edn, rev. H. Darbishire, Oxford: Clarendon Press.
——(1963) *Lyrical Ballads*, ed. R.L. Brett and A.R. Jones, London: Methuen.
——(1974) *Prose Works of William Wordsworth*, ed. W.J.B. Owen and J.W. Smyser, 3 vols, Oxford: Clarendon Press.
Yaeger, P. (1989) 'Toward a female sublime', in L. Kauffman (ed.) *Gender and Theory: Dialogues on Feminist Criticism*, Oxford: Basil Blackwell, 191–212.
Yarlott, G. (1967) *Coleridge and the Abyssinian Maid*, London: Methuen.
Young, Edward (1989) *Night Thoughts*, ed. Stephen Cornford, Cambridge: Cambridge University Press.

INDEX